The Publican's Handbook

WE WOULD LIKE TO THANK ALL OUR ADVERTISERS AND IN PARTICULAR OUR SPONSORS:

HM Customs
& Excise

P^{The}ublican's Handbook

Second Edition

Consultant Editor:
Ted Bruning

KOGAN PAGE

in association with

First published in 1997
This second edition published 1999

Kogan Page Limited
120 Pentonville Road
London N1 9JN
kpinfo@kogan-page.co.uk

© Kogan Page and Contributors 1999

British Library Cataloguing in Publication Data

ISBN 0 7494 29089

Typeset by JS Typesetting, Wellingborough, Northants.
Printed and bound in Great Britain by Bell & Bain Limited, Glasgow.

CONTENTS

Foreword   xiii
Mary Curnock Cook

Introduction   xv
Ted Bruning

List of Contributors   xvii

Part One: Entry Level

1   Choosing Your Pub   7
Barry Gillham

2   Training for the Trade   24
Andrew Palmer

Part Two: Stock in Trade

3   Beer and Cider   38
Ted Bruning

4   Profit from Wine   76
Martin Straus

5   Spirits   91
Ted Bruning

6   Glassware   101
Ted Bruning and Paul Cooper

Contents

7   Catering   106
Tony O'Reilly

Part Three: Personnel

8   Staff Training and Recruitment   141
Andrew Palmer and Ted Bruning

9   Hiring and Firing   145
Christine Bradley

Part Four: Operations Management

10 Bar Design and Merchandising   161
Paul Cooper

11 Marketing, Publicity and Promotion   172
Danny Blyth

12 Maximising Machine Income   184
Ian Chuter

13 The Family Trade   194
Ted Bruning

14 Adding Value   203
Paul Cooper

Part Five: Business Systems

15 Stock and Financial Control   225
Paul Adams

16 Information Technology for Publicans   241
Jill Upton

Part Six: For Your Comfort and Safety. . .

17 Fire Safety   249
Glen Gorman

18 Security in Licensed Outlets   256
Brian Taylor

19 Smoke Signals   268
Oliver Griffiths

Health and Safety Footnotes   73, 104, 137, 155, 170, 200, 220
Teresa Miller

Legal Footnotes   21, 75, 90, 100, 105, 138, 158,
Anthony Lyons   171, 193, 201, 221, 240, 267

Appendices

Appendix One: Licensing Justices and Licences   275

Appendix Two: Gaming   278

Appendix Three: Disability Discrimination   280

Appendix Four: Alterations and Refurbishments   282

Appendix Five: Notices You Must Display   284

Appendix Six: Useful Addresses and Phone Numbers   286

Appendix Seven: Checklist of Essential Contacts   289

Index of Advertisers   290

MAKING PUBMASTER'S
BUSINESS YOUR BUSINESS

For many people, running a pub is a romantic dream. Having a laugh with the regulars who become your friends...taking pride in the range of drinks and food you serve...and playing an important part in the local community. A PUBMASTER tenancy offers opportunities for those who have already have some experience in the trade opportunities for those who already have some experience in the trade, and those coming into pub retailing for the first time.

As one of the largest independent pub retailers in the UK, with over 1,600 pubs in its estate across the country, PUBMASTER can offer a wide choice of locations. Whether it is:

- In a rural area or village - ideal for both the country pub at the centre of village life, and for those in popular tourist areas, benefiting from passing trade;
- In a town or city - ideal for the more traditional pub, and those aimed at the younger customer, thriving on busy lunchtimes and/ or evenings; or
- In a residential area - ideal for both a local community pub in a popular suburban area, and for those on thriving housing estates.

Some excel at catering, others have adapted to a family environment. With many different character pubs across the country, there is something for all prospective licensees.

The Pub, the great British institution, has always been the bastion of business and social communities - the hallmark of tradition and heritage throughout Britain. Little has changed over the years, pubs are still social centres, meeting places and providers of entertainment and nourishment. The way we lead our lives, however, has changed quite dramatically over the last century, with the advancement of technology, greater mobility and the development of a vast leisure industry. No longer can a pub just rely on regular and passing trade to earn a living. The services a pub has to offer must be flexible to adapt to changing customer needs and requirements.

Customers are demanding higher standards, greater choice and improved levels of service. They are also insisting that pubs sell high quality food and drinks, cater for families and children and provide good quality accommodation. There is a growing need to have attractive products and services than other leisure pursuits. It is this notion of change and adaptability that PUBMASTER understands.

PUBMASTER is committed to matching the right people to the right locations, giving them the professional back-up to deliver a top quality service to their customers, which meets their customers needs. It has developed an approach that promotes teamwork and creativity with this understanding of their customers. Tenants receive support services from a team led by experienced licensed trade professionals. These include:

- marketing and promotional support;
- cellar management training;
- financial guidance,
- business development; and
- day to day assistance from regional managers and surveyors.

PUBMASTER'S independence gives it the freedom to choose the beers that it wants to sell in its pubs - freeing its pubs, its licensees and their customers from the constraints of a brewery tie, and widening the range of beers available in its pubs. PUBMASTER'S experience, along with its considerable financial strength, gives its licensees an unrivalled level of support, whilst retaining the freedom to run their own business.

Interested? For further information call the nearest PUBMASTER Office:
BROMSGROVE - Carol Reed - 01527 577222
IPSWICH - Jenny Barnicoat - 01473 280280
WAKEFIELD - Hilary Jackson - 01924 825260

FOREWORD

Leisure is the growth industry of the new Millennium. It will provide one in five new jobs and the sharpest growth within the leisure industry will come from satisfying soaring demand for food, drink and hospitality.

Responding to this the pub industry has expanded and diversified into three basic sectors; the 'local' providing a social asset for its community; the food-led outlet (pub-restaurant) and the buzzing young persons' venue seen in town centres.

High levels of competition plus a multitude of regulations covering food and drink services, licensing law, health and safety and employment law have transformed the role of the licensee, be he manager, tenant/lessee or freetrader, to an all-round business professional. There are terrific careers to be made in licensed retailing for people at all skill levels and entrants will be pleasantly surprised to find an emphasis on life-long training to ensure professionalism. Not surprisingly, as the body setting national standards, the British Institute of Innkeeping has seen soaring demand for membership as well as for its acclaimed range of training packages and qualifications.

Membership of the Institute from Graduate to Fellow status, in addition to its qualifications, are respected throughout the industry as well as by licensing magistrates and police licensing officers.

This handbook provides a clear guide to the careers in licensed retailing as well as more details on how the British Institute of Innkeeping supports success.

Mary Curnock Cook
Director, *British Institute of Innkeeping*

INTRODUCTION

Ted Bruning

The pub trade has always been a lot more complicated than people imagine. Even in those far-off days when police officers and servicemen could dream of retiring to a pub with roses round the door, there were all the complications of licensing law and bookkeeping to deal with, as well as less technical but equally daunting problems such as under-age drinking and brewery relations.

But the changes of the last 15–20 years have made the whole business even more complicated. The virtual collapse of the traditional short-term, low-rent, tied-on-everything brewery tenancy has left publicans with a bewildering array of long leases, discount agreements, quasi-franchises and heaven knows what else to cope with!

The market-place, too, is much harder than it was. Country pubs and town tenancies alike are going bust at an alarming rate, and no publican can simply assume that when he opens his door there'll be customers waiting to come in. They have to be found and fought for.

There's been an amazing explosion in the range of beers licensees need to know about, as well. Few publicans are entirely tied, and even those who are have a much wider range of tied products to choose from than their predecessors. Food service, increasingly an essential contributor to turnover, brings its own complications: you don't just have to be able to cook, you also have to be able to operate within one of the most regulated business environments on the planet.

And then there's crime. From drug-dealing to extortion, today's pubs are a magnet for criminals. They're places where people can meet and do business in relative anonymity, and where cash is available. Both facts attract criminals like moths to a candle.

This book does not, could not, answer every day-to-day query a publican might have arising from these and other issues, although I hope it can answer most of them. It has a more important function: to let the self-employed publican share the experience of people who have been involved in the licensed trade – some of them as hands-on doers, others as intimate observers

– for many years, and to help him focus on the issues that really matter in establishing a profitable and enjoyable business.

In journalism we have a precept that, while we can't be expected to know all the right answers, we should be expected to ask all the right questions. I hope this book helps you to do just that.

LIST OF CONTRIBUTORS

Paul Adams is a chartered accountant of 25 years' standing. His first experience in the leisure industry was in Ladbrokes' casino division. After moving to Ladbrokes' head office he was in charge of corporate planning and involved in projects such as the expansion of the Hilton Hotels chain.

In 1984 he joined David Bruce as Financial Director of the Firkin pubs. His first taste of the pub business – within a week of joining – was the bank's bouncing the VAT cheque. Once the finances were sorted out he played a major part in expanding the chain to 11 pubs, taking responsibility for all operational matters in the pubs.

When the Firkins were sold in 1988 he converted the old buffet at Kew Gardens Station to create the Pig and Parrot – still a highly successful pub now trading as a Firkin.

Having been involved with a further three pubs with David Bruce, he bought a one-third share of the Wychwood Brewery in 1992 with the specific intention of starting a pub chain. In November 1992 the first Hobgoblin opened in Staines and since then the chain has grown to 27 pubs spread throughout the south of England.

Danny Blyth is a journalist and publicist specialising in the licensed retail, leisure and travel industries. He regularly contributes to trade publications such as the *Licensee & Morning Advertiser* and *The Publican*, and has his own column in Free House. He also contributes regular features to in-house publications of companies such as Inntrepreneur, Whitbread and Bass Leisure.

Danny has also presented leisure features on London News radio and is regularly published in a range of other publications, from *Fish Restaurant International* to *Travel Trade Gazette Europa* and *Garden Answers*.

In addition he has acted as a publicity consultant on specific campaigns and product launches to firms like Allied Domecq, Scottish Courage and Hop Back Brewery. He has recently published his own guidebook to outside bar and function business, sponsored by Wadworth 6X.

Christine Bradley, a partner with leading northern law firm Pannone & Partners since 1985, specialises in employment law (all aspects, contentious and non-contentious). Christine heads the Employment Unit, which regularly presents workshops and seminars designed to provide a practical approach to current employment law problems.

The range of clients for whom Christine acts is broad, from very large plcs with nationally recognisable names to smaller high street businesses. Many of Christine's clients are in the licensed trade.

Ted Bruning is a freelance journalist who worked for seven years on the *Morning Advertiser* – then the licensed trade's daily newspaper – before becoming a contributing feature writer for *Brewers' Guardian* and *Caterer & Hotelkeeper*. He is also deputy editor of the Campaign for Real Ale's monthly newspaper, *What's Brewing*. His books include *Historic English Inns*, the *CAMRA Guide to Real Cider*, and *Historic Pubs of London*.

Ian Chuter is Rank Leisure Machine Services National Accounts Director, responsible for key accounts including national retailers, regional brewers, motorway service stations and licensed betting offices. With more than 16 years' experience in the amusement machine industry, part of his brief is to develop existing business, as well as explore opportunities for potential new business in what is a dynamic sector of the leisure industry. A company within the Rank Organisation Plc, Rank Leisure Machine Services is one of the UK's leading operators of amusement machines and electronic leisure products.

Paul Cooper runs Licensed Retail Consultants which provides services in food development, purchasing, marketing, human resources and new unit openings to Publican's, brewers and independent retailers. The company provides an objective view of a business through a range of cost-effective specialist facilities. Its services are geared to complement in-house departments or to serve as a surrogate department for those without an in-house operation. They provide creativity in their ideas, whilst working within the overall aims of a business and are able to offer either an integrated package of services or undertake one-off projects to suit a client's needs.

Paul Cooper's industry experience has included two years as Commercial Development Manager at Unicorn Inns Plc with responsibility for marketing, brand management, human resources, unit openings and purchasing. He was Specialist Retail Brand Manager at Wolverhampton & Dudley Breweries Plc where his role incorporated the marketing and evolution of YPV and liquor led branded operations.

Throughout his career, he has successfully developed both individual units and retail concepts, driving them forward to the leading edge of UK licensed retailing. His considerable management skills are backed up with substantial operational and practical experience and in-depth knowledge of the industry.

Barry Gillham, FRICS FSVA PPAVLP ACIArb, joined Fleurets in 1964 at the age of 16, passing his chartered surveyor's exams by the age of 19. At just 21 he was made an Associate Partner, becoming a full partner in 1974 and senior partner in 1979. He became Chairman of Fleurets in 1995.

In 1976 he became Secretary of the Association of Valuers of Licensed Property, a role he performed for 13 years before becoming President from 1989 to 1994 (its centenary year).

Fleurets is the oldest firm of chartered surveyors to specialise nationally and exclusively in the sale and valuation of hotels and licensed property. Founded in the 1820s, it had only one office, in Bloomsbury, until 1979. Since then it has opened offices in Birmingham, Brighton, Bristol, Leeds, Manchester, and Suffolk to cover the country.

Barry continues to be involved actively in the sale, letting and valuation of public houses on a nationwide basis.

Glen Gorman started his fire service in Lancashire in 1984. During his ten-year service he completed a four-week fire safety course to enable him to carry out inspections of pubs, hotels and other businesses under the 1971 Fire Prevention Act. Soon after winning promotion to sub-officer he completed the nine-week Watch Commander's Course at the Fire Service College at Moreton-in-Marsh.

In 1994 a transfer to the London Fire Brigade brought further promotion to the rank of Station Officer and a position as Inspecting Officer in what must be one of the country's busiest Fire Safety Departments: City of Westminster. A large proportion of the premises in the area are high risk, from small, privately owned backpackers' hostels to five-star international hotels – many of which have benefited from the advice the author has provided over the past three years.

Glen has also completed a 12-week Specialist Fire Safety Course at Moreton-in-Marsh, one of the highest national qualifications available in this field.

Oliver Griffiths is responsible for running the Atmosphere Improves Results (AIR) initiative, which identifies and promotes good practice in handling the issue of environmental tobacco smoke.

Oliver started his career in marketing at Procter and Gamble before moving on to wholesaling wines and spirits for Allied Lyons. He then set up and ran two award-winning target marketing companies before setting up the CSL environmental communications consultancy.

Anthony Lyons is the specialist licensing partner in Manchester law firm Pannone & Partners. He previously ran his own firm, Copeland Lyons – one of only two in Britain to specialise in liquor and entertainment law. His client list includes major names such as Café Inns and Peter Stringfellow, and he is legal adviser to the Federation of Licensed Victuallers' Associations.

Teresa Miller, BSc MA MCIEH, qualified as an environmental health officer in 1987 and has specialised for the most part in the areas of food hygiene and workplace health and safety. She currently works for a local authority in the Home Counties and is primarily concerned with food businesses and associated environmental health issues.

Tony O'Reilly was born in Dublin, Ireland. He was classically trained as a chef in the Isle of Man and has worked in many prestigious establishments in London including the City of London Club, Threadneedle Street and Earl's Court Exhibition Centre. As well as lecturing for 16 years he is an accomplished writer on all aspects of the catering industry and author of two cookery textbooks: *Food Preparation and Cooking* and *The Complete Cookery Manual.* He gave up lecturing in 1997 to become a Food Consultant and Development Chef for British Meat. A regular columnist for *Pubfood* magazine, the leading pub catering magazine, as well as contributing articles for principle trade titles.

Andrew Palmer is an award-winning business journalist who edits *New Innkeeper,* the monthly business journal for career licensees and staff and the official magazine of the British Institute of Innkeeping.
   A judge of the prestigious National Innkeeping Training awards and *The Publican* awards, Andrew was the award-winning editor of *The Publican* newspaper after its relaunch as a weekly title. He is also a director of the Publican Conference. As well as editing *New Innkeeper,* he runs a communications and copywriting agency operating in licensed hospitality.

Martin Straus has been associated with the Wine Trade for some 20 years. He joined Hedges & Butler (then the market leaders) in 1980 as a Hotel & Restaurant Division salesman. He was subsequently promoted to Area Sales Manager and finally National Accounts Manager responsible for all Bass Group national catering operations, including Holiday Inns, Crest Hotels, The Toby Restaurant Group and Bass regional brewery companies. His qualifications include the Wine & Spirit Education Trust Diploma and the Hotel & Catering Training Board Group Training Techniques Certificate.
   In 1988 he established his own wine consultancy, Winecraft. As well as advising a variety of hotels and restaurants, his many clients have included Sopexa (Food and Wine from France), CERT (the Republic of Ireland training agency) and the Association of Licensed Free Traders. He set up the Wine Appreciation Certificate for City & Guilds, and was National Assessor for three years. For the British Institute of Innkeeping, he piloted the Wine Retail Certificate, was a contributor to the training pack and was one of the first accredited trainers. He has also tutored the Wine & Spirit Education Trust Certificate and Higher Certificate courses for many years, primarily in association with Hertfordshire colleges.
   Martin's current activities include wine tastings, courses, seminars and tours, and specialising in wine and food pairing. He is also Consultant/

Business Development Manager for Bon Appetit, a French restaurant in St Albans, Hertfordshire.

Brian Taylor is group security adviser at Scottish & Newcastle. A Geordie by birth, Brian joined Newcastle City Police as a cadet and became a constable in 1959. In the early 1960s he graduated to the Northumbria Police CID, serving in the City Division, the Regional Crime Squad, and the Club and Vice Squad.

As a Detective Inspector he served in the Fraud Squad, and was promoted to Detective Chief Inspector in the Newcastle City West Division.

He was then appointed to help launch the 'Community Approach to Policing' before becoming superintendent in charge of crime prevention at police headquarters. He returned to operational duties as sub-divisional commander, deputy commander, then chief superintendent divisional commander of South Tyneside Division, retiring in May 1991 after 32 years' service.

He joined Newcastle Breweries as security manager before being appointed to his present position in the group.

Jill Upton has been in the IT industry for 20 years, first with the Granada Group and then Grand Metropolitan before joining IT Works of Maulden, Bedfordshire, five years ago as Managing Consultant.

IT Works is an independent computer systems consultancy helping small and medium businesses to analyse their business needs; select the right systems; implement systems. At the moment we are helping clients check and resolve their year 2000 problems.

IT Works also runs a support desk to help customers resolve their problems. Jill can be contacted on 01525 862266.

PART ONE
ENTRY LEVEL

Choosing Your Pub

During 1997 hundreds of people picked up the gauntlet and became pub lessees across the UK. Whitbread Pub Partnerships, the UK's leading leased pub retailer, has been helping people to change career for a number of years now and has seen all kinds of people enter into the public house arena. From newsagents to seamen, men and women from all walks of life decide to start a new career, and year after year potential lessees are still queuing up to accept the challenge of running a pub. The hours are long and the work is hard, but still you come. So, what possesses someone to take the leap of faith and become a pub lessee?

First, although running a pub is not an easy task, there can be many rewards. As many existing lessees will testify, much satisfaction can be derived from running your own business. Not only can it be seen as a great personal challenge, but it also provides an opportunity to innovate and implement business plans that reflect personal aims for the pub in question. Then, of course, once the plans come to fruition and the pub starts to bring in revenue, there are the financial rewards which can be substantial. Changing career abruptly can be a daunting process, but with the support of Whitbread Pub Partnerships, many new lessees have found the transition to be relatively painless and ultimately very rewarding.

One of the key reasons why so many people choose to become Whitbread Pub Partnerships lessees, rather than working with anyone else, is the massive level of support that the company offers. Whitbread Pub Partnerships builds genuine working relationships with its lessees, with the common aim of making the pub and the partnership an outstanding success.

The network of Business Development Managers provides key contacts and assistance when required, but they do not interfere with the day to day running of the pub. It is seen as the lessees business and it is generally the lessee who comes up with and runs with ideas, or puts together proposals for developments and refurbishment. Running a Whitbread Pub Partnerships pub is a partnership, but one where the lessee takes the lead.

Case Study One
Hazel Johnson-Ollier, The Letters Inn, Tattenhall, Cheshire

I've always wanted to be my own boss,' explains Hazel Johnson-Ollier, lessee at The Letters Inn, in Tattenhall, Chester. "I looked at several other possible businesses but I think it was always going to be a pub for me."

The pub in question is a 300-year-old former sorting office and a far cry from Hazel's previous work surroundings as an airhostess. "Of course there are many differences between the two jobs, but there are similarities too. I'm used to working long and unsociable hours, although it's

been a bit of a shock working for six months without a night off! I'm used to dealing with people and communicating on different levels, and I think I'm pretty good at handling stress as well."

Hazel worked in pubs as a student and remembers that standards were not always what they should have been. -Originally when I took over the pub, it was very tatty but it did have character and I could see the potential. It's very easy to let a pub go like that because there are so many pressures on your time. What I've tried to do is concentrate on the basics such as clean glasses and toilets, and people appreciate that, which is a good start,

"But my ultimate aim is to offer the standards of a five start hotel but without the prices,because not everything has to be expensive."

At first everyone presumed Hazel's husband had bought her the pub but they now accept her as the boss. Even her business development manger had his doubts until she presented him with her business plan and he could see how professional she was.

Hazel is a firm believer that little touches are important, which is why she presents guests with a small box of chocolates on special occasions, or gives out helium filled balloons to kids. It creates a good impression, she says, and you can tell people appreciate it by the size of the tips they leave.

Cleverly the balloons have a picture of the pub on, matching the pub logo which adorns the side of a her jeep. 'All advertising is important," she adds. "I don't like to think that I miss out on any opportunities.'

As with most landladies, Hazel deals with trouble herself, and she points put that the only time the police have been called to the pub was when she was away on holiday

Her main problem is with staff. 'My biggest day to day hassle is the reliability and attitude of the staff. People see working in a pub as a stop-gap and don't take it seriously enough. I do expect a lot from my staff and training is hard in such a small team, so most of it is carried out on the job. 'But I've got a very loyal team in general, and one of chefs has worked here for 14 months and never had a weekend off because he knows how important he is to me,' she continues.

"You don't go into business for a fast buck - it's a commitment, with long term-benefits, plus the thrill of the challenge to make it work. That's what ultimately makes it interesting.'

Case Study Two
Bill Davidson, The Morning Star, Lowestoft, Suffolk

For 33 years Bill Davidson rode the waves on the high seas, 26 of those as a Tug Master. He was responsible for the safe passage of vessels in and out of Lowestoft Harbour. However, in March last year he made a dramatic decision to come ashore and take the assignment of the Morning Star in Lowestoft, Suffolk. Bill and his wife Maureen are revelling in their new role, although Bill's tug boat experience is still called upon by his former employers, Klyme Tugs. He works from their office during the week, sorting out crews for tugs and acting as a general advisor.

Bill doesn't get out onto the sea much nowadays and after 33 years he felt that it was time to become a landlubber. "I did want to come ashore at last", says Bill. "However, it needed to be for the right reason. Secretly, I'd always wanted to run my own pub, so when this chance came along, I grabbed it. My role here does offer me some of the freedom I enjoyed at sea and I still do occasionally get out on a tug myself. Old habits die hard, as they say.'

Case Study Three
Joe and Margaret Briggs, The Black Horse, West Boldon, Tyne

Joe and Margaret Briggs spent 15 years rising early to open their newsagent shop and getting the news out to a waking world. Then, around Christmas 1996, they took on their first lease with Whitbread Pub Partnerships, at the Black Horse in West Boldon, Tyne and Wear. The couple have made a great success of their new career and even took on a special project to rejuvenate another local pub, the Hobson Hotel, increasing weekly turnover sixfold.

Now solely concentrating on the Black Horse again, they are keen to develop the food side of the business.

Joe has always been keen to take on new challenges: "I've long thought that you become stale in what you do unless you introduce an element of variety. Before I was a newsagent, I did a milk round for five years and I've also owned a fruit shop, a fried fish shop with cafe and a delicatessen. But I've sold the lot now and am really enjoying this new challenge."

In fact, running a pub is something that Joe had often contemplated: 'I'm a trained chef, so it often occurred to me that I could make success out of managing a pub. Now I've taken that leap, I'm really pleased with the results - it's been a great move.' The Briggs, like Whitbread Pub Partnerships lessees countrywide are thankful they made the decision and took the fateful jump into a new career.

For further information please contact:
The Lessee Recruitment Department
Whitbread Pub Partnerships
Whitbread House
Park Street West
Luton LU1 3BG
Tel: 01582 396 085   Fax: 01582 396 986

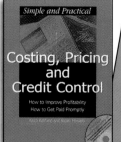

CHAPTER ONE

CHOOSING YOUR PUB

Barry Gillham

WHAT DO YOU EXPECT FROM PUB LIFE?

So you've decided to run a pub. Why? I have been in the pub business for more than 30 years, buying, selling and valuing. I think I have visited, in a professional capacity, maybe one-third of the 65,000 pubs in the country. Yet I have never had the urge to run one.

I am big and fat and cheerful – your archetypal publican if ever there was one – but there's a serious stumbling-block to my ever becoming one. You see, when I'm in a pub I like a drink – and if I drank too much, I'd be a lousy publican. But I couldn't bear to remain sober, either, when everyone around me was enjoying a few drinks, forgetting the punchlines to their jokes, spilling their drinks, sometimes even being sick in the toilets. So if I were sober, I'd still be a lousy publican.

That's why I shouldn't run a pub. How about you?

You need to analyse, thoroughly and honestly, the reasons why you would like to run a pub, and make sure you don't have rose-tinted spectacles. I find that 80 per cent of the people who enter the licensed trade leave within three years, never to touch the pub business again. The other 20 per cent love the life and stay in it until they retire – sometimes at the same pub, sometimes moving two or three times, sometimes even building a small chain.

There is virtually nothing in between. You either love the job or hate it: very few people stay seven or eight years and then change career.

The trick, therefore, is to make sure you are one of the 20 per cent before you make the mistake of entering a trade to which you are not suited – or perhaps going into the wrong branch of a trade in which you might have been successful had you received the right advice and training.

I always advise people to work part time in the trade before deciding. Before the days of comprehensive training courses, this was the only way to gain entry. I believe it is still the best way, although I accept that, today, more formal training is a must.

One advantage of working evenings and weekends in addition to a full-time job and spending any spare moments traipsing the country looking at potential pubs of your own is that you will get a foretaste of what it's like to work a 100-hour week. This is the best training for entering the licensed trade because it will prove you have the stamina. Your legs and feet will take the strain of standing for hours on end. You will have to survive on six hours' sleep a night and, most important, you will have to work with your spouse for long periods of time and resist the twin temptations of alcohol and the opposite sex. (Many of the 80 per cent who fall by the wayside do so either because they drink too much or because sex rears its ugly head. There are many combinations of husband falling for the barmaid or wife running off with the captain of the darts team. Sometimes suspicion alone is enough to break a marriage under pressure).

If you are still keen to take a pub after six months' work at your local, in addition to a full-time job, including a holiday relief and two or three long weekends on your own, you are more likely to succeed in this trade.

The demands of the lifestyle will, of course, vary from pub to pub. Often the smallest pubs (or those with the lowest turnover) are the hardest work because the licensees have to do it all themselves. Don't be fooled by the number of staff you see in the Rover's Return in Coronation Street or the Queen Vic in Albert Square: in fact, it may only

be on the busiest two or three nights plus a night off that any staff at all are employed in a typical local.

In most backstreet locals the day begins with the licensees doing the cleaning, glass washing and bottling up from the previous night. During the day one partner will run the bar while the other does the cooking. Any spare time is taken up with the books, the VAT, the ordering and the cellar.

If you have children, time must be devoted to them (not to mention the domestic housework). Most licensees of low volume businesses are also odd-job persons, unblocking toilets, unsticking window frames, clearing gutters and replacing the odd tile or slate (most pubs are over 100 years old – some of the best are 500 years old – and need constant doses of tender loving care).

Many pubs now open all day, offering little chance of an afternoon nap. Even if trade is quiet, it will still require one person in the bar between 3pm and 8pm, so at best each partner will get two or three hours away from serving.

Usually, the busier a pub is the more staff it can afford and, hopefully, the shorter the licensee's working week. Recently one of the major chains operating the biggest and best town centre pubs announced that its managers will only be required to work a 50-hour week, four days on and three days off. In this sort of pub the manager will be required to 'manage' – ie interview staff, compile working rotas, go to company training days and implement the trade-boosting ideas they are given. They won't have to clean the toilets, cook or even pull pints. They may have very little time to talk to customers. This may not be your idea of how you would like to run a pub.

There are many different lifestyles between these two extremes. Possibly the most successful (and I would say enjoyable) is where one partner is a chef who is also good at paperwork and the other partner is a front-of-house manager good at chatting up customers and motivating staff. If this describes you to a T, you need to find the right pub, on the right terms.

HOW DO I BECOME A PUBLICAN?

What sort of pub would best suit your means and ambitions? There are many ways into the pub trade, and many types of pub – managed, tenanted, leasehold, and freehold. Are you aware of the distinctions?

Managed houses

Breweries and other pub-operating companies tend to run the biggest and best of their pubs directly, employing managers and staff on salaries and bonuses and keeping all the profit themselves. Most managed houses – which account for a little over one-third of the country's pubs – have a turnover topping £6000 a week. Some, such as steak bars and theme pubs, have turnovers of well over £1m a year. Most managed house companies have their own training schemes. Prospective managers will be expected to work first as trainee managers then relief managers before they are given their own pub.

There are also many small companies running marginal pubs under management. Often these offer the worst of all worlds. Training is scarce or non-existent; there is tight control of costs because there is not really enough profit to warrant management; and promised bonuses never materialise because unrealistic targets have been set. This sort of pub is often the first step on the ladder for many entrants to the trade. Sadly, it produces a high proportion of the dropouts. There are many good small managed house companies, but there are probably more poor ones.

Traditional tenancies

Traditionally, brewery-owned pubs with insufficient trade to warrant management, ie turning over £2–4000 a week, were let on tied tenancy.

At its simplest, a tied tenancy is a short-term agreement (usually three years, but sometimes less and occasionally more) whereby the tenant rents the pub and buys beer, and sometimes other products, from the brewery. The tenant is responsible for all the expenses of running the pub, ie staff wages, gas and electricity, business rates, and some repairs and decoration. If the business makes a profit, the tenant keeps it. If the business makes a loss, the tenant bears it.

The degree of tie, ie whether it is on all beers, whether a guest beer is allowed, whether the tenant is tied on certain wines and spirits or has to share takings from gaming machines or juke boxes, varies from company to company. Generally tenants are required to pay the full list price for products on which they are tied. Naturally the price at which

EVERARDS - A FAMILY BUSINESS WHICH BELIEVES IN PEOPLE

Founded in 1849 Everards, the Leicestershire based independent family brewery, has a proud history of combining a progressive outlook with the best of tradition. From their current brewery at Castle Acres, Narborough, the family-run business takes great pride in the quality of its largely traditional estate of 156 pubs. These are based mainly in Leicestershire and surrounding counties. The company seeks to retain the best aspects of its long heritage but also to harness new developments where these can complement and enhance its standards of operation. What resolutely remains unchanged is the belief that people lie at the heart of the success of the business. Everards understands that good and consistent service is paramount and that this stems directly from high quality people. The recent award of "Investors in People" is a tangible recognition of their commitment. The selection and retention of excellent pub managers and tenants depends upon finding and properly rewarding the right type of licensees. Whether people join the business as managers or tenants, Everards carefully matches the right people with the right pubs. This simple approach ensures that licensees and customers bond well together. There are just over 100 tenancies in the estate and the remainder of houses are run under management. Says Chris Faircliffe, Managing Director - Trading, "We recognise that we are in a very competitive business and that if we are to attract the very best of staff then we have to offer the right kind of encouragement, training and rewards. We believe we can do this with greater sensitivity than many of the bigger pub companies because of the scale of our

operation. A lot of our managers and tenants have come to us from bigger breweries. Very few express any desire to return. They feel they have a real opportunity to express their views here and that they play an active part in developing their own roles. Creating a strong relationship with the people who run our pubs allows us to get closer to meeting our customer's needs and this gives us yet another way of establishing a competitive advantage." Whether joining the Company's 12 week in-house scheme for trainee managers or arriving as experienced licensees, all new employees receive a personal training programme to ensure they are equipped and prepared to reach their full potential. Modern Apprenticeships and National Vocational Qualifications (NVQ's) as vehicles for those seeking a career in the Licensed Trade, have been enthusiastically embraced by Everards. A link with Wilmorton College at Derby means they now have some 200 retail employees involved in extensive programme of vocational education. This is linked directly to pay awards and from this system Everards hopes to develop an increasing number of "home-grown" managers. Everards tenancies are operated under traditional, three-year agreements. The company takes pride in the relationship it maintains with its tenants and provides a wide range of support to help them to develop their businesses. Ambitious individuals, seeking a career with an established brewery, which demonstrates a long-term attitude to business and a positive attitude towards managers, staff and tenants, would find it hard to find a better partnership than Everards.

tenants buy in supplies will affect the profitability of the business and needs to be carefully assessed.

When the government investigated the licensed trade in 1988 it made various recommendations. This resulted in most of the national brewers giving up on traditional tenancies, although most regional and local breweries still have large numbers of pubs run on tied tenancy. A number of new companies were then set up to buy the large numbers of pubs that the national brewers were selling (these companies are colloquially known as 'PubCos'). In the main, they also run their pubs under tied tenancy. They are not brewers, but have trading agreements with one or more brewers and their tenants are given a list of products that they must buy via the 'PubCo' in a virtually identical manner to the traditional brewer's tied tenancy.

Modern long leases

The national brewers, and some regionals, have all followed the trail blazed by Grand Metropolitan in 1988 when it created the 20-year Inntrepreneur full-repairing leases. These vary from traditional tenancies in a number of important ways. The tie is generally only for beer (with provision for a guest ale in some cases), although some are totally free of tie. The lessee is free to buy wines and spirits where he wishes, and there is no tie in respect of gaming and other machines. The most important difference, however, is that the lessee, as well as being responsible for the profits or losses of the business, is able to sell the

business for what it is worth – good news for the successful licensee, but bad news for the unsuccessful lessee who has to find someone to take a loss-making business off his hands! (With a traditional tenancy it is the brewery's job to find your successor when you decide to go.)

The average leasehold pub turns over £3–5000 a week, and leases sell for an average of around £50,000, although the majority sell for £20/30,000 and a very small number for over £100,000.

Free houses

A little under one-third of the country's pubs are owned outright by the licensee, creating the stereotype of the thatched country pub with roses round the door. However, there are now many urban free houses as well – remember, the Rover's Return was owned by Newton & Ridley until Jack and Vera bought the freehold. Similarly, the Mitchell family bought the freehold of the Queen Vic in 1993.

Free houses are generally, but not always, the lowest-trading pubs because their barrelage does not warrant them being owned by a brewer or a PubCo. Average free house turnover is between £2–4000 a week.

HOW DO I GO ABOUT LOOKING FOR THE KIND OF PUB THAT WOULD MOST SUIT ME?

Managed

There are many avenues to try. The two licensed newspapers, *The Publican* (weekly) and *The Licensee* (Mondays and Thursdays) carry recruitment advertising; they can both be ordered through your news-agent. The bigger companies run their own training schemes; their addresses are published in the *Brewery Manual*, published by Hampton and available through your local library. Or you could approach local pub managers, who will be able to give you the name and address of their head offices.

Tenancies, leases and free houses

Again, the two main publications carry advertisements, as do *Dalton's Weekly* and *Caterer & Hotelkeeper*. Most of the advertisements, however, will not have been be placed by brewers and PubCos but by agencies, some-times known as brokers.

Tenancy brokers have been around for over 150 years. Brewers and Pub-Cos generally give letting informa-tion to around half-a-dozen brokers, who disseminate it to interested parties. Applicants for pub tenancies generally first attend an interview with one or more brokers. As well as completing an application form they will be given basic information as to how the system works, how to draft a business plan, and how to present their ideas and personality to the brewer or PubCo when they find a pub they like. The broker will also act for the tenant on his 'ingoing' to the pub. Brokers generally take their fee from the ingoing tenant.

Agencies which deal with the sale of freehold pubs are generally different firms. Agencies generally act for the vendor, preparing details in much the same way as an estate agent but in addition supplying information on the accounts of the business, licencing, planning, etc. Most free houses are sold by a relatively few well-known agencies that specialise in the trade. They therefore have a wide variety of pubs on offer and can supply good advice to the uninitiated. You are recom-mended to visit the offices of two or three agencies, by appointment, to take advantage of this advice.

The sale of leases is handled both by tenancy brokers and free house agencies, although increasingly it is seen as a marketing job to be given to the larger specialist agencies: my own company, Fleurets, is one of the few to deal with freeholds, tenancies and leases.

HOW CAN I TELL, FROM THE INFORMATION I RECEIVE, WHETHER I'VE FOUND THE RIGHT PUB?

Managed

You will be an employee. Your main income will be paid as wages. It will be up to you to obtain as much trading information as you can so that you can decide whether your bonus is likely to amount to some-thing or nothing.

Tenancies

When you take a tenancy your only relationship is with the owner of the pub. You do not 'buy the business' from the previous tenants, so you have no right to see their books, accounts or VAT records. Often the only information you will be given will be in the form of 'barrels' of beer supplied by the owner of the pub to the previous tenants. These supply figures may be up to 12 months out of date (and most businesses drop off once the tenant has decided to go). They may not include guest beers, wines and spirits, food or machine take.

A prospective tenant will need to construct a shadow profit-and-loss account and would do well to take advice at this stage. His broker will be able to give basic advice like how to calculate the conversion of a barrel of beer into takings. But with many pubs now doing as much as 50 per cent food trade, guesstimates could be way out. Prospective tenants would therefore do well to take advice (at the appropriate fee) from a professional licensed property valuer, accountant or stocktaker. At the very least he should be guided by an experienced publican or compare the pub on busy and quiet nights to two or three others where trading figures are available and which might provide reliable guidance.

Free houses and leases

Where these are being sold by a publican you will generally be asked to pay a price that includes goodwill – that is, you are buying a business as well as a building. The better the business, the more you will be asked to pay. If you are paying more than the building (or lease) and the trade furniture is worth, you have a right to be provided with up-to-date proven accounts. However it is up to you to ask for them and to have them vetted carefully by an accountant or valuer.

If you are borrowing money the lender will generally commission a Business Appraisal Report. The valuer preparing this will look at existing accounts and make a shrewd judgement as to whether the business ought to have been making more or less money than shown in the accounts. The lender will only be concerned to know that the business is worth more than he is lending, but even if you are borrowing little or nothing you should consider having your own Business Appraisal Report carried out (Fleurets does these for a fee starting at £600 plus VAT. This could prove a very wise investment).

If the accounts are out of date you should consider carefully whether business is likely to have fallen since they were completed, and by how much. You may consider asking to see recent VAT returns, or insist that later accounts are prepared and audited before you commit yourself.

Some pubs are sold or leased by breweries or PubCos without the benefit of accounts (often because the pubs were previously let to tied tenants and no accounts are available). These will generally be cheaper because you are not paying for goodwill. They may look like a bargain, but remember that it may take a while to build up the business, during which you may make losses which must be weighed against the savings in capital cost.

WHAT TRADING INFORMATION DO I NEED TO EXTRACT FROM ANY BOOKS I WILL BE SHOWN?

The most important figure is turnover. Everything stems from how much is put into the till to begin with.

Accounts are always shown with VAT excluded. But weekly takings are often shown inclusive of VAT as the amount paid into the till. This is a most important point to remember. If you are shown accounts a year out of date with a turnover of £100,000, and then takings for the last 12 months showing a weekly turnover of £2200 you may think that turnover has risen (52 × £2200 = £114,400), whereas in fact it will have fallen to a net-of-VAT figure of £97,362.

You also need to consider if the accounts show the full turnover. Often catering is a separate business run by a spouse. Sometimes staff or a window cleaner are paid out of the till. Sometimes, heaven forbid, a licensee may even pay for his gambling, holidays or new shoes out of the till. The gross profit margin often gives a hint as to how much should be shown on the takings line, as most operators are keen to claim all their 'inputs' against tax even if they don't always show all the takings.

Beware the seller who has more than one business and who may artificially inflate the takings figures of the business he is selling with money from one he is retaining. An astute adviser will be able to give you pointers on the amounts spent on major outgoings such as wages, light, heat, rent and rates compared to what he would expect to see for an average business.

This could direct you to the consideration of a business that has an excellent turnover but poor profits due to a 'pile it high, sell it cheap' policy or perhaps rent, rates and other costs that impinge on profitability.

Often accounts are prepared with the main aim of depressing profits and thereby saving tax. Quite legitimate expenses such as depreciation, private use of car, wages and pension payments made to the owners can be added back. Unusual levels of outgoings for major repairs may need to be averaged over several years. Out-of-date accounts may show a rent that has since been increased. A valuer will produce what is known as an 'adjusted net profit' to reflect what the purchaser is likely to achieve as opposed to what the audited accounts actually show.

HOW CAN I TELL IF THE PRICE IS RIGHT? WHO SHOULD I TURN TO FOR ADVICE, AND WHAT SORT OF ADVICE SHOULD I RECEIVE?

Managed houses

Other than a security bond (possibly), you should not expect to have to make any investment.

Tenancies

You buy furniture and stock at valuation, and you pay a security deposit that earns interest and is refundable (subject to your having paid all your bills) at the end of your tenancy. The tenancy details you are given will also have an 'estimated ingoing' figure that may include fees or working capital. Once you are accepted as the 'ingoing tenant' your broker will act on your behalf in negotiating the best price for the furniture and stock.

Leases and free houses

Before you rush into anything you are best advised to look around.

After four to six weeks looking at three or four properties each weekend, you will establish a 'feel for the market' – ie, what you will be expected to pay for the sort of pub you wish to buy.

Essentially, price is determined by demand. A pretty pub with good living accommodation in a sought-after area will command a high multiplier of the adjusted net profit.

But don't be fooled by asking prices. Different agents have different policies. Agencies which ask the vendor to contribute to the cost of advertising can afford to have large numbers of properties on their books at prices dictated by the vendors, however unrealistic. But the vendor is committed because he has spent his own money, and eventually the pub will sell for a price the market will bear. Others, including my own company, charge on an all-inclusive, no sale/no fee basis. Since these agents pay for the advertising they are keen to get properties on to the market at or very close to a price they believe will be achievable.

Your mortgage broker is often a good source of advice, in that he will tell you whether you can afford to buy the pub of your dreams. This is not the same as telling you what the pub is worth, but it will save you wasting your time. A valuer acting for your lender, for you, or for both, is the only person who can really tell you if the price is right. Some agents, including Fleurets, have separate valuation departments that can advise you in respect of pubs being bought through other agents (although do beware of conflicts of interest).

If you intend raising a mortgage be sure that your valuer is approved by your chosen lender or lenders, or you could end up paying for two valuations, and be sure your chosen valuer really specialises in pubs in the area. But remember, a valuation is not a building survey and you will probably need a report on the building from a building surveyor as well (both the surveyor and the valuer are likely to be members of the RICS – Royal Institution of Chartered Surveyors – but it is unlikely that one person will have the necessary expertise to do both jobs properly).

WHAT MARKET DOES THE PUB I HAVE CHOSEN SET OUT TO SERVE? HOW WELL DOES IT SUCCEED? IS THE PUB APPROPRIATE TO MY AMBITIONS? HOW DO I ASSESS THE LOCAL MARKET?

If we think back to our 80:20 success ratio, there is another big mistake to be avoided. That is, trying to turn a successful pub into something it is not.

If you take a pub that is the successful hub of the village's sporting life, you will have paid a price or a rent that reflects the trade enjoyed. It is very high risk to try to create a food trade either in addition to or instead of beer-bashing laddish trade.

Pubs have changed over the years, and these changes have all been made by licensees who have taken risks. However those risks are minimised if you either take a pub which is run down (with an accordingly low price or rent) or seek to develop a theme which is already in its infancy. If the pub you are looking

at has not already been operated in the way you have in mind, you should consider carefully whether you will be able to make a successful transition. It may be just too well known in its existing incarnation for you to be able to change it. Would you be better off seeking an alternative pub more to your liking?

Look at what is already being provided in the area. Every area needs a variety of pubs: some young people's music venues, some older folks' venues for food or games, some for gays, some for bikers, maybe even some for gay bikers. But the narrower the market you want to target, the better you must be. You also need to be very good to provide 'yet another pub specialising in . . .' in an area already overloaded with similar outlets.

I have always found assessing the local market one of the most enjoyable parts of my job, involving as it does sitting on many barstools chatting up many barmaids (politically incorrect as this may be!). A 'market' can vary according to the type of pub and its location. For a quality food house it can be some dozens of villages over a 15-mile radius, the whole of a market town, or a number of backstreets in a large city.

When 'assessing' you are checking on a number of factors: what is being well provided locally and where are the gaps in the market; which pubs are 'over-trading', from which you could expect to take trade; which pubs are currently poorly run, decorated or furnished but which may provide stronger competition in the near future; what prices can be sustained by the local economy.

You will also be looking at your target market. How many potential customers are there? Is potential custom growing or shrinking? Are local employers taking on staff or rumoured to be closing down?

This is a job you may share with professional advisers. You may have access to invaluable local knowledge. A professional valuer may have access to trade figures at local competitor outlets that could assist in your estimation of the potential of the pub you are interested in. An expert valuer could also use publicly available figures from the rating authority to provide an estimate of recent trade at all the pubs round and about.

HOW DO I SET ABOUT FINANCING THE COST OF MY PUB?

Tenancy ingoings

Most brewers and PubCos expect the ingoings for a tenancy to be financed from unborrowed cash. As I say, you are only buying furniture and stock. You are not acquiring a business that can be sold and will have no previous accounts to go on, so a bank is unlikely to lend money in any event. The average ingoing is £10–20,000 – not much more than the cost of the average new car, yet it will provide both a home and a business. Potential tenants should have a minimum of £5000 cash.

Lease premium

New-issue leases direct from brewers or PubCos work just like tenancies, in that the lessee buys inventory and stock and sometimes pays a deposit. Old leases coming up for assignment are sold at prices negotiated by the incoming and outgoing lessees. It is difficult but not impossible to raise a bank loan against a pub lease. It is more usual to put up some form of security (perhaps a second charge against a private house) while using the accounts of the pub business as proof to the bank that the borrower can afford to repay the loan. Brewers of course will not be interested in lending against tied leases, although there are some free-of-tie leases that could provide security for a free trade loan.

Leases can be had for very little money. Most sell for £20–30,000; a few fetch over £100,000, but these are likely to show a potential income of £50-100,000 a year.

Free house purchase

Freeholds have traditionally sold at one and a half times turnover because, depending on interest rates, a business can generally support a loan of around one to one and a quarter times turnover. Banks have aimed to loan only around two-thirds of the purchase price, with the balance coming from the purchaser's own resources. In addition to funding the other third, the purchaser will need money for stock cashflow and possible improvements. It does not pay to be underfunded when starting a business.

Let us consider two alternatives. Thus it can be seen that, on paper at least, the buyer of a run-down pub needs more cash than the buyer of an existing success. In practice such pubs are often bought by people who are able to do much of the renovation themselves, and will be funded over a period of time, per-

haps taking a second loan from a brewery. I have made no allowance for the VAT payable as this is refundable to the business; although it has to be found on day one it can be reused as working or development capital when it is reclaimed.

Finance for buying a free house mainly comes from banks, which require a business viability study as well as a building survey. Brewers still provide free trade loans, but increasingly these are used to 'top up' bank loans or for development capital when the owner wishes to build an extension. Brewery loans for the purchase of free houses are most prevalent in the north of England, where a higher proportion of sales will come from beer.

WOULD A LOAN TIE BE APPROPRIATE FOR A FREE HOUSE?

When interest rates are low and available discounts on beer are high, it is unusual for a free trade loan to be the best source of finance for the purchase of a free house. There are exceptions, but brewery finance is more usually used in small doses over short periods.

In our first example above, the prospective purchaser may only have £90,000 cash. To enable him to buy he would borrow £16,000 on second charge from a brewery but would aim to pay this off as soon as possible because he will be better off claiming discounts on beer supplies. However, without the brewery loan he would either have been unable to buy or would have started trading in a dangerously tight financial position.

(a) An immaculate, well-maintained, furnished and decorated free house with a current proven turnover of £200,000 and a net profit of £50,000.

Purchase price 5½ times net profit	=	£275,000
Bank loan of 70 per cent	=	£192,500
Cash required by buyer	=	£82,500
Plus stock	=	£5,000
Plus fees for solicitor, survey	=	£8,250
Plus cash in hand	=	£10,000
Purchaser's total requirement	=	£105,750

In this case, the buyer needed cash resources amounting to 38.5 per cent of the purchase price.

(b) Run-down pub being bought from a brewery. Needs £30,000 spent on structure, £20,000 on new inventory, £10,000 on decorations. Likely to take £150,000, but will take 12 months to reach this level.

Purchase price	=	£100,000
Bank loan of 60 per cent	=	£60,000
Cash required by buyer	=	£40,000
Plus stock	=	£2,000
Plus fees	=	£5,000
Improvements as above	=	£60,000
Six months' losses	=	£30,000
Living expenses for a year	=	£10,000
Purchaser's total requirement	=	£147,000

BUSINESS PLANS, CASHFLOW FORECASTS, AND INDEPENDENT FINANCIAL ADVICE

All lenders will require business plans and cashflow forecasts. Even if you are fortunate enough not to need other people's money or are taking a tenancy or a low-priced lease, you would be well advised to prepare these plans for your own use. In any event, landlords are likely to want to see them from applicants for tenancies and leases.

There are professional firms that will produce business plans and cashflows for you, but many are 'off the peg' financial models that you will have to adapt to the business you intend to run. It is also import-ant that you understand what has been produced for you and what to do to turn paper into profits. Training courses will tell you the basics so that you can work with the professionals to achieve results.

A good mortgage broker will usually work through a business plan with a potential buyer as it will form part of the application for the loan. Otherwise you will do well to get a recommendation on a stocktaker and/or accountant who specialises in the licensed trade. Your agent, mortgage broker or even a friendly local licensee should be in a position to recommend one.

Accountants often specialise: you want one who already handles a large number of public house accounts.

Similarly, a good stocktaker can be a provider of good, relatively cheap advice both before you buy and, most important, in the first few months of running your business.

WHAT SOLICITORS TO USE?

I think you've got the message by now: use specialists. You need specialist valuers, agents/brokers, accountants, mortgage brokers and stocktakers. Similarly, the solicitor who was jolly good for your mum's holiday claim or your brother's fraud case is unlikely to be much use when you are buying your pub.

Solicitors charge by the hour. One who doesn't know what he's doing is likely to take twice as long – and charge twice as much! Solicitors need to know how to tie in the dates of the transfer of the licence with exchange and completion of the sale. Regular dealings with those providing mortgage funds will also smooth the path.

At Fleurets we have two or three solicitors in each region who we are able to recommend on the basis of a combination of speed, efficiency and cost. Agents are probably in the best position to judge these factors.

CONCLUSION

I trust I have given you food for thought. Most of what I've said may sound off-putting. If you still want to run a pub you should be much better equipped to do so once you have read this book. But don't forget, it is no use just seeking advice – you must act on it. Good luck! I hope you buy your first pub through Fleurets.

Legal Notes

Without doubt anyone interested in acquiring a public house should seek guidance from professional advisers experienced in the area of licensed premises.

You should consult:

- ◆ a surveyor who will check out the property
- ◆ an accountant to assess the viability of the figures and prepare cash flow forecasts and a business plan

- ◆ a solicitor to handle the lease/conveyancing formalities and the transfer of the Liquor Licence.

Ask as many questions of the seller as possible. If your questions are not answered to your complete satisfaction, then walk away.

Visit the premises as much as possible prior to making any commitment. Watch carefully what trade is like. Ensure that you visit at different hours of the day and different days of the week to get an overall feel for the business and to assess the pub's potential. Ask locals for their views. Ask the police if they are aware of any problems. Consult representatives of the local authority to establish whether there are any noise complaints or concerns of a similar nature. Weigh up the opposition and carefully consider what the potential is and whether your future plans for development are realistic.

APPLYING FOR A LICENCE

Where an application is for a new licence, the recommended approach is to consult a solicitor familiar with liquor licensing. Be careful, as this is very much a specialist field, so seek out the licensing specialists in your area for the best advice.

Where there is already a licence you can apply for a transfer of the licence. Application must be made in prescribed form to the Clerk to the Licensing Justices, the police, the local authority and any parish or district council (Schedule 1 Licensing Act 1964).

You will have to satisfy the police and court that you are a fit and proper person to hold a Justices' Licence. Typically this will involve a meeting with the local police licensing officer, who will check for any criminal convictions and carry out an interview with a view to establishing whether you are familiar with the licensing laws. Criminal convictions may or may not be a

bar to obtaining a licence, depending upon when and in what circumstances the convictions arose, the severity of the matters involved and the attitude of the local police and justices. But failure to disclose immediately any conviction (no matter how irrelevant you may consider it to be) is always fatal to any licence application. The police will expect you to be frank and truthful.

If for any reason your application is opposed you can present your application to the magistrates, who will listen to the arguments both for and against. They will then decide whether or not to grant a transfer. There is a right of appeal against refusal to the Crown Court within 21 days of the date of the decision.

TRADING DURING THE TRANSFER OF A LICENCE

When a licensee leaves, then under new flexible arrangements introduced to aid the continuity of the business an application can be made to the Magistrates' Court for an Interim Authority which, if granted, lasts for 28 days. Provided that the application is made within seven days of the licensee leaving the premises, the applicant on making the application will automatically possess 'deemed' authority to run the premises – effectively becoming the licensee immediately. This authority will last for up to 14 days provided the police do not object.

Once granted, the Interim Authority means that the applicant is treated under the licensing laws as if he were the holder of the licence.

Unlike the protection order, an Interim Authority may be sought by a person – probably a brewery area manager or a relief manager – who does not intend to apply for a transfer of the licence to himself. When application for transfer is made following the grant of an Interim Authority, the Interim Authority will not cease until the transfer is completed. It does not matter that the holder of the Interim Authority is not the person who applies for the transfer of the licence.

An application for an Interim Authority, as it is often to cover a sudden departure, does not have to wait for a Licensing Justices' transfer session: it can also be heard by a Magistrates' Court or may even be granted in certain circumstances by the Clerk to the Licensing Justices.

Another new procedure now available to Licensing Justices is to approve a person as a Prospective Licensee of named premises. The justices need to be satisfied that the applicant is a fit and proper person and is not disqualified from holding a Justices' Licence. Once approved, then should an event occur which would allow the Licensing Justices to transfer the licence, for example the licensee leaving the premises, the approved Prospective Licensee may serve a notice on the Clerk to the Licensing Justices and also the police and may take over the running of the premises without a court hearing, effectively becoming the licensee.

Application for approval of a Prospective Licensee is made to the Licensing Justices by giving 21 days' notice of the application. The notice must be displayed on the premises to which the application relates and in a newspaper circulating in the district prior to the hearing of the application.

TRAINING FOR THE TRADE

Andrew Palmer

Licensed retailing can give the right people – young or mature, male or female – a hugely varied and fulfilling career; and if you prove yourself, you can be offered challenging responsibilities at an early stage.

But it's training that makes the difference between success and failure; and the industry has seen a sea change in recent years in its attitude towards training and the delivering of business skills to licensees and staff. Training provides the tools for success in a happy, rewarding career in a challenging, people-oriented industry.

The current upsurge in the availability of highly pertinent training, with qualifications recognised throughout the country, is revolutionising the industry and has been driven by the professional body for licensees, staff and industry suppliers, the British Institute of Innkeeping (BII).

Traditionally, the public has never understood what is involved in

running a pub, and in-depth training has not been thought of as necessary.

In fact just about everybody who hasn't tried it thinks they instinctively know how to run a great pub. It would be difficult to find a single regular of the 60,000 or so pubs up and down the country who does not sincerely believe that if only they were handed the keys to a pub – any pub – it would be a right money spinner. And what a cosy life, too!

'All you've got to do is smile, keep the beer fresh and the loos clean, stick the wife in the kitchen, and recruit an attractive bar maid,' goes the myth. 'Then you open the door and watch the trade roll in.'

Anyone who still believes that has an interesting three months or so to look forward to: bankruptcy, marriage break-up, poor health. . . None of these consequences is unusual among those who, before taking a pub, didn't research the local market, sweat over a realistic one-, three-, and five-year business plan, train the staff in customer care, or use all the training support available to learn motivational techniques and gain exemplary staff performance.

Time was when you retired to a pub. Many licensees would be ex-forces or policemen who had picked up their gratuity, done the minimum of training offered by brewers (a bit of cellarmanship and general book-keeping).

Times have changed. The hard economic climate and growing competition from high standard leisure alternatives mean that licensees now work in one of the harshest and least forgiving trading climates any sector of commerce has seen.

Rents are at a historical high, yet people are drinking less beer – consumption has declined almost annually since 1978 due to the decline of heavy industry, the trend towards home entertainment and concerns about health.

Business rates, excise duty, wages, the cost of compliance with health and safety and employment legislation all cheerfully rise each year. Pub professionals from junior staff to licensees must master every retailing discipline – purchasing, recruitment, financial control, marketing – to ensure they run a profitable unit.

THE RESPONSIBILITY

How many careers are there where almost immediately you may be put in charge of an established business with annual sales of £200,000-plus?

You have total responsibility for purchasing everything, from beer to dry goods to garden furniture. You must recruit and motivate staff, you must know, or at least know where to find out the basics of food costing and control, food hygiene and processing procedures, drinks product knowledge, cellar skills, licensing law, gaming and betting legislation, rights of entry, refusing entry and service, weights and measures, and a host of other specialist topics.

You are the financial director, and must understand cash flow and working capital, cash control, VAT, budgets, stocktaking and information systems.

Employment issues are of prime importance to licensees, with their high proportion of casual staff and staff turnover. What are the rights of employees; how do you draw up their statement of terms and conditions; are part-time staff entitled to the same conditions as full-time (yes, due to recent legislation), what about disciplining staff and unfair dismissal, with all the problems of possible claims against you? Do you understand the laws on racial, disability and sexual discrimination and how to stay within them? What about statutory maternity benefits and transfers of undertakings?

We haven't even covered marketing, merchandising and best practice in selling. Nor have we looked at the intricacies of health and safety procedures, Control of Substances Hazardous to Health Regulations 1988, the reporting and recording of accidents, risk assessment for employees and customers, the regulations concerning electricity, noise, fire and first aid.

In short, there's a great deal to running a pub that is profitable, where customers actually enjoy parting with their hard-earned cash, and where staff are happy and productive.

In licensed retailing you must prepare for success, and that means training. Training makes the difference between failure and an enjoyable and rewarding career. It is the key to success.

WHAT TRAINING IS AVAILABLE?

If you want to understand more about a successful career in licensed retailing then consult the BII. It exists to guide people towards pertinent training and provide a network that may support you.

The BII has varying levels of membership, from Graduate Member upwards. It has worked with the industry, the Home Office and Licensing Justices' national bodies to develop a widely recognised and admired progressive series of qualifications which arm licensees with the knowledge and skills required for success. These include the following.

The BII Certificate of Induction Examination

This is a three-day training course that provides a knowledge of the basic technicalities and skills required in running a pub. It consists of two parts, and candidates must pass both to be certificated and allowed to apply for graduate membership of the Institute.

Part one tests the candidate's knowledge and understanding of:

◆ the health and safety legal framework, and the particular responsibilities placed upon licensees and staff by various Acts and Regulations

◆ the practical and legal requirements of employing paid staff
◆ the essentials of bar service
◆ the essentials of cellar and stock management
◆ the administration and operation of a catering service
◆ basic principles of financial control and legal financial liabilities
◆ maximisation of sales/profits through the appropriate marketing of the house and its products
◆ the importance of customer service to the business.

Part two (the National Licensee's Certificate) tests the candidate's knowledge and understanding of:

◆ Justices' Licences and other types of licence; permitted hours; young persons; employment of young persons; gaming, betting and lotteries; exclusion orders; public entertainment; the Weights and Measures Act (Intoxicating Liquor) Order 1988 and other related laws; sale of tobacco; credit; notices
◆ the social responsibilities of licences covering alcohol, drinking and driving, prevention of and dealing with violence, proof of age, drugs, door staff, pubwatch.

The National Licensee's Certificate is also available as a stand-alone qualification. Many Licensing Justices prefer new applicants for licences to hold this certificate as proof that they understand basic law and responsibilities.

The NLC is also available as a stand alone qualification, obtained by sitting a short multiple choice exam. Those without access to

Enter A Winning Partnership

If you are professional and ambitious, ready to apply innovative marketing ideas and techniques, plus sound business practices in running your pub, Morland is your ideal partner.

As the second oldest independent regional brewer in the country, Morland has a long history of helping licensees to serve their community and profit from their investment. The Tenancy Division is currently made up of 300 pubs situated in the South East, the majority of which trade under Morland's attractive 21 Year Lease. An experienced team of Business Development Managers support the tenanted estate. Their personal commitment and attention to detail give Morland tenants the confidence to carry their businesses forward which is essential for success in today's competitive market.

There are many recent examples of entrepreneurial licensees putting their confidence in Morland and its lease with fantastic results. The partnership offered allows both experienced licensees and those new to the trade to maximise their potential as profitable operators. We've spoken to Gerald Wolfenden, licensee of Morland's current Pub of the Year - The White Hart, Chalfont St Giles, to get some first hand advice for those considering a career in the licensed trade.

Learn the basics......

Gerald begins by saying, "I think the first thing that anyone who is considering running a pub for a living should do is to spend some time working for a licensee and living on the premises. Even if it is just for a week, it will give you a good feel for what is involved. I found that, despite having worked on the sales and marketing side of the licensed trade for 12 years, I was still surprised by just how hard you have to work to build up and maintain a successful pub. Lots of stamina and enthusiasm are called for and if you don't like dealing with people then a pub is certainly not the right place for you to be."

Plan rigorously......

Having experienced pub life from behind the bar, and assuming you haven't changed your mind in the meantime, you are now in a good position to start pulling together your business plan and talking to brewers about prospective pubs.

Gerald stresses that, "Attention to detail is critical at this stage. Your plans should be detailed so that you can start as you mean to go on. Pay particular attention to choosing a pub and a brewer (I can personally recommend

Choose a pub that can meet your expectations

Morland!) who can meet your expectations and be just as critical when it comes to recruiting staff and suppliers."

"To achieve the goals you have set for your business you will inevitably have to invest and you will need to make sure you have enough money to realise your pub's potential. In today's market you cannot, in my view, ignore the role food has to play in your offering. Decide who you want your pub and its menus to attract and then make sure that everything else you do helps to bring your target market through the door."

Be there......

Successful licensees do not work hard for a couple of years and then fade into the background leaving the running of their pub to paid employees. Nobody will be as passionate about your business as you are and it is therefore vital that you keep a close eye on how your pub is developing. It is also worth remembering that you, as the landlord and owner of the business, are one of the main reasons why customers choose to visit your pub. Gerald explains, "Unlike most modern businesses where the branch manager is the most senior person on the premises, the pub is special because very often the first person the customer sees is the licensee, the owner of the business. I think being there for your customers is key. Regulars do expect to be greeted by you and they will be disappointed if you are seldom there."

Take time out......

This is not to say that you must chain yourself to the bar every single night of the week. Gerald ends by saying, "Quality time away from your pub is a must. It allows you to recharge your batteries, enjoy some of your hard earned profits, and pursue interests that are totally unrelated to the pub trade. If you strike the balance correctly you will be quite capable of running a busy, successful business which will reap both financial and personal rewards for you and your staff. It is an exciting business which I can thoroughly recommend to all those who enjoy hard work and thrive on people."

If you would like to know more about becoming a Morland lessee, please phone Cathy Dean (01235 540486) for an information pack.

As a licensee you need to be there for your customers

company training schemes can take a short course leading up to the exam, or simply buy a handbook from the BII.

The *Handbook for the National Licensee's Certificate*, published by the National Licensee's Certificate Awarding Body (NLCAB) at the same address as the BII, can be used in conjunction with a training course or as a self-study aid for those who simply wish to sit the exam.

The Qualifying Exam

The Qualifying Exam (QE) of the BII is a more in-depth qualification, with laying emphasis on management skills and their application.

The QE consists of five parts and requires a minimum of five days training followed by an exam. Candidates who fail one of the tests have to retake the failed test only.

Part one tests the candidate's knowledge and understanding of health and safety at work; drinks service; financial control; cash control and security; cellar management; storage and stock control; food service.

Part two is the National Licensee's Certificate (see above).

Part three tests the candidate's knowledge and understanding of selling skills; merchandising; customer care; management of internal and external areas; employment legislation; staffing; marketing; management skills.

Part four tests the candidate's knowledge and understanding of food safety and hygiene.

Part five is a practical exam and consists of tests in recruitment, training and cellar fault identification.

Advanced qualifications

The BII has developed a series of pioneering business-building qualifications aimed at helping licensees and senior staff in pubs and pub/restaurants run a more profitable business.

These new qualifications will for the first time achieve a set national standard in their disciplines and will be recognised by employers throughout the hospitality industry.

The new qualifications are:

1. Catering Management Certificate
2. Financial Management Certificate
3. Business Development Certificate
4. Advanced Leadership and Motivation Certificate
5. Customer Service Management Certificate
6. Cellar Management Certificate
7. Spirits Retail Certificate
8. Wine Retail Certificate.

Although courses in these disciplines have long been widely available, the BII's new accredited courses address the need for a uniform standard set and approved by the industry.

In order to maintain high standards the BII is accrediting individual named trainers – not organisations – to run each of the courses. The trainers must be re-accredited each year.

Pitched at management level, the Advanced Qualifications have been developed by the BII in conjunction with licensees and management from leading brewers and pub groups. Each course has been developed by subject experts guided by an industry steering group, and will usually take two or three days. The emphasis is on practical exercises and participation by delegates, and each course concludes with a certificate based on assessment and/or an exam.

Let us look at each certificate in detail.

Catering Management Certificate

This certificate is suitable for licensees new to catering operations or experienced practitioners wanting to improve the business. It is not about improving cookery skills, but about managing all aspects of developing and running a profitable and effective pub catering operation.

The three-day course is specifically written for pubs and is based on an understanding of pub catering, not other catering establishments or hotels.

Licensees will learn how to improve the quality of food, speed of service and use of equipment. They will understand key marketing techniques and be stimulated into better menu planning and providing new ideas for food.

Spilt into four key areas, the course covers:

◆ introduction to the business
◆ production management
◆ sales, service and promotion
◆ overall management.

Financial Management Certificate

Often the closest licensees get to financial management is when they compile figures or paperwork at the end of a quarter and pack them off to the accountant to produce something to satisfy the bank manager. This is not financial control.

This three-day course demystifies a complex subject and gives licensees confidence in using financial controls to run a better business. It will equip licensees with the basic financial skills needed to manage the entirety of a cash-based business and the emphasis is on efficient financial control and planning, and reducing financial service charges (banking, accountant's fees).

Components of the course include:

◆ calculating VAT and completing your own returns
◆ recording weekly revenue and expenses sheets and dealing with invoices, machine takings and till receipts
◆ calculating gross profit, cost price and retail prices on products
◆ putting together your own profit and loss account and setting budgets
◆ stock control and how to identify stock loss and take preventative measures
◆ setting sales targets and analysing the success of promotional events
◆ understanding break-even analysis and how to calculate revenue levels to cover your costs.

Business Development Certificate

This will give licensees the basic tools to help them assess the potential of their business and produce a strategy to achieve realistic objectives.

Starting with the widely-used SWOT analysis (strengths, weaknesses, opportunities, threats), delegates will over three days appraise the positioning of their pub and be made aware of demographic information available from key sources that gives a factual understanding of their local market and its potential needs.

Delegates write a concise business plan that includes realistic goals, strategy, timetables and resource planning. Intensely practical, the course aims to simplify business planning and strategy so that it can be used effectively in day-to-day management to achieve business goals.

Advanced Leadership and Motivation Certificate

The two-day intensive course aims to give practical skills in leading a workforce to achieve greater sales and profitability. Licensees focus on:

◆ the introduction of skills to encourage the formulation of precise business objectives and a system to measure success or shortfalls
◆ how to encourage the team and individuals through positive leadership and motivational skills to take ownership of those objectives
◆ managing performance in areas ranging from the good to the more difficult, eg attitude, and the specific, such as achievement of sales and profit targets.

Advanced Qualification in Cellar Management and Beer Quality

Serving better beer, cutting unnecessary costs and introducing a proven cellar hygiene system that eliminates the danger of infection are three huge benefits experienced by licensees who have tested the new Advanced Qualification in Cellar Management and Beer Quality.

Designed to make money for licensees by focusing on specific areas of business and setting nationally agreed standards of professionalism, the course lasts one and a half days, and BII members receive a 20 per cent discount off the exam cost of Advanced Qualifications.

With the pivotal importance that quality beer holds in good pubs, it is believed that even experienced licensees will want to take this course as a 'refresher' and to benefit from new procedures developed since their induction training. And, of course, it is a must for newcomers, says the BII.

Advanced Qualification in Spirit Retailing

Experienced licensees and business development managers have warmly praised the practical benefits and profit potential learnt from the BII's new one-day Advanced Qualification in Spirit Retailing. Spirits are the most profitable unit of drink a pub can sell, but the real skill for the successful licensee lies in increasing total wet sales, not simply increasing spirits at the expense of beer or wine.

Like all the Advanced Qualifications, Spirit Retailing addresses a specific area of business and will help even experienced licensees make more profit. In a trade dominated by beer it is important to remember that spirits are a great source of profit, and small, simple adjust-

ments to the back bar can make a huge difference.

Advanced Qualification in Customer Care

The two-day AQ in Customer Service Management is unique. Unlike other customer care courses, the AQ in Customer Service Management does not attempt to prescribe a general formula – not all pubs are branded operations. This AQ will help licensees create a specific customer care strategy that matches the personality of each individual pub and its customer base. If there is one single area of operation that can impact on the bottom line it is customer service. This AQ is an invaluable business tool that aims to help professionals build a better business.

Wine Retail Certificate

This qualification focuses on providing the skills and information required by licensees who wish to promote wine sales in their pubs or bars.

The two-day course includes:

◆ basic product knowledge and wine tasting
◆ how to discern quality from the label
◆ where to buy wines and how to store and serve them correctly
◆ how to compile a wine list and match it to your menu
◆ merchandising and selling techniques
◆ how to pick the most appropriate pricing strategy for your business and your market

◆ eight steps to planning a staff training programme.

To find out more, contact the British Institute of Innkeeping, Park House, 22–24 Park Street, Camberley, Surrey GU15 3PL; tel: 01276 684449.

In a move which makes the Institute the only professional members' organisation to put its reserves back into the market place, from 1998 a minimum £250,000 of Advanced Qualification training will be given free to around 1,500 members over the next five years.

In the first year around 350 members will take the three-day Business Development Certificate worth approximately £250. Other AQs will be covered by the initiative as it is rolled out through training centres across the country. The Better Business Initiative is open to members of the British Institute of Innkeeping.

PART TWO
STOCK IN TRADE

THE UK'S LEADING DRINKS DISTRIBUTOR

Tavern is the largest independent drinks distributor in the UK and supplies beers, ciders, wines, spirits and soft drinks to any outlet that has the freedom to determine its own source of supply.

The company offers an extensive and flexible portfolio of products, backed up by a comprehensive delivery, support and customer service package The company has a distribution network covering the length and breadth of the UK and is a genuine one-stop shop for drinks retailers of all sizes. One delivery, one invoice and with increasingly hectic lifestyles, having just one reliable supplier is a real benefit to the vast majority of businesses. The reasons for this are many, not least the fact that people now need to spend more time focusing on other areas of their business

instead of working the extra hours required to order products from several different suppliers and await deliveries.

Tavern is structured in order to make it the perfect seamless link between customers and suppliers, a link that provides the former with the best service. Its distribution operation serves in excess of 23,000 individual customers throughout the UK enabling the company to achieve a turnover of over £220 Million per annum.

Understanding the needs of the client is the key to a successful business relationship. A Tavern Sales Executive will work with a client towards these needs and goals. Once they are defined, the Sales Executive will assist in the design of a customised and effective strategy.

This can include steering retailers in the right direction in order to provide them with a range of products that will help build their business. That means getting behind established, well supported brands which have a strong consumer loyalty, as well as stocking emerging new brands that are driving the value of the market.

The danger to the independent retailer is that they may end up stocking a whole range of duplicate products all trading on price and ignoring the real opportunities which lie in offering a well balanced range. This demonstrates the need to re-assess their range and cut out the dead wood, slow selling brands and duplications, thereby freeing up valuable shelf space for the 'movers and shakers' in the market which add interest and value to their businesses. This is an area where Tavern can make an enormous difference to a

customer's business, improving the bottom line and ensuring more repeat custom.

Tavern's 47 depot base gives national coverage and can be thought of as an amalgamation of around thirty different businesses, each of them bringing their own specialised local knowledge and expertise so whilst Tavern operates as one highly efficient company, it has not lost that unique awareness of the community and the people that they deal with on a regular basis.

Tavern intend to build on the success that has already been achieved over previous years with a commitment to improving customer service, both through it's employees and systems technology.

Indeed maintaining its focus on a changing market place will ensure that the needs of Tavern's customers, large and small, continue to be met now and into the new millennium.

TAVERN GROUP LIMITED

MERCURY WAY, BARTON DOCK ROAD,
TRAFFORD PARK, MANCHESTER M41 7LQ
TELEPHONE: 0161 864 5000 FACSIMILE: 0161 864 5050

CHAPTER THREE

BEER AND CIDER

Ted Bruning

BEER

Beer sales may not be as high a proportion of turnover as they used to be, but beer is still Britain's most popular alcoholic drink and is still at the very heart of the pub trade.

But what is beer? Put simply, it is the fermented result of adding yeast to a syrup derived from a cereal, usually malted barley, which has been dosed with hops. However, the number of variations in both ingredients and process makes for an almost limitless variety of beers.

Few things say more about a publican than the range and quality of his beers, and nobody should know more about beer than the publican who deals in it. All publicans should make a point of visiting a brewery, and several if they can, until they have a better than working knowledge of the business of brewing: the publicans who really know how to work their beers to best advantage are those with a deep understanding of what is, admittedly, a vast subject.

And it is a truly vast subject: gone are the days when a tied landlord had to stock his brewery's beers and only his brewery's beers, with no reason to know about anything else, and when local people happily drank whatever beer their local pub happened to serve. Today there is a huge range of lagers, bitters, milds, stouts, porters, ice beers, dry beers, even wheat beers, fruit beers, and beers brewed by Belgian monks, to be had from four national brewers, 60-odd old-established regional and local brewers, 300 (and rising) 'micro' brewers, and a growing band of independent importers and wholesalers. There are still pubgoers who ask for 'a pint of lager' or 'a pint of bitter', whatever the weather, the occasion, or the season; but they are fast being outnumbered by knowledgeable consumers who know their beers and choose from a wide repertoire.

Remember: there are few things more galling than facing a customer who knows more than you do about what is supposedly your specialist subject – it happens!

One of the most advanced brewing facilities in the world

Germany is renowned for producing some of the World's finest beers and Henninger - brewed in Frankfurt since 1869 - is one of the German beer industry's top ten selling brands.

In fact, the national drink of Germany is beer, it is rooted in the lifestyle and culture of the people and two out of every five breweries in the world are located there. Although there is no one dominant brand in Germany and competition is intense, Henninger continues to be a successful mass market producer.

The secret of this success lies in the marriage of proven brewing tradition with advanced brewing technology. A traditional emphasis on quality, along with the company's progressive management, is expressed in one of the most advanced brewing facilities in the world. Since 1961, Henninger's brewery tower - a 16,000 ton capacity barley silo - has dominated the Frankfurt skyline and serves as a constant reminder of the town's impressive history of beer production.

The popularity of Henninger can largely be attributed to the ability to meet the high levels of quality demanded by consumers and publicans alike and they realised early on that this could only be achieved by controlling the whole brewing process.

Through a massive investment programme in its Frankfurt brewing facility, Henninger has gained control of the supply and manufacturing chain, a policy which is echoed by the companies mantle - "we do everything ourselves". Quality control starts at the beginning of the brewing process with the selection of the barley seed by the farmer and doesn't end until the beer has been served to the customer.

High levels of quality, purity and taste

Only the purest ingredients are used in the brewing process - the best brewing barley grown under carefully monitored conditions and stored in Henninger's own malthouse, carefully selected hops, pure culture yeast and crystal water - to ensure the consistent high standards of their beer*.

Henninger builds its success on the resulting unique, full-flavoured taste and smooth character that has made it so popular the world over. The famous black label of the brewery is known as a symbol of quality in more than sixty countries world-wide. The beer is

brewed under licence in seven and has already proven itself internationally, with sales of over 3.5 million hectolitres from domestic and export production.

Driven by the popularity of premium German lager and an increased demand for authentic imported products, the prize winning Henninger Premier Pilsner, which launched into the UK in 1997 is well set for commercial success. German beers have long been attributed with high levels of quality, purity and taste and this has created a demand which has enabled Germany to treble its export beer sales. In the past 20 years, sales have risen to 7.75 million hectolitres globally, while the 1.42 million litres** which are sold in Great Britain account for an incredible 27.4% of all UK beer imports.

This incredible success for the German beer industry in the international market demonstrates that there is growing consumer demand for authentic German beers in the UK.

Within months of its UK launch Henninger achieved national off-trade listings with Asda, Bargain Booze and Kwiksave and is continuing to build on that achievement.

Consumers attach a great deal of credibility to German beers and Henninger Permier Pilsner certainly helps to confirm their beliefs.

Publicans are discovering, that by serving high quality beers, they are adding value to their offering and thus helping to encourage repeat trade. A growing number of them are turning to traditional and authentic products, like Henninger.

Supporting publicans

Henninger's commitment to quality and eye for detail is mirrored by

support for their customers. "Satisfying the needs of our customer helps to build loyalty for the brand," says Sarah Shepley, Marketing Director of the UK distributor Shackleford Sales Ltd, "and on-going Henninger promotions will help to increase sales in the longterm as opposed to generating ad -hoc demand."

This dedication to sustained growth is supplemented by on-site and account specific support. The brand is supported with a range of stylish merchandising and POS materials featuring the black and red colour scheme for which Henninger is globally known. The range of support materials includes branded bar trays, wall plaques, glasses, coasters and t-shirts as well as a number of other promotional items.

Henninger is available in loose packed cases of 24 330ml long necked bottles, available direct through Shackleford Sales Ltd.

Henninger complies with the Reinheitsgebot purity law - formed in 1516 - that stipulated that only malts, hops, yeast and water can be used in beer production.

**Source: Foreign Trade Statistics 1995*

TYPES OF BEER

Lager and ale are generally accepted as being subdivisions of beer, so the often-heard term 'beer and lager' is not strictly accurate.

Lager

'Lager' is not a term commonly used on the Continent: most of the beers we British call lagers are descendants of the golden beers first brewed in the early nineteenth century in Pilsen, now in the Czech Republic, and are described in Europe with varying degrees of accuracy as Pilsners or just plain pils.

Good Pilsners are normally around 4.5–5.5 per cent alcohol by volume (abv) and are characterised by the floral aromas and soft, fruity flavours derived from Continental malt and hops. Long conditioning at low temperature should create a smooth, spritzy drink without the metallic tang evident in hastily made examples. A characteristic of matured lagers is that they are well attenuated – that is, all or nearly all the sugar is digested by the yeast, leaving a strong, dry beer suitable for diabetics. Holsten Pils is probably the best-known example.

One of the best lagers, however, does not derive from Pilsen at all, but from Ceske Budejovice or Budwar, another brewing town now in the Czech Republic. Budweiser Budwar is not to be confused with its American namesake (whose lack of taste comes from the use of rice in the mash), and its success in Britain has opened the way for a flood of Czech beers such as Zamek, Radegast, Bohemia, Staropramen, and Pilsner Urquell.

There are many differences between lager and ale. Lagers traditionally use poorer quality strains of barley for malting, so a much more complicated mashing process is needed to extract the fermentable sugars. Traditional lager hops have lower levels of bitterness-producing alpha acids than British hops, and lager yeasts ferment at lower temperatures than ale yeasts. Lagers should mature or condition for much longer than ales ('lager' means, very roughly, 'kept'), and at much lower temperatures, which explains the difference in serving temperature.

These variables all have their effect on flavour characteristics, although they have always been very approximate, and the edges are blurring all the time: many ale brewers now use lager-type hops, for instance; some ales are brewed with lager yeasts; nitrokeg ales and stouts are served at near lager temperatures; and many British lagers condition for less time than a premium bitter does. Nevertheless, the differences in materials and process should add up to appreciable differences in flavour and appearance. Lagers are generally very pale (although there are dark variants) and should have a soft, fruity taste without the long, dry aftertaste common in, say, bitter.

Ale

Ale was the dominant type of beer in Britain until lager (which has been brewed here for well over a century) started being heavily promoted in the 1970s. Pilsner-style lagers now account for around half the British beer market; of the various ale varieties, bitter dominates.

Bitter derives its derivation for the addition of high-alpha hops to the malt syrup or 'wort' early in the brewing process. Hops serve a dual purpose: they confer a whole range of flavours, depending on variety and the point at which they are added to the boil; they are also a good preservative. Standard bitter ranges from 3.5–4 per cent abv, premium or best bitters from 4–4.8 per cent abv, and there are even stronger ales these days which seem to fit the 'bitter' category better than any other, Morland Old Speckled Hen at 5.2 per cent abv being a prominent example. The rise of the guest ale market and the general trading-up process have given premium bitters such as Fuller's London Pride, Marston's Pedigree and Wad-worth 6X dominance over standard bitters.

Mild, sweeter, weaker and less hoppy, was once the favourite of workers both in agriculture and in heavy industry, being a cheap, quenching beer that can be consumed in bulk. Milds – Scotch Ales in the north-east – are usually dark, although there are pale variants including 60/- in Scotland and 'boy's bitter' in the West Country. They usually vary from 2.8–3.5 per cent abv, although there are much stronger variants. Brown ales were originally bottled mild, and since the 1920s there have been two distinct styles – sweet or small browns, such as Mann's, and much stronger north-eastern browns: Newcastle, Maxim and High Level.

Setting The Standard for Automated Line Cleaning

Bill Richardson

It is revelationary that, as we rocket into the 21st Century, the majority of our homes and businesses benefit from the technology that has become such a part of, and eases, our everyday life (such as microwave ovens, dishwashers, and computers) yet a huge number of intelligent Publicans are still trudging up and down to their cellars in their Wellington boots with buckets, goggles and aprons manually flushing out their beerlines in a desperate attempt to pull the perfect pint.

As all Publicans are aware, to get the perfect pint is one thing but to keep it's continuity is another. While there are many influences on the beer one of the most important has to be the integrity and cleanliness of the beerline. Not only is it a hygiene requirement to keep the lines regularly cleaned but also critical to the quality of the beer and, unfortunately, it needs to be undertaken every seven days. Surely, in this age of high technology, the time has come to throw the buckets, goggles and aprons away and apply our time to more rewarding and pleasurable pastimes.

Historically, beerline cleaning has been a time consuming and mundane exercise manually undertaken by the Publican himself and which wasted many pints of perfectly saleable beer. Manual cleaning is not only highly time consuming and frustrating but necessitates the handling of hazardous chemicals and, if not properly controlled and supervised, can lead to prosecution under the Health and Safety at Work Act with Publicans facing fines of up to £20,000 per offence!

For many years various manufacturers (and Publicans themselves) have tried to develop automated beerline cleaning systems to overcome the manual procedure but, until recently, there has not really been one that totally fulfils the needs of the industry. However, this has all just changed whereby automated beerline cleaning has just come of age with the introduction of the most straightforward, manageable, 'no- nonsense' line cleaning system available today from Advanced Beerline Cleaning (ABC), a subsidiary of Cellar Myzer Trading Limited.

Launched at the recent Pub and Bar 98 Trade Exhibition at Olympia the ABC line cleaning system received accolades from the industry. The show proved to be a fantastic vehicle for the launch of the new system with the industry praising the technologically improved approach to automated beerline cleaning systems. The company has already received orders from both the local and international trade far in excess of expectations.

The ABC system provides a simple solution to the age-old problem or beerline cleaning through the installation of a simple yet highly automated unit. The unit's operation is absolutely straightforward in approach whereby (and without the aid of fancy gizmos, gadgets, magnets or magic tricks) it is the only system that automatically cleans and flushes up to 36 beerlines at once with the facility to clean a single line on demand. The unit is totally self-contained and even the chemicals are safely locked within it overcoming the potential risk of visitors to the cellar having an encounter of the caustic kind.

As a self-contained, automated unit the system meets both the COSHH and pressure regulations and effectively and safely replaces the buckets, wellies and goggles. In addition to scrupulously cleaning up to 36 beerlines, the unit provides an intelligent link to the pub's computer system telling the publican when the lines need cleaning, monitoring ullage and providing a complete audit trail of events for stocktakers, management, accountants or Inland Revenue.

The ABC unit has been developed in consultation with brewers and provides a highly cost effective option when compared to other systems. As an example of cost efficiency ABC's system for 4 taps is less than £1,500 fully installed whereas the nearest comparable competitive product is £140 per month (for only 4 taps) and needs commitment to a seven year lease equating to a total cost of £11,760!

Many units have already been successfully installed and Publicans are in agreement that the ABC system requires minimal staff training and eliminates the wasted hours of labour involved in traditional line cleaning, leaving them free to attend to concentrating on the overall profitability of their businesses.

ABC has recognised that many Publicans have their own manual cleaning procedure whereby they have developed different soak times and flushings to give an almost personal touch to the pint. With this in mind the ABC system is almost infinitely programmable to automatically follow the Publican's own methods and routines should he so wish. The system does everything that you could ever do only probably better and definitely without you having to stand around wasting endless hours.

As a highly versatile system, ABC boasts an extensive choice of operations and ensures that lines are cleaned thoroughly, meeting industry standards. The unit is very competitively priced and available in varying options covering basic installations of only one tap and one coupler up to huge establishments with multiple lines and couplers. One of the more expensive options, covering 24 taps and the longest drops, the ABC system will only need the Publican to make an investment of £2,115 for a fully installed system. Most other systems available have to be leased at exorbitant monthly rates far in excess of the amounts that can ever be recouped through claimed savings on beer wastage and, in many cases, after a few months end up being decommissioned. In fact beer wastage claims are viewed as a very cloudy issue by most Publicans as many are able to achieve minimal wastage even when manually cleaning through applying sensible management techniques.

The ABC system can also incorporate Cellar Myzer's unique beer recovery system which genuinely saves up to 95% of the beer in the lines - this alone can save the publican a small fortune when compared to the beer lost with traditional cleaning methods. Traditional methods of line cleaning can lose up to ten pints per line and bearing in mind that the average retail price for a pint is £1.85, licensees are literally flushing money down the drain every week. This is particularly true for larger establishments where long term losses of revenue and potential savings are considerable. Chris Reid, Stock Control Manager of the well-known Buzz Bar, Leicester Square, London has recently had the Cellar Myzer system installed and estimates a saving of £35,000 per year.

Whilst ABC's product is new to the market the company's founders are hardly new to the trade sharing over 60 years experience, both working for major breweries in a technical support environment and the 'pub and club' trade. As such, ABC fully understand the need for service support for the product and is committed to providing service excellence.

Mild sales have declined to no more than 2 per cent of the national market in the 1990s, but there is evidence of a comeback.

Stout was originally 'Stout Porter' – not a fat bag carrier, but a stronger version of porter (see below). Today, though, the term stout means either the dry or Irish style of around 4.5 per cent abv, typified by a strong flavour of roasted unmalted barley, or the much weaker, sweet style of which Mackeson (3 per cent abv) is the principal survivor. The Irish stouts, Guinness, Murphy's and Beamish, account for over 5 per cent of the market but have been slipping in recent years: in response, Guinness has reduced its recommended serving temperature to arctic levels.

There are also many **speciality beers**, both British and Continental, appearing on the market.

Many British brewers, especially the newer micro brewers, have started reviving old-fashioned styles, often in bottles. They include old ales, exemplified by Theakston's Old Peculier at 5.7 per cent abv, and porter, the dominant beer style of the eighteenth to nineteenth centuries, killed by malt rationing in World War I and revived in the 1980s. There is endless argument as to what porter was really like: since it was the first ale purpose-brewed for widespread distribution (the term has nothing to do with London market porters, it simply means 'portable', and the best modern rendition is 'export'), it would have been very hoppy and highly alcoholic. It would have left the brewery in an incomplete state, the continuing fermentation and CO_2 production giving further protection during transit. Modern porters, however, tend to be only mid-strength. India Pale Ales (IPAs) were also developed for export, and exactly the same rules of strength and hoppiness apply as for porter, except that as IPAs were a later development they benefited from advances in the malting process and were therefore pale and clear. Today IPA, if it means anything, means 'best bitter', although some breweries apply it to their standard bitters.

Another traditional speciality due for a revival after years of decline is **barley wine.** Traditionally the strongest of ales, barley wine is so called because by the time the yeast has struggled up to 9–10 per cent abv, it has also created a raisiny, vinous flavour. Whitbread Gold Label and Marston's Owd Roger are the only national brands today, but in times gone by brewers prided themselves on their barley wines, and the revival of the bottled beer market gives fine barley wines such as Fuller's Golden Pride a shot at national distribution.

The British market is also becoming increasingly receptive to quirky Continental specialities, many of them technically ales. First among these is wheat beer, that is, beer brewed from at least 50 per cent malted or unmalted wheat. These beers are brewed chiefly in Belgium and Bavaria, with Hoegaarden the best-known example. They are soft and spritzy like lagers – although they count as ales, being top fermented and warm conditioned. The many odd flavours generated by wheat include cloves, banana, and even bubblegum. Belgian fruit beers, mainly cherry and raspberry (*kriek* and *frambozen*), are also building followings, as are Flemish strong ales such as Duvel and the Trappist ales brewed by monks, of which Chimay is perhaps best known. Be warned: these beers can be immensely strong – the strongest Chimay is 9 per cent abv!

DRAUGHT BEERS

Cask-conditioned ale

Traditionally, all draught ale in Britain was cask conditioned or 'real', having gone through a gentle secondary fermentation in the cask and arriving in the pub with a proportion of living yeast, which generates an entirely natural head and creates a prickle of carbonation in the body.

Cask ale today accounts for only about one-quarter of draught beer sales – and a great deal of comment, publicity and argument. It needs special handling in the cellar before it can be served and, because it is perishable, it has to be sold within three or four days of tapping.

Most publicans want to offer as much choice as they can, but this is a temptation to be resisted, at least as far as cask ale is concerned. Attractive as a forest of handpumps may be, product quality will suffer badly if throughput is slow. Few things dishearten the customer, especially the discerning customer, more than discovering a pub that serves a dozen favourite ales, only to find none of them drinkable. For most pubs, three or at a pinch four cask ales are ample – a standard bitter, the brewery's own best bitter, a guest ale (see below), and the brewery's current seasonal special. (A cask mild is a fifth option in some pubs.) The public thirst for novelty is just as well served by constantly changing the guest ale and the seasonal special as by trying to stock seven or eight cask beers at once.

This is as true of wholly tied regional brewery tenants as it is of publicans under a more liberal regime. For instance, a Greene King tenant has a choice of a mild (XXD), a standard bitter (IPA), a world-class premium ale (Abbot), and a complete range of seasonal specials, as well as two world-class strong bottled beers (St Edmund's and Strong Suffolk). Greene King has been under consumer pressure to stock a 'foreign' premium bitter alongside Abbot, and some tenants have been given a limited menu of guests to choose from; but tenants cannot really complain that their options are unduly restricted, even without foreigners.

Publicans who do decide to stock an unusually wide range of real ales should be confident of their cellar skills and should also give specially deep thought to the question of cask size: the firkin is ideal, especially for guest ales.

(NB: Since the Beer Orders of 1990 tenants, lessees, and loan-tied free trade customers of national breweries – that is, breweries owning more than 2000 pubs – have been entitled to stock one cask ale of their choice above and beyond the beers supplied by their own brewery. Selecting from the brewery's own list of foreigners does not disqualify a tenant from stocking one other cask ale not on the list. Any disadvantage arising from a decision to stock a guest ale such as the threat of a rent rise, or withdrawal of discounts on brewery-supplied lines, should be reported to the Office of Fair Trading.)

Since 1995 the cask ale market has been in decline, and one reason given by the industry has been poor quality. Whether this is true or not, in today's competitive cask market quality is essential, and the publican's contribution is top-notch cellar management. All breweries these days offer comprehensive courses in cellar skills, and no one should go behind a bar without a solid grounding.

To a great extent, keg and nitro-keg ales and lagers will look after themselves: they are designed to be stable on leaving the brewery, and the mechanical skills required on the publican's part to operate the dispense equipment satisfactorily can (and should) be learned and applied pretty much by rote.

Matters are very different when it comes to cask ale: to get the best out of the beer, the publican needs to be something of an engineer, something of an obsessive, and something of a connoisseur. This not the place for an A–Z of cellar skills: all publicans are offered cellar training and should seize the opportunity; but there are some areas which may have been insufficiently emphasised on some courses but which cannot be repeated too often.

Never serve green beer. Many breweries these days send out ale which only needs to be vented and soft-spiled for a few hours before it is ready to be tapped, but this is not true of all beers. If you are serving unfamiliar brands, take the trouble to find out if they have any peculiar conditioning characteristics (ring the brewer – he's a nice man!) so that you can serve them at their best. Avoid floating filters and other devices that enable you to pull pints off the top of the barrel while the sediment is still sinking to the bottom: (a) you may get some of the top breaks coming through, which will do nothing for your reputation, and (b) the beer may be bright, but its flavour will still be immature.

Never return beer to the barrel. The financial savings are not worth the time and trouble involved – and they are certainly not worth the risk of infection and tainting which could end up with the waste of a whole barrel and unhappy customers.

Choose the right cask size. Few real ales last more than three or four days after tapping, and few publicans these days would expect to empty even an 18-gallon barrel (kilderkin) of any but the best-selling brand in that time. Don't be afraid to order in nines (firkins) or elevens: the effort involved is well worth the return in terms of reputation, especially if you stock the width of range expected today.

Never flash-chill real ale. It should be served a few degrees below ambient, and although the trend today is for ever-cooler beers, publicans should resist the temptation to serve real ale too cold. As well as killing many of the flavours, it prevents the release of CO_2, making the beer too gassy. Temperature fluctuations, direct sources of heat and draughts can have equally harsh effects, and too high a temperature is even worse. Maintain the cellar at a constant 52–55°F and the ale should be

Kegmiser

for
accurate stocktaking
improved stock control
measured beer returns

Contact: **COMWARE TECHNOLOGY LTD**
(01383) 820680

Cellar Safe and Sound

Anyone who has flicked through the pages of the pub market cannot have failed to see the plethora of adverts offering cask stillaging, racks and lift trucks. What's it all about?

Well it's certainly an important issue and one which should be given full consideration by anyone with responsibilities for profitability, maintenance of the cellar or the well being of the cellar staff. In terms of stillage systems the issue divides into three core subjects

1. Health and safety
2. Profitable use of casks
3. Maximising cellar space

Health and Safety

The following is an extract from *'The Manual Handling Operations Regulations 1992'*

Interpretation

Any duty imposed by these regulations on an employer in respect of his employees shall also be imposed on a self-employed person in respect of himself.

Duties of employers

1) Each employer shall
a) so far as is reasonably practicable, avoid the need for his employees to undertake any manual handling operations at work which involve risk of their being injured; or
b) where it is not reasonably practicable to avoid the need for his employees to undertake any manual handling operations at work which involve risk of their being injured
(i) make a suitable and sufficient assessment of all such manual handling operations to be undertaken by them,
(ii) take appropriate steps to reduce the risk of injury to those employees arising out of their undertaking any such manual handling operations to the lowest level reasonably practicable, and
(iii) take appropriate steps to provide any of those employees who are undertaking any such manual handling operations with general indications and, where it is reasonably practicable to do so, precise information on -
(aa) the weight of each load, and
(bb) the heaviest side of any load whose centre of gravity is not positioned centrally.

(2) Any assessment such as referred to in paragraph 4(1)(b)(i) of this regulation shall be reviewed by the employer who made it if -
(a) there is any reason to suspect that it is no longer valid; or
(b) there has been a significant change in the manual handling operations to which it relates;
and where as a result of any such review changes to an assessment are required, the

relevant employer shall make them.

Duty of employers

Each employee while at work shall make full and proper use of any system of work provided for his use by his employer in compliance with regulation 4(1)(b)(ii) of these Regulations.

These extracts should not be used for guidance without reference to the entire document. Reproduced with kind permission of Her Majesty's Stationary Office

Of course reducing or even eliminating heavy work in the cellar has benefits that extend far beyond simply complying with regulations, even if the regulations do not apply, the increased ease and speed with which casks can be moved around the cellar and loaded to the stillage will bring surprising relief to even the most ardent proponent of strong arm tactics. Consider the flexibility, with a few minutes instruction anyone can quickly easily and safely stillage casks, so it is no longer necessary to seek muscle bound cellar sitters every time you take time off, so the freedom one can gain can be very important and very profitable.

Consider your own health and the health of others, the safety regulations were introduced to help prevent personal injury, they are not there simply to cause a nuisance to pub and bar owners, a back injury incurred by lifting a heavy cask could be with you for life, and may have a serious effect on your future ability to work.

Profitable use of Casks

One of the main motivators for people to invest in a stillage system is the self tilting feature built into each stillage, there are various mechanisms to raise the cask but in it's simplest form a pair of torsion springs overcome the weight of the cask as it's contents is extracted, the stillage will gently tilt the cask to a pre-defined or adjustable stop. The period over which the stillage comes to full tilt will depend on the mechanism, but in nearly all cases the achievable angle of tilt is much greater than that generally possible by chocking. Of course it's not always desirable to tilt the cask to a steep angle, the optimum angle of tilt will vary with the brand of beer, but in a majority of cases it possible to extract more saleable beer from the cask than by normal stooping practice, and in many cases this can mean two or three pints extra per cask.

The methods employed to tilt the cask have been the subject of much debate in brewery circles, and has been the subject of misinformation propagated by equipment suppliers to gain commercial advantage. There are a couple of important points that the purchaser should consider and which will guide him to a decision he will be happy with. If we start by describing the two most common means of 'powering' the tilt and examine the advantages and disadvantages of each, then selection will be more obvious. The first

and most widely used is the torsion springs (as mentioned above), these are low cost and reliable, the number of coils will determine the quality and longevity of the spring. Basically, the more coils the less work each has to do, hence more consistent results over a longer period, good quality multi-coiled springs will never grow tired. Torsion springs will act perpendicular to the moment of load, that is to say, the spring pushes in the direction you wish to move the cask, this ensures a consistent force which will raise the cask gently over a several gallons of beer dispensed. Slow tilting has the built in advantage of being able to roughly determine the contents of a cask just by looking at it.Torsion springs cannot be overloaded, if a heavy cask is dropped suddenly on to a stillage the springs will simply recoil in the normal way, albeit a little faster, successive banging of casks will not damage torsion springs. Torsion springs will if the cask is severely knocked, cause the cask to 'bounce', this of course could lead to disturbance of the beer, in point of fact the likelihood is very small.

Gas springs. The main advantage of gas springs is that they are damped, that is to say they cannot move quickly, this is particularly useful when casks are on the back bar and where they are continually being served from, this can put them at risk of disturbance if not damped. Gas springs have a linear action, therefore unless they are positioned perpendicular to the force, the actual force on the cask will not be consistent. The length of gas springs prevents perpendicular mounting on low profile stillages, therefore the spring must be placed at an angle to the force which results in increasing spring force as the cask rises, i.e. at the same time as the cask grows lighter. The combined effects cause the cask to rise quickly from the point at which the cask first starts to move, and although the action is smooth it would normally tilt quickly and not over the course of several gallons as a purchaser might expect. Manufacturers of gas springs will not normally guarantee their products as they cannot control the environment in which they are used. Unlike torsion springs, the damping in the gas spring will resist the weight of a falling cask, this by definition puts the gas spring under load, a load which they are not designed to take. Only shock absorbers are designed to take shock loads, it is therefore unlikely that a stillage maker will offer a warranty on stillages operated by gas springs when used in the cellar.

Other pointers to consider when selecting an autotilting stillage. Can the spring(s) be easily changed or re-positioned to suit other cask sizes? Metal to metal surfaces will wear regardless of surface finishes, wear will lead to rust and possible seizure. Only select stillages with properly bushed hinges and protected wear points. Ask for a lifetime warranty, if the manufacturer has any confidence in his product he will be happy oblige. Ask about metal finishes, some plated finishes look great in the photos or the exhibition hall, but the first sight of beer may result in unsightly staining or even strip the finish off. Flexibility is paramount, cellars change and people change cellars, it is important that your stillages change with you, what is the point of floor standing stillages which become useless the day you want to put them on a rack to save space.

There are of course no guarantees on savings and no supplier of stillage systems should be believed in their claims, whilst there certainly can be savings and these will define an often short payback period, a potential buyer should look to the pub operators to see the buying patterns. Almost all pub operators will have experience of stillage systems and many have specified the equipment as standard for the whole estate. Of course there are different motives at play, when looking at equipment to save beer it is not necessarily in the beer sellers interest to recommend or invest in equipment that will in effect reduce his sales.

Maximising Cellar Space

If it's not on a shelf it's on the floor, a basic truth that explains how floor space can be increased when casks and for that matter crates, mixers and wines are stacked in an organised fashion on purpose made shelving. Cellars are often small-with low ceilings which can make organisation difficult and by combining cask or keg racking with shelving for other things normally stored in the cellar, cellar space can be much better used and the floor space significantly increased.

It should be stated at this point that the two issues of autotilting and cask racking are not necessarily interlinked. There are low cost cask racking systems which allow for mechanical lifting but retain manual tilting. These systems have the advantage of improving cellar space, complying with the manual handling regs, keeping with the traditional methods of cask stooping, and saving money in the process.

55–57°F in the glass, which is about right.

Think before using a cask breather. These devices, which fill the cask with CO_2 as the level of beer sinks, protect slower-selling beers from infection or oxidisation, and as the CO_2 is at atmospheric pressure it should not dissolve in the ale. Critics say they stop the beer maturing and conceal laziness in the cellar; but it is surely better to secure the survival of slower selling lines, especially mild, in cask form by use of the cask breather than that they should be available only in keg format or, worse, withdrawn altogether. An alternative is the autobreather, a simple valve in place of the spile. This traps the naturally occurring CO_2 in a protective blanket and admits air only as beer is pulled off.

Recently, the brewing industry has launched a special initiative, the Cask Marque Scheme, aimed at assuring the quality of cask ale and promoting pubs where a tested and proven standard is maintained.

Cask Marque was established following a study which revealed the poor quality of cask-conditioned ale in many pubs. The study itself was a sign of the anxiety the industry felt at a cask ale sales slump which has been running at 15 per cent a year since the hot summer of 1995.

The scheme was the brainchild of Adnams, Marston's, Morland and Greene King, which jointly invested £30,000 in an independent survey of 1000 pubs in spring and summer 1997.

The surveyors found 23 per cent of the pints they sampled to be below an acceptable standard. Many were simply too warm, showing how widely the industry had ignored the lessons of the summers of 1995 and 1996. A disproportionate number of the bad pints were served in free houses with five cask ales or more on tap.

Former Adnams sales director Paul Nunny, who is running Cask Marque, said that in the boom years publicans had been quick to add to the number of handpumps on the bar, but when consumption began to fall they failed to cut back on what they stocked. As a result, they often did not have the throughput necessary to maintain quality.

Most breweries have cask ale quality programmes of their own. But Cask Marque is a recognition of the fact that only a nationwide, independent scheme can restore public confidence in cask ale.

At the heart of the scheme is the award of a plaque – the Cask Marque – to publicans whose real ales can stand up to repeated samplings by qualified inspectors. The plaque and its associated merchandising material should be prominently displayed and may also be used in advertisements, letterheads, etc. Cask Marque is also promoted on the Internet.

Publicans have to apply to take part, and each applicant is inspected twice in three months. If the ale measures up on condition, appearance, taste, temperature and character, a plaque is awarded. If it fails, the inspector will make a written report and the publican will be retested.

The plaque is awarded to the publican rather than the pub in

Getting a good pint every time

With the increasing emphasis on beer quality more and more publicans are realising that the proven Alevator system can actually help them deliver what they and their clients want - a good pint of real ale - every time.

The Alevator can be supplied as a single unit or as part of a complete cellar system designed to suit individual requirements.

The well-proven advantages of the Alevator are obvious - the saving of money, space and effort being the formost.

The Inn Profit Systems Cellar Management System begin as soon as the dray arrives. The cellar trolley takes casks to your cellar effortlessly, avoiding lifting, rolling or manhandling in any way.

Simply engage the trolley hook into the lip of the cask, and you're away! And there's achoice of wheels to suit your floor.

The revolutionary IPS Alevator is at the heart of the system. Load any cask - from nine to 36 gallons - on to the Alevator - and position it in your cellar (or behind the bar). Then let it do your work for you!

It will gently tilt the cask as ale is drawn leaving less than a pint of ullage in the cask. Sediment remains undisturbed, giving clear, high-quality pints right to the end of the cask. (For heavy sediment ales, use the IPS tilt fine tuner).

Meanwhile the IPS fork truck, like all IPS equipment is designed specifically for cellar work. The loaded Alevator simply connects to the truck which raises it to

racking height. The Alevator and cask is then gently lowered into position - and no further handling is required until the cask is empty!

Choose from a manually operated truck - or the hydraulic version with 360 degree turning circle for smaller cellars. The IPS stacking and racking system is designed to be used in conjuction with the Alevator.

It can be customised to fit your cellar exactly, and once in place will eliminate many of the problems traditionally associated with cask storage. Even more muscle - even less waste.

Contact IPS for more details of a free demonstration.

recognition of the fact that skill and care are more important than facilities, but a publican who moves pubs will have to be retested.

A third inspection follows the award of the plaque, with two inspections every year thereafter. The plaque can be withdrawn if standards slip, and customers will be able to complain.

The publican pays £140 in the first year and then £100 a year to cover the cost of inspections, but in most cases the pub's main supplier will pay half.

Cask Marque sees itself as a purely commercial scheme intended to increase cask ale sales. Improving the overall quality of cask ale will slow the decline in cask ale volume, prevent delistings, and preserve choice.

Cask Marque has the support of the Brewers and Licensed Retailers Association, the Independent Family Brewers of Britain, the British Institute of Innkeeping, and the Campaign for Real Ale (CAMRA).

For an information pack, ring Antony Hawkins on 01254 668104.

Another area of controversy with cask ale is dispense. Keg, nitrokeg and stout fonts and Keating pumps (keg taps dressed up to look like handpumps) are delivered by the brewery; they should be operated in strict accordance with brewery instructions and their maintenance should be left to the brewery's technical staff. Things aren't so simple with cask ale – but then, they never are!

Northern bitters such as Boddington, Tetley and John Smith's in their cask version are correctly pulled through a quarter-pint piston, a swan-neck, and a tight sparkler. This gives the ale the dense, creamy head prized by northerners but knocks much of the CO_2 out of the body of the pint and drives off some of the hop aroma. Northern beers are formulated to withstand the battering with their flavours intact; most southern beers are not and are traditionally served through a flat spout with no sparkler to produce a beer with a smaller, looser, head but more hop aroma and more life in the body of the beer.

Sadly, since northern-style ales arrived in the south, many publicans and breweries have decided that one type of engine must serve all ales, and the flat-spout kit has been discarded. Some brewers, though, have resolutely clung to their traditional beer engines; CAMRA has pitched in; and so controversy has arisen.

There is no need for argument, though, so long as the publican is prepared to respect the opinion of customers who express a preference. By all means install swan-necks and tight sparklers, but simply instruct staff to loosen the sparkler on request. It takes very little trouble and pleases the customer which is, after all, what matters. (There is now a dual-spout pump on the market that can give northern or southern dispense at the flick of a switch; it was invented by Bateman's Brewery of Wainfleet, to whom enquiries should be addressed.)

Handpumps are not the only method of dispensing real ale. Until recently, metered electric pumps were common in the Midlands and north-west. They have the advantage of delivering an exact pint, but

Was the barrel in "**Roll Out The Barrel**" full of Budweiser Budvar?

Composed in 1929 by the Czech Jaromír Vejvoda.

Original premium Czech lager

Contact B.B. Supply Centre Ltd. on 0171 247 1252

many customers think they are keg taps. Metered or otherwise, electric pumps are necessary where there is an unusually long pipe-run between cellar and bar. The quality of the beer should be unaffected.

Another form of cask ale dispense gaining favour is the simplest: gravity, with the ale being poured straight from casks on stillages behind the bar. Many connoisseurs say this produces the best results of all: it is visually highly appealing; and it eliminates all the waste of line-cleaning, pulling off, etc. However it does lead to problems of temperature control, atmospheric taint (although there is little evidence that this really occurs), and stock management. It is not really advisable as the usual means of dispense, but it works well in alehouse operations like Whitbread's Hogshead pubs.

Lager and keg ales

Lager and so-called 'keg' or brewery-conditioned ales are matured in tanks at the brewery and then filtered, pasteurised and infused with carbon dioxide before being put into kegs. They last a good deal longer than cask ale, and there is no 'ullage' – the unusable barrel-ends – but they have to be given another dose of CO_2 in the pub cellar as a propellant.

This method of processing beer was adapted from bottling technology in the 1930s, with the original aim of making draught exports (knocked for six by the World War I), possible on a commercial scale again. However it was soon found that the most eager customers for these stable new products were sporting clubs, which might only open once a week, and usually found – especially in the days before refrigerated storage – that any beer left unsold was spoilt by the next time it was wanted.

The first national brand of keg ale was launched in the 1950s by Flower's of Stratford-upon-Avon. Its advantages to the brewer were immediately obvious: having a long shelf-life, it could be widely distributed; and it would remain fresh without a high alcohol content and consequently without attracting a punitive level of duty. Its advantages to the publican were equally apparent: no fiddly cellar work, no unsaleable sediment, and far less spoilt beer in hot weather.

It wasn't until the very hot summer of 1959 that keg ale started to appeal to pub customers, though. In record temperatures, the deficiencies in quality control standards at Britain's many small local breweries and the primitive cellarage arrangements of most pubs became painfully evident; and in an era that was, anyway, far less cynical about technological developments than we are now, keg ales were welcomed as consistent and reliable.

Keg ales quickly caught on in working men's clubs, mainly for ease of service, and the big brewers – then in a volcanic period of growth by merger and takeover – soon started developing national keg brands, such as Worthington E, Ind Coope Double Diamond, Courage Tavern, Whitbread Tankard and the now notorious Watney's Red Barrel, which they could dispatch to far-flung depots on the nation's expanding motorway network.

The keg dream soured, however, partly because of the greed of the brewers in increasing the price while reducing the strength of their keg brands to the point of national scandal – a series of *Daily Mirror* exposes in the early 1970s revealed that some keg brands would have been legal in America during Prohibition yet cost several pence a pint more than regional brewers' cask brands – and partly because of a largely middle-class backlash. The Society for the Preservation of Beers from the Wood slightly predated the Campaign for Real Ale, whose formation coincided with the revival of small-scale craft brewing, and also with the publication of Chris Hutt's influential book *The Death of the English Pub*. This all happened at the same time as Richard Boston's Beer and Skittles column in the *Guardian* and Ian Nairn's writings on beer in *The Times*. By the late 1970s, cask ale was firmly re-established.

By this time, however, keg technology had also made possible the growth of lager sales in Britain. Lager had been brewed in small amounts, mainly in Scotland, for over a century; returning World War II and British Army of the Rhine personnel brought with them a fondness for Holsten; and the package holiday generation of the 1960s learnt to drink Pilsner-type beers on the Spanish Costas. The economics of lager were the same as the economics of keg ale – it was cheap to brew, it attracted less duty, it travelled, it kept, there was no unsalable sediment – but, unlike keg ale, it wasn't a distress purchase; being foreign, it was aspirational in its own right. Lager's growth has proved unstoppable, even though the same charges have been levelled against it as were levelled against keg ales 25 years ago. It now commands a good half of the British beer market.

As far as stocking draught lagers is concerned, most publicans will find their options limited by the tie. It has become common to stock three: a session lager such as Carlsberg or Carling Black Label; a premium lager of European extraction such as Kronenbourg or Stella, and a premium, non-European lager: say Foster's or Red Stripe. Sales of the session lagers are beginning to slip, but they are still must-stocks.

Carlsberg-Tetley, the UK's

largest independent brewer and wholesaler, re-launched its premier lager brand, Carlsberg Export, in the summer of 1998, with a major promotional and advertising campaign. Since then, the new taste lager has rapidly gained converts across the country.

The new formula Carlsberg Export has a significantly increased ABV, from 4.7% to 5%, stylish new packaging and a new and distinctive flavour.

Explains Bernie Ray, Managing Director of On-Trade Sales at **Carlsberg-Tetley**: "From the beginning we set ourselves the objective of creating a product that was at least as good as, if not better than the competition, and we have achieved it. To create our new recipe we threw away everything except the Carlsberg yeast, examined everything from ABV level to bitterness.

"This will be a hat-trick for **Carlsberg-Tetley** – the tried and tested re-launches of Carlsberg Lager in 1996 and Tetley's Bitter in 1997 paid dividends and we are confident that this success has been repeated with the new recipe Carlsberg Export."

Carlsberg Export is the third best selling premium draught lager in what is the fastest growing sector of the beer market. Blind tests during research saw scores for the brand exceed all premium category competitors with regard to taste and people's intent to purchase.

Carlsberg-Tetley have invested significant sums in promoting the new Carlsberg Export. A completely new illuminated font, which is stylish, eye-catching and modern, has been designed and installed in outlets across the country,

and a distinctive 275 ml NRB bottle is also available.

A comprehensive multi-million pound advertising campaign hit the small screen in late summer to promote the premium lager's new packaging, taste and ABV to consumers. The campaign was seen an average of 11 times by 93% of 18-34 year old men.

The Carlsberg Export television advertisement appealed to the British sense of humour whilst drawing on the beer's Danish origins, portraying the pressure put on a marriage by the husbands new job – as a lorry driver for Carlsberg Export.

Carlsberg Export's TV advertising was backed up by the brand's sponsorship of the Reading Festival in August, which offered up to 100,00 music fans the opportunity to sample the new beer in heavily branded surroundings.

However, the on-going Carlsberg Export campaign will also involve promotional activity, as witnessed by the first promotion for Carlsberg Export since it's re-launch, "Nothing Else To Declare", which built on Carlsberg Export's international heritage. Uniquely, **Carlsberg-Tetley** tailored the prizes on offer to two specific markets, traditional pubs and bars and clubs, aiming at drinkers in a range of age brackets and offering prize-winning odds of one in six.

Concludes Bernie Ray; "It is quite clear that there is a growing consumer preference towards higher strength premium lagers. For the trade, the new strength Carlsberg Export, with its proven success in consumer research tests, offers high level profit potential for all who choose to stock it."

CARLSBERG-TETLEY

Probably the best Export in the world.

There is now a fourth option as well: the 'authentic' European lager. Authentic draught imports – including Czech lagers such as Budwar, Pilsner Urquell and Zamek, and Belgian speciality beers such as Hoegaarden – confer the stamp of quality on a pub just as cask ale does.

Yet a fifth option open to some publicans is a mixed-gas variant such as Bass's Carling Premier and Guinness's Enigma. Being smoother than carbonated lagers, it should be possible to drink more of these brands; they are also brewed to be served at a lower temperature, which is all the rage. However, they seem to be catching on only slowly.

Mixed-gas or nitrokeg ale is processed in exactly the same way as old-style keg, except that the gas added in the cellar is not straight CO_2 but a mixture of CO_2 and nitrogen.

The technology was developed by Guinness in the 1980s and adapted in 1994 by Bass, which was seeking a product with the economic qualities of keg and lager but the delivery of cask ale. The advantage of mixed gas, they found, was that nitrogen was not as soluble as CO_2, so nitrokegs would be less fizzy than CO_2-only keg. Nitrogen also makes smaller bubbles, so the head on a nitrokeg ale would be deep, dense, and long lasting – just the presentation qualities made popular by the national launches five years earlier of northern-style ales such as Tetley, John Smith's and Boddington.

Coincidentally, while the chemists at Burton were working on this project the brewers at Bass's Belfast plant (previously Caffrey's Brewery) were experimenting with a tradi-

tional Irish beer style, red ale, that was sweet and lightly hopped. The final version proved the ideal beer to be given the nitrokeg treatment, especially as, having little hop character, it suited the low serving temperatures that Bass's marketing department deemed desirable.

Caffrey's was launched in 1994, and providentially, 1995 proved to be another 1959-style hot summer. It went straight into 6000 pubs and sold over 150,000 barrels in its first year: at 25-30 barrels per house, not quite the phenomenon it seemed at the time but, given that it had no above-the-line support, a more than encouraging start.

Caffrey's was quickly followed by Kilkenny from Guinness and a whole host of regional brands, mostly with an Irish slant (such as Greene King's Wexford and Usher's Milligan's Mist), and mostly at the premium end of the strength scale favoured by younger drinkers. Sales of these 'stand alone' nitrokeg brands were tailing off by the end of 1997, although new brands such as Sam Adams' Boston Beer from Whitbread continued to appear and for now, at least, one or other of these brands is a must-stock.

Less high profile but likely to be more enduring is the mixed-gas variant of the cask brand: Thwaites Smooth, John Smith's Smoothpour and so on. Many breweries now offer nitrokeg versions of their top sellers rather than the all-CO_2 keg. Most keg drinkers seem to prefer the temperature and delivery of nitrokeg to old-style all-CO_2 kegs, and the commercial advantages of keg beers generally over cask ale apply equally to nitrokeg ales.

'From Suffolk's Oldest Brewery, Britain's Finest Beer' -
for further details contact Angie Hewitt on 01502 727268.

Northern-style ales suit this treatment particularly well because they traditionally have a lower hop character and a less lively body than their southern counterparts, and even some beer experts have been unable to tell the difference between a very cold pint of cask Tetley and the nitrokeg version.

One bad practice that has become common, though, especially in the north, is to regard the nitrokeg variant as the pouring brand, offered to the customer who expresses no preference. The logic of this is simple – it's where the profit is, so seek actively to sell more of it – but shortsighted. If the cask is perishable and the nitrokeg has the longer life, it makes sense to use up the perishable variant first. Otherwise the quality of the cask will suffer thanks to slow throughput, and much of it will become unsalable. If you want to keep the cask variant, make it the pourer; otherwise, it's a waste of money to keep it at all.

One interesting fact you should note before deciding to do without cask ale altogether is that cask ale drinkers are more regular pub users, drink more per session, and tend to be more loyal to a favourite pub than other drinkers. It's up to you, with your knowledge of your own clientele, to balance this against the greater profit per pint of nitrokeg.

BOTTLED BEERS

Bottled beer sales have started growing again after a long period of decline since their 1960s' heyday, when the mixture of a bottle of light ale – dependable but expensive – and a half of draught bitter – cheap but often a bit off – made a reasonable compromise pint. The difference this time round, though, is that the main growth is in non-returnable 500ml bottles – the kind that people buy in supermarkets to take home.

Publicans, however, can use their range of bottled beers to extend customer choice comparatively cheaply and easily. The minimum outlay for an experimental new line in bottled beer is far less than for a draught equivalent, while the long shelf-life of bottled beer is another plus: if you try a new line and it flops, there's no rush to get rid of the leftovers. A good array of different labels in the chiller cabinet is a low-cost way of maintaining an exciting range of beers and gives the flexibility to suit individual customers: for instance, you can economically keep a stock of bottled Marston's Low C for a diabetic regular, but you couldn't if it was draught.

These advantages also offer the opportunity – subject, of course, to tie requirements – of low-risk promotions such as stocking a range of US beers for 4th July; a special offer on San Miguel and Keo in that post-holiday blues period; a big display of Christmas specials in November and December. In short, the huge range of bottled beers on the market today gives flexibility to the creative publican.

Bottled premium lagers such as Holsten Pils and Grolsch have been with us for a long time, and ice beers have become must-stocks. Now bottled ales, for too long a choice of light, pale, brown, and stout, are catching up in the style stakes. Until recently almost all bottled ales were pasteurised and artificially carbonated, with the exception of a small number of specialities such as Worthington White Shield which were bottled with enough live yeast to generate natural CO_2 in exactly the same way as cask conditioning.

The number of these bottle-conditioned ales (BCAs) on the market has increased enormously in the last three or four years, thanks mainly to the micro-brewing sector, and tenants and lessees of national brewers are now allowed to stock one guest BCA in addition to one guest cask ale. BCAs have a number of advantages for the publican: they are premium products and command a premium price, and they offer an opportunity to stock a wide range of 'real' beers without the risk of stocking too many cask ales.

A drawback is that being alive they do change, sometimes but not always for the better. Careful keeping in a cool, dark and vibration-free cellar and sensible stock management should be enough to ensure they are served at their best, but an open attitude to customer complaints is essential.

CANNED BEERS

Canned beers, by contrast, are all pasteurised and artificially gassed. Carbonated canned beers are now giving way to so-called draught-in-can versions that, like nitrokeg, contain both CO_2 and nitrogen. Draught-in-can beers contain nitrogen in solution, which is released upon opening by a plastic device dubbed a widget, producing a sudden gaseous surge settling to a dense head.

Publicans have traditionally been wary of stocking canned beers unless strictly necessary, as they invite an invidious comparison with take-home prices. However there are opportunities for stocking canned beers: many Japanese imports are only available in cans and are quite stylish; and canned beers might even be considered suitable for serving at barbecues for the simple reason that no glass need change hands.

CIDER

It is always puzzling that cider should be classed alongside beer, since by any practical definition it is a wine, being no more than the fermented juice of apples or, in the case of perry, pears. Be that as it may, cider is usually served draught by the pint like beer or in bottles that mimic premium lager; and it is as an alternative to beer that it has enjoyed the fantastic success of the last 30 years.

Until the 1950s draught cider was rare outside its western homeland, and even bottled cider was a minority drink. Many people didn't bracket it

with other intoxicating liquors at all, despite an alcoholic content of anything up to 8 per cent by volume; until 1976, it wasn't even taxed as such.

In the 1950s keg technology gave the biggest cidermakers the ability to despatch supplies of stable, consistent cider all over the country, and at the same time the decision was made to reduce the alcoholic strength of mainstream brands to that of premium beers. The fast-growing national brewers soon got involved in the ownership of potentially extremely profitable companies: Bulmer's remained independent, but Taunton was bought by a consortium of brewers including Bass and Courage, and the Showering's group, which included Coate's, Whiteways and Gaymer's, was bought by Allied. Given the national promotion the new generation of keg ciders received, and their relative cheapness thanks to the favourable tax regime, it's no surprise that sales started growing; and barring one or two hiccups whenever duties were raised, they have been growing ever since.

Cider has succeeded largely through good marketing, tracking developments in the beer market

The very best in gas dispense

BOC Sureflow offers an unrivalled service nation-wide in the supply of both carbon dioxide and mixed gas for dispensing beer and soft drinks.

Mixed gas is a combination of carbon dioxide and nitrogen in three different proportions – 30% carbon dioxide for ales and stouts, 50% carbon dioxide for ales and lagers and 60% carbon dioxide for highly carbonated lagers and ciders.

Mixed gas offers a number of benefits over traditional carbon dioxide:

■ *Beer wastage through fobbing can be significantly reduced*

■ *Beer is dispensed faster with mixed gas which enables more customers to be served in a given time period*

■ *The pint's presentation can be consistently improved with a longer lasting, tighter, creamier head*

■ *Slower moving draught beers can be kept in good condition for longer*

■ *Mixed gas avoids the need for unnecessary and complex electric pumps*

The sort of dispense equipment required is largely dependent on the level of throughput. For those outlets dispensing under eight barrels a week the traditional 14lb cylinder is popular and cost effective.

For pubs using more than eight standard 14lb cylinders a month BOC Sureflow offers three further options:

The Large Cylinder Package

The large pre-mixed cylinder has a capacity five times greater than standard 14lb cylinders. Gas is piped into the ring mains. Up to two or four cylinders of any mixed gas or carbon dioxide can be connected together via a manifold providing the equivalent of up to 20 traditional cylinders.

As the cylinder empties a simple switch changes from empty to full. BOC Sureflow will deliver the new cylinders to the point of use and connect them up. The Large Cylinder Package will save time. For customers using more than eight standard cylinders per month the Large Cylinder Package saves between 20-30% in gas costs.

Gasgen 2000

An air separation unit is an on-site nitrogen generation and carbon dioxide gas blending system for mixed gas dispense. Gasgen 2000 can generate up to four mixtures of gas thereby enabling the dispense of a wider range of drinks from a single gas source. In addition the wall mounted unit is ideally suited to the cellar environment and has the added advantage of using free nitrogen to dispense wines and fruit drinks as well as blanketing for cask conditioned ales. Carbon dioxide can also be used for post mix. For larger users the Gasgen 2000 offers an average saving of up to 10%.

BOC GASES
SUREFLOW

BOC GASES

SUREFLOW

The guaranteed dispensing gas service **03**

Bulk Liquid Carbon Dioxide Tank

The liquid tank provides the equivalent to 32 traditional 14lb carbon dioxide cylinders. It is an ideal solution for high volume soft drink or beer dispensing. It is particularly convenient and cost effective if the usage is greater than eighteen 14lb cylinders per month.

THE BOC SUREFLOW PROMISE FOR EQUIPMENT

■ We will not require customers to commit to a contract.

■ BOC Sureflow will carry out a free site and safety survey.

■ Installation and maintenance are usually free of charge.

■ We have an emergency call out service should your BOC installed equipment break down where service engineers will arrive within four normal working hours.

■ Full training on the use and operation of the systems is provided by BOC Staff.

AND A SPECIAL GUARANTEE OF RELIABILITY

If through any fault of BOC Sureflow, you run out of gas, we will provide you with £20 worth of free gas.

FOR MORE INFORMATION ON BOC SUREFLOW

call **0345 302 302** quoting ref: ADV64

The BOC Sureflow Service Charter

■ Free emergency service seven days a week to supply extra gas within 24 hours

■ Reliability – we will deliver the quantities required on the days it is needed so that gas supply does not run short

■ Cylinders are delivered to the point of use and connected as part of the service

■ Collection – to ensure a safe and clutter free area, we will remove our empty cylinder promptly

■ Free leak tests – if you wish, we will ensure that gas is not being wasted by undertaking leak tests on your dispensing equipment

■ Free replacement – our cylinders are well maintained, and filled with the highest quality food grade gas. Any cylinder that proves to be faulty will be replaced free of charge

BOC GASES
SUREFLOW

what our custome
say about us

"The confidence of working with the leading dispense gas supplier in the country means we know we will have the best products and the very highest standards of quality and safety" Mike Constable, Ushers' Managed House Director.

"BOC Sureflow has been superb - the deliveries and collections happen at agreed times, the delivery people actually take the cylinders down into the cellar - and take away the empties - which saves me having to carry them up into the yard. On top of all that the lower gas costs mean that effectively I now 'buy one get one free'". Mike Tucker, George Inn, Chideock, Palmer's Tenant.

"BOC Sureflow's expertise and advice for safety in the cellar has proved invaluable" Jean Harris, Head of Technical Services, King & Barnes.

"BOC Sureflow offered the best products and services as well as the best value for money". Louise Prynne, SA Brain.

"Introducing BOC Sureflow's new Gasgen system was arguably the best business decision my brother and I ever made." Matt Shaw, licensee of the Red Lion, Stourbridge.

"We have worked with BOC Sureflow for a number of years and know we can rely on them to provide us with a first class and professional service." Ian Hose, Commercial Manager, NAAFI Leisure Division.

Committed to your business, dedicated to your needs

For further information call: **0345 302302**

BOC GASES

Balloons, Balloons Balloons...

Balloon decorations made simple

BOC Gases has teamed up with the UK's leading latex and custom print balloon supplier, Pioneer Europe Ltd, to offer an unrivalled service for supplying balloons for events of all sizes from a one off pub opening to 300 functions and product promotions at venues all over the country.

With one phone call to BOC Gases all the arrangements for individually branded balloons and the helium cylinders can be organised. If necessary a specialist balloon decorator can also be booked to add a distinctive touch to any event.

Complete packs can be tailored for special occasions, which include both latex and foil balloons with suitable logos and weights, ties, filling kit and instructions - in fact everything needed to decorate a venue for that particular day.

Balloon Vending Machine

BOC Gases has launched a unique helium balloon vending machine which is ideally suited to family-friendly pubs, clubs and other leisure outlets. It's easy to use, self-contained and a high revenue generator.

The customer puts a £1 coin in the slot and selects one of four balloon designs - then the machine does the rest - inflating and releasing the balloon (with a ribbon and weight attached) for the customer to take away. Each machine can generate a minimum of £1000 profit per annum for the outlet

Call **0345 302302** for further information

and using the price advantage derived from its tax status to gain an edge. Thus Diamond White was developed by Taunton as the cider version of premium bottled lager, and what a success it proved to be. Only occasionally have the marketeers been caught on the hop, most notably in 1995–6, when they were ambushed by alcopops – and even then they were able to turn things round by using highly processed and fairly neutral ciders as the base of alcopops of their own.

The commercially successful ciders were a long way removed from the farm produce from which they were developed. But farm ciders have persisted, and in recent years have been enjoying something of a renaissance. Many real ale pubs like to have a polycask of farm cider in evidence on the bar in summer, when pints are passed across with many a bucolic wisecrack. These drinks have their place, and thanks to their tax advantage can make a very good margin. But they have to be actively sold, and they are sensitive to the environment. Oddly enough, they are most appreciated well outside their traditional heartlands, where sales are if anything declining.

 ## Health and Safety Notes

There are particular health and safety issues associated with the cellar. The first of these, the safety of the access, has already been referred to with regard to trap doors behind the bar. Alternative access arrangements such as steps can also be hazardous. They should be properly maintained, adequately lit, kept clear and provided with a handrail.

The cellar is where the majority of manual handling takes place, ie the lifting and moving of kegs, crates, etc. The conditions sometimes found in beer cellars – low ceilings and/or limited space – often make manual handling tasks more awkward. Specific legislation applies: the Manual Handling Operations Regulations 1992.

It is important that where manual handling cannot reasonably be avoided the risks of injury are assessed and appropriate measures taken to reduce them as far as is reasonably practicable. Appropriate measures include, for example, training in the correct way to lift and move loads and, possibly, rearranging the layout to reduce the amount of lifting and manoeuvring needed. Some pub cellars are fitted with a lift or hoist to help reduce the level of manual handling. Particular requirements exist for lifts and hoists under the Offices, Shops and Railway Premises (Lift and Hoists) Regulations 1968. These include ensuring that the lift/hoist is checked every six months by a competent person covering specific aspects. (Where a lift is hand operated the check needs to be done every 12 months.)

The Control of Substances Hazardous to Health Regulations (COSHH) have particular significance to the cellar. These Regulations require that no person at work be exposed to substances hazardous to health unless the health risks have been assessed and the necessary precautions have been identified and implemented. It is useful to clarify the difference between 'hazard' and 'risk': a 'hazard' is the potential to do harm and a 'risk' is the likelihood that harm will arise. Where and how a substance is used may mean that the risk is low despite the hazard. You need to identify what activities involve exposure to hazardous substances and what risks to health may arise (short term and long term). For a cleaning chemical such as beer-line cleaner the information on the label and that available from the supplier or manufacturer will enable risks to be identified. The appropriate measures include informing, instructing and training whoever does the job and, in addition, the provision and use of suitable protective clothing (eg gloves, goggles and apron).

COSHH also applies to carbon dioxide, an asphyxiant gas in a pressurised container. It is important that relevant staff are aware of how to safely store and use carbon dioxide cylinders and for cylinder restraints, etc to be provided. It is also vital that people understand and appreciate the dangers, know how to identify a leak and are aware of what to do. Anyone working in the cellar must always be able to make a quick exit. Further information and advice can be obtained from suppliers.

In some pubs asbestos lagging may still be apparent on pipework in the cellar. If such lagging is damaged or disturbed there is a risk of asbestos fibres being released and, therefore, a risk of asbestos-related disease. If there is any cause for concern in this respect professional advice must be sought: your local environmental health officer will be able to assist. You are obliged to protect your employees (and yourselves) from such exposure.

Finally, the procedure for deliveries and collection of empties may give rise to health and safety risks. The potential for injury to passers-by when the cellar flaps are open needs to be considered and appropriate measures implemented to ensure that the risk is addressed.

(See also the health and safety issues raised under 'Staff').

Legal Notes

The sale of draught beer and cider must be made in measures of either one-third of a pint or half a pint or multiples of a half-pint. There are exceptions for bottled or canned beer or cider.

Where brim measure glasses are used, a measure may consist of liquid and a reasonable head. The recommendation of the Brewers & Licensed Retailers Association (BLRA) is that the liquid content of beer and cider, once the head has collapsed, should not be less than 95 per cent of any of the permissible measures. According to BLRA guidelines on draught dispense, a top-up should be given 'with good grace' to any customer who wants one, but the measure should still not be passed to the customer with less than 95 per cent liquid. These guidelines have no legal force, but proof that you and your staff are aware of them and follow them should be a sufficient defence against conviction for serving short measure.

However, the government has promised legislation that will require a full pint of liquid to be served, and it may be advisable to start replacing stocks of brim-measure glasses with lined, oversized glasses – hopefully, the near-elimination of spillage will recoup much of the 'extra' beer the new legislation will force publicans to serve.

The law requires that price lists are clearly displayed in order that customers may know what the prices are for food and drink offered for sale. Where there are 30 items or less on a menu or list, the prices of all items must be shown. However, it is sufficient to display the prices of 30 selected items from a larger range. There are separate rules in respect of categories or items listed together, and in respect of the listing of wines and mixed drinks: see Price Marketing (Food and Drink on Premises) Order 1979. All prices must be VAT inclusive. Any service charges or other extra charges must be indicated.

CHAPTER FOUR

PROFIT FROM WINE

Martin Straus

'Wine in pubs is a disaster area!' – that's the perception of the vast majority of consumers, *Which* and the media.

Sadly, with notable exceptions, the sentiment is still difficult to refute. Pubs offer the last great surviving opportunity for wine development in the UK today, and with the Millennium almost upon us – what an opportunity!

Yet with the demise of the Wine Promotion Board (previously the Wine Development Board) almost a decade ago there is no longer a national body consistently promoting the sale of wine in the licensed on-trade. That is not to say that there is no wine promotion; simply that it is now very fragmented. The opportunity for virtually *all* on-licensees to enhance their bottom line and put bums on seats (pardon the pun) is still undoubtedly there; only the strategy must change.

Even the most traditional beer pub will have customers who want the occasional glass of wine, and at the other extreme the pub with a high food trade is an obvious wine market. What they have in common is a need for wines that are fitted to their context, stored and served in prime condition – just as a conscientious licensee would select and treat his beer.

THE UK WINE MARKET TODAY

Annual wine consumption has more than doubled, to around 16 litres a head, over the last 20 years. Although this is less than in most other European countries, the UK and Ireland are the only markets in the European Union where wine sales are increasing.

This figure compares to around 123 litres of beer and 12 litres of spirits and represented around 7700 million litres of wine sold in 1996, of which about 17 per cent – 1309 million litres – was in the on-trade. Are you getting your share?

Table wines made up just over 90 per cent of wine sold in British pubs, clubs, hotels and restaurants, with fortified wines making up 9.3 per cent, and sparkling a meagre 0.4 per cent, albeit of relatively high value.

In terms of colour, the British wine market breaks down into: white – 60 per cent, red – 38 per cent, and rosé – 2 per cent. There has been a constant increase in the shift from white to red recently. Contributory factors include increased European travel, medical opinion that red wine in moderation is good for the heart, and a generally more mature wine market. Many women now drink red wine, whereas at one time the vast majority drank only white. Dry rosé wines, although a tiny part of the market, are an interesting growth area – in Continental countries they are extremely popular, and more rosé wines are becoming available here.

Table 4.1 Top 10 countries shipping wine to UK market

Still light wines under 15 per cent alcohol by volume (millions of litres)

	1995	1996
France	213.6	216.4
Germany	105.8	87.3
Italy	87.1	82
Australia	47.8	66.8
Spain	47.8	49
South Africa	26.1	33.9
Bulgaria	30.5	33.3
USA	18.1	27.2
Chile	12.8	24.4
Hungary	10.7	11.8

Source: Wine & Spirit Education Trust, Summer 1997

FRANCE

France is not only the largest importer of wines into the UK, but is second only to Italy as the biggest producer of wines in the world at 5561 million litres.

It has been a major achievement to maintain its position in the face of massive competition from the New World. France has done this by responding to consumer demand and producing good, price-fighting wines in the Vin de Pays category to supplement its classic Appellation Controllée wines.

French wine labels tell us the official quality level of the wines, but it is important to remember that this is only a guide. There are two main categories of wine in France – table wine and quality wine. Table wine is further divided into Vin de Table (which can come from anywhere in France, or be a blend of different areas or grapes) and Vin de Pays (where the label specifies its geographical origin, and the wine has to meet more stringent quality standards).

Quality wine is divided into VDQS – *Vin Délimité de Qualité Supérieur* (the lesser subdivision); and AC – *Appellation Controllée* or AOC (*Appellation d'Origine Controllée*). Most VDQS wines have now been upgraded to AC.

Vin de Pays

Usually AC indicates a better wine than Vin de Pays, especially now that the regulations have been tightened up. However, in some instances, Vin de Pays may indicate a style of wine which, however good the product, simply does not comply with the AC regulations. An example comes from the Languedoc-Roussillon region in the south of France. AC Minervois must comply with regulations concerning specific, traditional grape varieties, but in the same vineyard one might find Cabernet

Sauvignon or Merlot, which cannot be included in the Minervois blend. The wine of these vineyards will therefore be labelled, for example 'Merlot, Vin de Pays d'Oc', which is not necessarily inferior to the same estate's AC Minervois, simply different.

Vin de Pays wines are one of the fastest expanding categories of French wines, and are often more 'international' in style than AC wines. Because of competitive pricing this sector is proving an excellent alternative to New World wines, and the range is now huge. In some instances wines are made by New World winemakers – usually Australian – and several vineyards are now owned by Aussie companies.

Vin de Pays wines are an ideal choice for pubs as they can be priced competitively and are usually of a consistent standard. Apart from Languedoc-Roussillon mentioned earlier, other good regions from which to source Vin de Pays wines include the Loire and the Ardèche (part of the Rhone Valley).

The Ardèche in particular is one to watch for the future. Its wines have for many years been used by the major supermarket chains as own-labels owing to exceptional value for money and consistency.

Bordeaux

Bordeaux wines have been known in England for longer than any other region: in 1182 Henry II married Eleanor of Aquitaine, and for 300 years England and Bordeaux were one country. The best-known wine in the world is claret, a synonym for red Bordeaux.

Getting to know Bordeaux is a full-time occupation. There are various quality levels: generic (Bordeaux and Bordeaux Supérieur), districts (eg St Emilion) and communes (eg St Julien). To confuse matters further, different districts have their own classifications: in the Médoc, there is a system of what are known as 'Classed Growths' (eg Château Mouton Rothschild, a First Growth or Premier Cru) and Crus Bourgeois, which come between generic Bordeaux and Classed Growths. Few pubs will have a market for Classed Growths, but should still consider an easy-drinking red Bordeaux, possibly a St Emilion, depending on the local clientele.

Do not overlook white Bordeaux, which now represents outstanding value. If the wine is entirely made of the Sauvignon grape it is usually labelled Bordeaux Sauvignon and is a crisp style good with seafood; if it is just labelled Bordeaux or Bordeaux Blanc, it is probably a blend of Sauvignon and Sémillon grapes and is a more rounded style of wine.

Burgundy

In the UK white Burgundy is more popular than red, although Beaujolais – a district of Burgundy – is the exception.

Of the whites, do consider Chablis, especially if you have a more traditional market, but bear in mind these wines are particularly dry. More versatile – and cheaper – are wines from the Maconnais district. Pouilly Fuissé is regarded as the best, but is often prohibitively expensive. Look for good Macon Blanc Villages wines (eg Macon Peronne) and St

Veran, the adjacent village to Pouilly Fuissé (and far better value). The Chalamais district is another source of excellent value white Burgundy (eg Montagny).

Beaujolais Nouveau is ideal to launch the Christmas season (it is released on the third Thursday in November), but it is Beaujolais Villages that represents the best quality/price; if you want to go the whole hog and list one of the ten 'Crus', Fleurie is perhaps the best known, but can be expensive. If you want to be daring, and feel you have the confidence to promote what is in the bottle, Julienas usually represents particularly good value.

Loire

The Loire Valley includes a huge variety of wines from Nantes at the estuary to the 'Central Vineyards' district at the other. In the Nantes area the main wine is Muscadet, whose quality standards have been significantly tightened up recently. The best type of Muscadet is 'Sur Lie', a lovely, clean, fresh wine, which goes very well with seafood and also makes refreshing summer drinking.

The huge middle section is composed of Anjou-Saumur and Touraine, where many of the traditional whites have been made from the Chenin Blanc grape variety (described later). It produces a full range of wine styles – dry, medium and sweet – as well as sparkling wines such as Saumur and Vouvray. Sadly, these excellent French 'sparklers' have decreased in popularity, owing to their relatively high prices compared to Cava from Spain and other sparklers from the New World.

These districts are also the source of many less expensive wines including the AC Sauvignon de Touraine (white) and Gamay de Touraine (red) and varietal Vin de Pays wines. Whites from this northerly climate are generally good.

Some 60 miles along the river, we come to the Central Vineyards district, the best-known wines being Sancerre and Pouilly Fumé. Not cheap, but some would argue the best wines in the world from the Sauvignon Blanc grape variety. Whether one has a market for Sancerre in a pub depends on local circumstances, but there is a case for paying a little extra and buying a wine from a single reputable grower, rather than a 'negoçiant' wine, blended from several growers. This applies to many regions, not only the Loire but also Burgundy and the Rhone, for example.

Alsace

This region on the Rhine has been contested by France and Germany for centuries, and as a consequence has acquired a culture and dialect of its own. It is a centre of gastronomy, and has more Michelin-starred restaurants than any other part of France.

Its wines are unique. Almost all – and certainly its finest – wines are varietal, the most popular in this country being the Pinot Blanc and the Gewurztraminer, although the Riesling is regarded as the 'king of wines' locally. Most Alsace wines tend to be relatively high in alcohol, making them ideal with food. The Pinot Blanc is a good all-purpose wine, dry (or sometimes off-dry), full of fruit and flavour. The

Gewurztraminer is exceptionally good with spicy food and where there is a little sugar in the dish (such as Chinese cuisine).

The Riesling from Alsace is sometimes a little dry for English tastes, although some feel it is the ideal match with, for example, river fish. My personal favourite is the rarer but more versatile Pinot Gris, which is a little spicey (but less so than Gewurztraminer), and goes so well with a wide variety of dishes. Alsace wines are relatively less expensive than they used to be, especially those from the well-run cooperatives such as Turkheim. If possible it is worth paying the extra for a top producer, for example Josmeyer (available from Pol Roger Ltd; tel: 01432 262800).

Rhone

The Rhone is best known for its red wines. The northern Rhone is renowned for its single varietal Syrah wines, the same grape as the Shiraz of Australia. Perhaps the most widely distributed is Crozes Hermitage, but St Joseph is perhaps better value – if you can find it!

The southern Rhone is the home of the famous Châteauneuf du Pape, rich, red, peppery and often highly alcoholic! Particularly good as a winter wine, it goes brilliantly with stews and gamey dishes. Other, less expensive alternatives are such AC wines as Gigondas and Vacqueras – superb value. Côtes du Rhone can come from either the north or south subregions, but most comes from the south. A step up is Côtes du Rhone Villages, which comes exclusively from specified villages in the south.

Whether straight Côtes du Rhone or Villages, it is important to establish whether the wine is the traditional, full-bodied, heavier style, or the modern, light, easy-drinking style; both can be excellent, but the choice will depend on what one is looking for.

GERMANY

Germany is second in volume of UK imports but still has less than half the volume of France, and is in continual decline. In terms of wine production, Germany is far lower down the league table, currently sixth at 1105 million litres, but 10 per cent up on the previous year.

Its disastrous recent performance in the UK results from the lack of a consistent market-led policy on the part of many German producers. German wines have for many years suffered from labels incomprehensible to many consumers, complete with Gothic script. Many of the cheaper wines would never be consumed locally. Lesser wines destined for the UK have often been treated with every permissible additive permitted under European Union regulations, and in particular the use of sugar to the maximum allowable level to enhance the very low alcohol level. The fact that Liebfraumilch is classified as 'quality wine' illustrates why British consumers are so confused.

Instead of addressing the German wine industry's identity crisis, the current trend is to move still further from hallowed tradition and into gimmickry, such as the switch from traditional bottle shapes into either French or entirely new shapes along with international-style labels and brand-names like 'Devil's Rock'. The tragedy is that Germany's classic wines represent outstanding value for money, and many in the trade would like to see better promotion of the Riesling, one of the world's great grape varieties.

Germany is certainly a source of opportunity for the pub trade, with its modestly alcoholic wines which are so easy to drink both with and without food. Seek out well-made German wines and promote them – the drier wines have definite potential.

ITALY

Italy is a country of anomalies, and wine is no exception. The *numero uno* of wine production at 5929 million litres, Italy exported only 82 million litres to the UK in 1996, down 6 per cent on the previous year.

Italy offers everything from easy-drinking, inexpensive wines to top-end, niche-market specialities both traditional and international in style. The major off-licence chains are sourcing many budget-priced wines from southern Italy, particularly Puglia, where winemaking has been totally transformed.

Many of Italy's traditional names are now better value than ever, with less emphasis on the two- and three-litre bottles of boring, flavourless wines that have predominated in the past and done no good to the image of such great names as Chianti, Frascati, Valpolicella and Soave.

Italy invests too little to develop the image of its wines in this country. Many of Italy's finest wines have

been labelled simply 'Vino da Tavola' for ludicrous reasons, although this has to some extent been rectified by recent legislation. In terms of distribution, many quality wines have tended to be sold by Italian importers/wholesalers almost exclusively to Italian restaurateurs, but there are great opportunities to develop sales via pubs. Some of the more recent Italian wines are eminently drinkable on their own, but traditionally – especially in Italy – wines have shown their best with food.

Avoid big wines like Barolo, which tend if good to be fairly expensive, and take too long to breathe to be practicable in the pub context. Look for the simple Chianti, which can be inexpensive and delicious, and Frascati, which should be made from a high proportion of the Malvasia grape; also wines from the south – from Puglia and Basilicata.

Another area to watch is Sardinia, where wonderful value wines are made from the Cannonau grape variety (the Grenache of France).

SPAIN

Spain's imports to the UK have held their own, because their quality is constantly increasing.

The famous Rioja region represents better value than ever, with appealing, smooth, easy-drinking wines traditionally aged in American oak having a distinct aroma of vanilla. Much of the Rioja produced for home consumption is less expensive, with no oak ageing, and many of these are now available in the UK.

The adjacent region of Navarra offers really good value, as do many lesser-known regions such as Borba. The wines of Penedes are also good, the most famous producer being Torres.

PORTUGAL

Portugal is ninth in world production at 713 million litres, but tiny in terms of UK imports. Difficult to sell in off-licences, its wines are perfect for the on-trade, where they can be promoted and sold on a one-to-one basis. Make sure the wine is tasted before listing, as some Portuguese wines may be too esoteric for the particular local market. Others, however, will be delicious and inexpensive.

EASTERN EUROPE: BULGARIA AND HUNGARY

Bulgaria is seventh in UK imports at 33.3 million litres (up 9 per cent) and Hungary tenth at 11.8 million bottles (up 10 per cent). Both have been consistent sources for wines at keen prices in the off-trade for many years.

In simple terms, Bulgaria excels at highly drinkable reds, which tend either to be international varieties such as Cabernet Sauvignon or Merlot or the less expensive 'country wines' – blends of international and local varieties that are at worst sound and are sometimes superb value.

Hungary's whites are good value, particularly the Chardonnay and the little-known Irsay Oliver.

The difficulty for many pubs will be price comparison with shops, although opinions vary as to whether consumers are now more ready to accept a higher on-trade price if it is kept to a reasonable level.

AUSTRALIA

The great success story of the last decade, Australia has just beaten Spain into fourth place in the UK (up a staggering 40 per cent to 66.8 million litres).

Eleventh in world production at 503 million litres, the huge demand for Aussie wines in the UK has continued unabated. With recent production difficulties in Australia there may be a temporary blip, but the medium- and long-term trend is likely to continue. Why is this?

Australia got its act together some years ago by deciding where it wanted to be in terms of its export market and producing delicious, fruity wines at the right price. Its generic market research, marketing and promotion policy have been an example to the rest of the wine world.

The range of wines from Australia is now colossal, and we are regularly seeing higher quality wines selling at enhanced price levels – and higher cash margins for the retailer.

If price comparison with shops is a problem, it is often possible to source Australian wines with labels reserved for the on-trade.

NEW ZEALAND

New Zealand's wine industry in world terms is minuscule, both in terms of production and the UK market – nevertheless, by far its biggest export market is the UK.

What it does produce is generally of excellent quality, and includes producers such as Montana, Cooks and Nobilo, supplemented by top-end names such as Cloudy Bay and Nautilus. Most wines are sold under varietal labels, with the vineyard locality underneath.

The white variety most associated with New Zealand is the Sauvignon Blanc, although there has been a substantial increase in Chardonnay (also very good). A good, budget-priced wine is Nobilo's 'White Cloud', a medium-dry blend of Muller-Thurgau and Sauvignon Blanc. Owing to its vastly increased popularity, it is now listed by most of the high street chains, so look out for their 'vintage white' – almost identical, a little cheaper and targetted at on-trade.

Reds are growing in quantity from a far smaller base, and tend to be a blend of Cabernet Sauvignon and Merlot.

SOUTH AFRICA

South Africa has been a producer of high quality wines for many years, wine-growing having been established for over three centuries. However, the years of apartheid left the country out of the UK's wine boom of the last two decades.

Happily that era is behind us now, and the more friendly political climate in South Africa has led to production being increased and to their wines being far more widely distributed in the UK. Now ranking fifth in the UK at 33.9 million litres (up 30 per cent), South Africa is eighth in wine production at 755 million litres (up 4 per cent).

Varieties traditionally associated with South Africa include the white Chenin Blanc (usually either dry or off-dry) and the red Pinotage (a cross between the Pinot Noir and Cinsault). However, South Africa has also shown itself capable of making stunning Chardonnay and Pinot Noir, among others. Certainly consider including South African wines in a forward-thinking wine list.

USA

California is by far the largest wine region in the United States, and exports wines at all price levels to the UK. In 1996 it was the eighth largest importer, its imports having increased by 50 per cent to 27 million-litres.

California's less expensive wines tend to be very easy drinking and have proved very popular with the consumer, especially for barbeques. It also produces some very 'serious' wines, at prices to match, which are likely to be too expensive for all but the upper end of the restaurant market. Look out, however, for some of the mid-priced wines of Californian origin, such as the Zinfandel and Petite Sirah (both red), which go so well with a wide variety of modern dishes.

Other wine-producing regions of the USA include Washington State (excellent Merlot) and Oregon (famous for its Pinot Noir), but wines from these regions tend to be outside the price bracket for the pub sector.

It should also be noted that Cabernet Sauvignon and Chardonnay may be found at every quality level – and price point – throughout the United States.

CHILE AND ARGENTINA

Chile has for many years been a significant exporter to the UK and ranked ninth in 1996, having doubled its volume to 24 million bottles, almost on a par with the United States. Its wines are very good value, again very easy drinking, and there are now several brands on the market.

Argentina is an anomaly, being one of the world's largest producers but way behind Chile in terms of UK imports.

The Falklands War was almost certainly the major factor behind Argentina's failure to penetrate the UK market to any degree, but today this is not seen as a significant drawback. Indeed, Argentina produces some really superb, world-class wines (and by no means cheap), and only three years ago was the source of the International Wine Challenge White Wine of the Year – from an indigenous variety, the Torrontes.

Both Chile and Argentina are well worth bearing in mind for pub wine lists.

CHAMPAGNE AND SPARKLING WINES

Champagne is a very emotive subject, particular given the millennium hype. No, it simply is not worth laying down wine for the millennium, except for the very top wines which could well be in short supply. These wines are hardly likely to be of interest to other than a tiny proportion of wine drinkers, so it is the bulk of the Champagne market that needs to be examined.

Champagne in reality can be classified as follows

♦ Grower's Champagnes (code number on label: RM. . .)
♦ 'Own-label' 'negoçiant' (code number on label: MA. . .)
♦ Non-branded 'negoçiant' houses
♦ Budget-priced brands (eg Mercier, Lanson)
♦ Standard brands (eg Moet et Chandon)
♦ Premium brands (eg Bollinger)
♦ De Luxe brands (eg Krug).

All 'main wines' produced by each house will have a code number on the label starting with the letters NM. . .

In each category, there may well be a non-vintage (white), rosé, a vintage and possibly a 'special' blend.

It is well worth considering a house Champagne that is really good, irrespective of whether it has a well-known label, and selling it at a competitive price – perhaps £19.95 per bottle (or £3.95 per 12.5cl glass, where appropriate).

Sparkling wines are usually regarded as those 'bubblies' that are not produced in the Champagne region of France although, strictly, Champagne is included in the category.

The cheapest sparkling wines are produced by carbon dioxide injection, but the quality is pretty basic.

The next category up consists of those wines made by the tank method (also known as 'cuve close' or 'charmat'). Some very drinkable wines can be obtained by this method, including several of the less expensive French and Australian sparklers (eg Veuve du Vernay).

Above this category come sparkling wines produced by the 'Transfer Method', mainly from Australia – including Yalumba's Pinot-Chardonnay – where the first fermentation is in bottle, transferred to tank and then returned to bottle.

The top category is wines produced in the identical way to Champagne, and these are typically labelled 'Traditional Method' (previously 'Champagne Method'). The least expensive wines in this category are often Cavas from Spain, followed by sparkling wines from the New World – especially Australia, New Zealand, California and South Africa. A particularly good but more unusual example is Yarden Brut from Israel.

In this price range there is an overlap with the least expensive Champagnes, and although quality sparkling wines at this level may well be superior, the magic name 'Champagne' is often the consumer's choice. Nevertheless, for the enterprising establishment, it is well worth promoting good sparkling wines, as poor Champagnes taste just what they are – poor!

FORTIFIED WINES

Sherry and port are the main wines in this category, although there are others.

Sherry is having an extremely difficult time these days. There are some absolutely wonderful wines available, representing incomparable value, but with a very limited market, especially in pubs.

Still, it's a must-stock – but remember: sherry loses its freshness very quickly, and should really be consumed six to nine months

from the date of bottling and within seven days of opening the bottle – often quite impracticable in the real world. To minimise the risk of stock deterioration ensure purchases are as fresh as possible and, once the bottle is opened, extend its shelf-life by using the Winesaver (see below) and keeping the bottle in the fridge.

Port is also usually kept for far too long. Vintage port starts to lose its character within 24 hours of the cork being pulled, and should be drunk at one sitting for best results – almost certainly unrealistic except in very rare circumstances.

Late Bottled Vintage is often selected as an after-dinner port, and has the advantage of being more durable and far less expensive than vintage port. However, it is heavily filtered and produced for early maturation – so while it is technically a port from a single year, it bears no relation in taste to a true vintage port. You pays your money and you takes your choice!

TRAINING IN WINE SERVICE

The Wine and Spirit Education Trust (WSET) 5 Kings House, 1 Queen Street Place, London EC1R 1QS; tel: 0171 236 3551; fax: 0171 236 0298 is the nationally recognised body providing wine product knowledge at Certificate, Higher Certificate and Diploma levels.

The Certificate (minimum of seven two-hour sessions plus multiple choice exam) covers an overview of wines of the world including spirits, liqueurs and associated beverages; the language of wine; and elementary tasting technique. No preliminary qualifications are required.

The Higher Certificate (minimum of 15 two-hour sessions plus multiple choice exam) goes into much more detail concerning individual regions and grape varieties, viticulture (growing of grapes) and vinification (winemaking), together with tasting of a wider range of wines in more depth. The Certificate is strongly recommended before embarking on the Higher Certificate.

These qualifications are offered by several centres around the country (mainly colleges) and by the WSET itself in London. Colleges normally deliver the courses as weekly evening courses, and the WSET runs a range of options including half-days and full days.

The Diploma, delivered only by the WSET in London and provincial centres, is the wine trade's management qualification, and a Higher Certificate is required.

Costs vary according to the centre but, as a guide, fees for courses run by the WSET during 1998/9, including study materials, are as follows:

Certificate: £150 plus £26 exam fee
Higher Certificate: £285 plus £34 exam fee
Diploma: £1,950 including exam.

All courses may be studied by distance learning. For further information on this aspect, or any other information, contact the Wine and Spirit Education Trust on 0171 236 3551 (or Fax 0171 329 8712).

It is also useful to be aware of the British Institute of Innkeeping (BII) Wine Retail Certificate, launched in 1997. The qualification comple-

ments rather than replaces the WSET courses, because the emphasis is on wine skills rather than product knowledge.

The qualification breaks down into the following areas:

◆ introduction to wine
◆ tasting wine
◆ buying and storing wine
◆ serving wine
◆ pricing wine
◆ choosing wines
◆ compiling a wine list
◆ merchandising and promotions
◆ training staff.

The programme is delivered by BII-accredited trainers, usually in two full days, and includes well-constructed practical sessions. The cost varies according to who is carrying out the training, the number of participants and other variable factors. The number of delegates on each course is typically six to ten. For more information, telephone the British Institute of Innkeeping on 01276 684449 or fax 01276 23045.

DEVELOPING AND IMPLEMENTING A WINE STRATEGY

Like every other part of the business, wine sales should never be taken for granted. Whatever the trading profile of your pub, a little thought is sure to be rewarded. Whether you plan simply to make more of the wine sales you already have, or to develop them further, whether you sell a little wine or a lot, a strategy is essential.

Assessing your pub's existing customer profile is the first step. At one extreme is the traditional beer pub, with little perceived demand for wine. At the other end of the spectrum, the operation might include a substantial restaurant, banqueting, outside bars or an off-licence, and decisions concerning wine will be more wide ranging.

The next stage is to carry out market research to see whether there is greater potential. What is the competition offering? Is there an opportunity to offer an enhanced wine range?

Having reviewed existing wine sales and decided what direction to take for the future, you can formulate a simple business plan for wine development.

Sources of wine supply

Unless your tie extends to wine, there are various types of wine supplier (all with their advantages and disadvantages) for you to consider using. These include:

♦ the traditional shipper/wholesaler, offering a duty-paid, delivered service
♦ the cash and carry
♦ the independent local merchant/wholesaler
♦ the national wholesaler.

The wines offered by different types of suppliers will range from mass-produced blends at bargain basement prices to rare vintages from obscure vineyards. Shop around. Which of them seems to best understand *your* business's needs? Which of them will tailor an offering to your business, rather than try to talk you into stocking their promotional lines, relevant or not? And remember: it is essential to look at not only the cost of the wines but the quality, consistency and, in particular, the back-up service.

In most instances you will need a mixed-case facility from your supplier.

Pricing wine

There are various methods of calculating profit margins, but basically the cash margin may be applied either to the cost or to the selling price, ensuring that all figures are either inclusive or exclusive of VAT. Hotel buyers calculate margins their own way as 'beverage cost', which is simply the cost expressed as a percentage of the selling price rather than as gross profit percentage; both percentages total 100 per cent. Thus a gross profit on selling price of 70 per cent translates into a beverage cost of 30 per cent.

What should always be borne in mind, though, is that you can't bank percentages. Obvious as this may seem, many establishments price wines at the same percentage margins throughout the list, making the pricier wines prohibitively expensive, with the result that they sell in tiny volumes. Far better to calculate the gross margin on the house wine, then add a little in cash terms to all other wines up the cost scale. This results in wines being sold more evenly across the list, in a higher actual cash profit, in customers feeling they are getting value for money, and in more recommendations to their friends.

The wine list

Whatever the size, type or style of the list, it is essential for it to be balanced. The number of wines needs to be considered most carefully. On the one hand there must be a big enough range to provide a choice suitable to the context; on the other, the greater the range of wines the more storage/chilling space you need and the more cash you have tied up in stock.

Presentation of the wine list is another major consideration. Is it to be printed by a printer? (Not usually recommended these days – too expensive and inflexible.) Is it to be prepared on your own PC? (Time-consuming, but so quick to update.) Will your supplier prepare the list as part of the service? (Often the best way, but ensure a clear brief is given as to how detailed the wine descriptions are to be, and whether any reference is to be made to compatibility with dishes on the menu.) Or is the blackboard the best place? (Cheap and cheerful, but conspicuous and with a certain immediacy: blackboards are also an excellent medium for promotions.)

Wine by the glass (including wine preservation)

Even if the outlet has a predominance of male beer drinkers, there are often occasions where a woman might prefer a glass of wine, and it is important that the consumer can be confident that the wine will be sound. In the past, white wine would usually have been the choice in these circumstances, but the trend is increasing towards red, and in many parts of the country the split between red and white is now 50:50. This is because many people – both

men and women – prefer the fuller flavour of red; also, the influence of foreign travel and, perhaps most significantly, modern medical opinion that red wine in moderation is positively good for you.

Presentation is an area of wine service where the most basic boozer can score as highly as the poshest restaurant, and entirely without cost. Wine must be served in measures of 125ml (six glasses to the bottle, providing the basic single measure of alcohol) or 175ml (four to the bottle), using either lined glasses or a metered dispense device such as an optic. The latter is preferable because it helps avoid the commonest and least forgivable sin committed by publicans. This is to serve red wine in brim measure Paris goblets and white wine in brim measure flutes, and to wine drinkers it is heresy. Wine glasses need plenty of headspace in which the aromatic vapours, which are half the pleasure of wine, can gather. But when using oversized lined wine glasses staff tend to overpour, and in wine service this is more critical than in pulling pints of beer because a winebottle contains a precise number of measures. Overpour means the last glass out of the bottle is substantially short, so a new bottle has to be opened before the customer can be satisfactorily served – which is time consuming and looks sloppy. An optic or similar device solves all these problems.

Wine served by the glass *must* be in good condition. The maximum shelf-life of wine in bottles once opened and at room temperature is 36 hours. There are many different methods of preserving wine once it is opened.

At the most basic level, there is bag-in-box, and this might well be the preferred option for the pub that has only a limited call for wine.

It is also now possible to offer a small range of wines in a single-serve format. Available bottle sizes are 10cl, 18.75cl and 25cl. A minor benefit, if this is the only way that wines can be offered by the glass, is that it removes the requirement for lined and stamped glasses. Although the 10cl size is the cheapest in actual price, it is nevertheless very expensive when the quantity:price ratio is taken into account. For this reason 18.75cl is probably the optimum bottle size. One company offering a selection of over 20 wines from well-known producers, together with promotional material, is Reed Wines.

The range is marketed via a number of independent wholesalers across the country.

If wines by the glass are served from the bottle – and this is the only realistic option if a wide range of wine is to be offered – then there are various alternative methods of wine preservation.

Perhaps the best known is the Vacu-Vin, a handpump used to remove air from bottles, costing around £7. It is inexpensive, can be used on an unlimited number of bottles, and preserves wine for up to two weeks. However, it is hard to determine the level of vacuum: not enough and the wine will oxidise; too much, and the aromas and flavours will be adversely affected. It is not appropriate to sparkling wines and not ideal for large-scale commercial use (though the latter is unlikely to affect most pubs).

Another simple method is the Winesaver, a small disposable cylinder (80 per cent nitrogen and 20 per cent carbon dioxide), which is sprayed into the open bottle, displacing the air. With low initial cost (around £5), it preserves wines, sherry and port (in decanters as well) for up to two weeks. It is a more consistent and gentler method than the Vacu-Vin, but more expensive as it needs replacing every hundred bottles or so. Again, it is unsuitable for sparkling wines.

Le Verre du Vin is the most effective commercial wine preservation system, and can be used for still and sparkling wines. But at £2050 (excluding sparkling) and £2450 (including sparkling) for the basic unit, exclusive of delivery and installation, and with cooler units at around £500 extra, this is a serious investment. The system also needs plenty of space. Except for large-scale wine on-licence sales, this system is likely to be inappropriate, but if further information is required, contact Waverley Vintners (tel: 01738 629621; fax: 01738 630338).

Legal Notes

Wine when sold by the glass must be in quantities of 125ml or 175ml, and a statement must be displayed indicating the measures in use. It is acceptable to use both measures.

Wine when sold in carafes must conform to either 25 cl, 50cl, 75cl or one litre. All measures can be used in the same premises and again, a notice is required.

CHAPTER FIVE

SPIRITS

Ted Bruning

Unit for unit, spirits are the most profitable items in the pub. There are many interesting parallels between the beer and spirits markets in Britain's pubs.

Whisky, like ale, was the unchallenged king in the 1950s, when gin was drunk only by naval types, salesmen with social pretensions and aged flappers; brandy was more common at table than in the bar; and vodka was known only to the more effete members of the Diplomatic Corps.

The day Sean Connery first asked for a vodka martini, shaken not stirred, was a fateful moment for the Scotch whisky industry. The Bond films gave the first inkling to most English people that there was an exciting, cosmopolitan life to be lived beyond suburbia; that their aspirations could extend beyond a week in Bognor and a new Ford Popular; and that their boss need not be their social model.

From that moment white spirits – vodka and white rum, not poor old gin – began to challenge whisky, even as lager was beginning to challenge ale. (Is casting dark rum in the role of mild ale stretching the analogy too far?) Nevertheless, whisky is still the single most important category in the average pub's profile of spirits sales.

WHISK(E)Y

Whisk(e)y is basically distilled beer without the hops. It was invented by Irish or Scottish monks in the fourteenth or fifteenth centuries, using technology learnt from the Arabs, who had used distilling to make perfumes and medicines.

Whisky or whiskey? The spellings are etymologically interchangeable, but it has become conventional to describe Scotch and its Canadian and Japanese descendants without the 'e' and Irish and its American offspring with it.

Scotland is divided into four malt distilling regions:

1. Highland accounts for most production, best-known names being Glenfiddich, Glenlivet and Macallan

2. Island includes Islay, which produces characterful malts such as
Laphroaig
3. Lowland malts are becoming rarer
and tend to be less interesting as
singles, more used for blending
4. Campbeltown is reduced to two
distilleries, one of them the
supreme Springbank.

Single malt

The product of one distillery, generally aged for at least eight years,
although a five-year-old Balblair is
not bad.

Vatted malt

A blend of single malts, common in
the last century, but virtually extinct
until supermarket chains hit on the
idea of reviving it for their own-label
generic malts.

Grain whisky

Whisky made on a continuous still
rather than the traditional pot still.
Cheap, and until recently used only
for blending. A couple of single grain
whiskies have been launched in the
1990s to try and wrest market share
from white spirits.

Blends

By far the commonest type. A com-
pound of malt and grain whiskies,
whose price and cost rises along with
the proportion of malt. Standard
blends contain one-third or less malt
whisky, although there are no legal
definitions and some of them can
taste pretty malty. De luxe blends
such as Chivas Regal and Johnnie
Walker Red Label still occupy a small
place in the market, while export

blends such as Johnnie Walker Black
Label, Ballantine's and Cutty Sark
have increasing cachet in the home
market.

Irish whiskeys

These are made by a slightly different
process from Scotch and tend to
be smoother and sweeter. All the
common brands are blends, although
single malts are beginning to creep
on to the market.

American whiskies

In very broad terms, Canadian
whisky derives from the Scottish
tradition, and US whiskey from the
Irish. However, there has been so
much cross-fertilisation over the
years, and innovations dictated by
local conditions (especially in the
use of rye) that the distinction is
meaningless. Canadian distillers have
stepped in to fill the gap in the take-
home market created by the banning
of subnorm (less than 40 per cent
alcohol by volume) Scotches, but
Canadian Club is still an important
pub brand. One or more US whiskeys – Jim Beam, Jack Daniels, Wild
Turkey – are must-stocks, as is
the derivative Southern Comfort. A
connoisseurs' brand of US whiskey
is Maker's Mark.

Retailing whisk(e)y

Twenty years ago, a single Scotch
was 50 per cent more expensive than
a pint of bitter. Now it falls somewhere between a half and a pint. The
margin is still good, but more and
more pubs are finding that they
have to take their whisky range
upmarket. This is all part of the game

Berentzen

The Original Apfelkorn

For Further Information please contact:
Amberstone Trading Co Limited, Suite 13, Cortland,
George Street, Halisham, East Sussex, BN27 1QN.
Tel: 01323 842880/Fax: 01323 842830

Berentzen

The Original Apfelkorn

Light Fruit Schnapps is the fastest growing category among discerning consumers. Berentzen Distillers, Europe's market leaders in this field offer a range of premium packaged Schnapps in 10 smooth and easy to drink flavours. Since its establishment in 1758, Berentzen has proceeded to capture the imagination of consumers world-wide and is now available in over 100 countries.

Reflecting its fun loving roots Berentzen has become synonymous with having fun and partying to the earlier hours of the morning. Popular with both men and women in the 18-24 year old market, they can be drunk neat or with a variety or mixers.

Berentzen Schnapps support includes branded chiller units offered on a self liquidating basis, event nights and impactful point of sale.

For further information please contact: Amberstone Trading Co Limited, Suite 13, Cortland, George Street, Hailsham, East Sussex BN27 1QN. Tel:01323 842880 Fax:01323 842830

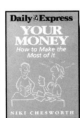

of balancing quality and afford-
ability; but with Scotch it is possible
for most publicans to stock one or
two really expensive whiskies, since
the entry price of even £2 a single
measure is still not beyond the reach
of many customers (especially as the
evening wears on).

Pub whisky has always been more
upmarket than take home whisky
anyway – you never saw subnorm
Scotches in pubs even when they
were legal, let alone supermarket
own labels. In fact, brand leadership
could be established by pricing up –
Bell's eclipsed Haig by increasing its
price to create the illusion of better
quality, and Famous Grouse has very
nearly eclipsed Bell's the same way.

Today Bell's, Teacher's and Grouse
are the lowest common denomin-
ators in pubs, and all pubs stock at
least one single malt (invariably
Glenfiddich). Any pub except the
most basic will stock two or three
malts: the United Distillers Classic
malts range is especially well presented, and you may have a market
for the new generation of 'designer
malts', such as Macallan aged in
Sherry casks. It has also become
common to stock two or even three
Irish whiskeys. The next step in going
up-market is to stock merchant-
bottled single malts. Cask strength,
single cask and over-aged malts from
the merchant bottlers – Gordon
& MacPhail, Cadenhead's, and the
Scotch Malt Whisky Society – are the
dernier cri in whisky snobbery: they
are not really for the average publican, but you never know. The joy of
whisk(e)y is that it's an area where
the publican has the flexibility
to stock a brand just for one good
regular.

OTHER SPIRITS

It may seem a little brusque, but with
all other spirits the rule is precisely
the same as it is for whisk(e)y: chase
the premium. It's the same as with
canned beers: people may have them
at home, but they want something
a bit posher when they go out.

For instance, French brandy in
pubs has to be Cognac (with Armag-
nac as a speciality). Even the most
basic boozer can't get away with
French grape brandies such as
Three Barrels: the handful of brandy-
drinking punters may quite happily
drink own-label, subnorm caramel-
ised grape spirit in the house but,
when they go out, it has to be the
real thing.

The same is true with gin: Gordon's
may be the most expensive gin
people take home, but it's the lowest
common denominator in pub terms,
and if you want to diversify it has
to be upwards into Booth's, Bombay
Sapphire and other premium brands.
Gin in the UK is today targeted
mainly at the 18–35 age group, and
it's a fair assumption that the brand-
leader, Gordon's, sees its main competitors as other white spirits – primarily Bacardi and Smirnoff Vodka
– rather than other gins.

What all these products have in
common is an alcoholic strength in
the UK of 37.5 per cent. Professional
cocktail bartenders prefer higher
strength white spirits to minimise
the effect of dilution from ice, tonic
and so on. Gin in particular is not
as effective at 37.5 per cent, because
at this level the botanicals (including
juniper, spices and citrus rind) lose
much of their aroma and flavour.
This is why Gordon's and Tanqueray

Krush is a NEW, exciting and profitable drinking experience. Made from real fruit juices, premium spirits and blended to give a unique COCKTAIL Experience.

Krush the UK's only pre-mixed ready to use frozen ALCOHOLIC cocktail, is guaranteed to give a 5% ABV. The drink comes pre-packed in a 5 Litre container and is ready to use with your Krush refrigeration unit, which is only available to the Licensed On Trade.

BIG PROFITS of 70% G.P. are easily achievable, pre-mixed and guaranteed to give a 5% ABV in fifteen exciting flavours. The only effort for your bar staff is to pour the contents of each 5 Ltr. Container into the Krush refrigeration unit and just switch on, no plumbing required.

Krush refrigeration units are lit and branded; a state of te art moving spiral churns and freezes the cocktails giving a highly visible effect. The units are free standing and can be placed on the back or front bar area. No plumbing is necessary, Krush refrigeration units simply plug into a 13 amp socket. There are three sizes of units available, single bowl, double and triple bowl units. Which can be purchased outright, lease purchased, or rented which comes with 12 month service contract.

Krush in the ideal route to additional profits and guaranteed to satisfy a thirsty market, which is ready for a NEW TASTE SENSATION. The range has been specially formulated for the UK and the FIFteen Flavours provide a combination of great tastes colours.

The history of COCKTAILS is nothing new and our classic range is taken from out long established names like Pina Colada, Marguerita, and a fabulous range of Daquiris. FROZEN Cocktails were originally developed in the USA and have been selling for the past 10 years. The concept was developed in Florida and spread to California, Spain, the South of France and ski resorts throughout the French Alps. The response from British tourists has been huge. Since the launch of the product two years ago in the UK it can now be found in venues of all shapes and sizes, from very large operators to the independent free houses.

The Krush Product range is fully supported by a range of Point of Sale materials, but clearly the main P.O.S. is the KRUSH Refrigeration Unit itself which is lit by its own internal light. With the churning of the colourful cocktails the dispensing unit becomes a main feature of the bar.

KRUSH - COOL PROFITS - *JUST A FEW EXAMPLES*

FEEDER BAR NOTTINGHAM

Selling Price per 6oz Serving	£2.00
Less Vat (if applicable)	£0.30
Sub Total	£1.70
Less Pre-Mixed Cocktail Cost	£0.46
PROFIT PER SAVING	**£1.24**
Average Number of servings per week	328
GROSS WEEKLY PROFIT	£406
Less weekly lease purchase price of Triple Unit	£19.54
Net Weekly Profit	£386.46
***NET FIRST YEAR PROFIT**	**£20,095.92**

VODKA BAR - SOUTH WALES

Selling Price per 6oz Serving	£2.10
Less Vat (if applicable)	£0.31
Sub Total	£1.79
Less Pre-Mixed Cocktail Cost	£0.55
PROFIT PER SAVING	**£1.24**
Average Number of servings per week	264
NET WEEKLY PROFIT	£327
*NET WEEKLY PROFIT	£17,022
Less purchase price - double bowl unit	£1,300
***NET FIRST YEAR PROFIT**	**£15,722**

Questions & Answers

(Q) Does the KRUSH Refrigeration Unit have to be left running 24 hours a day?

(A) No, the unit needs to be turned on 1½ hours before you wish to use it to allow it to freeze down and is then turned off when trading ends.

(Q) Is it difficult to maintain the units?

(A) The KRUSH refrigeration units are easily maintained and only need to be washed once per week.

(Q) Is it a fad?

(A) No, Cocktails have sold since the 1920's so there is no reason for them to stop now.

(Q) Is Krush just a summer drink?

(A) Frozen cocktails have sold in Ski resort all France for the last four years, and KRUSH is now into a second successful winter season in the U.K.

(Q) How many flavours are there?

(A) There is currently a range of fifteen cocktail flavours. Strawberry Marguerita, Sex on the Beach, Slow Comfortable Screw, Pina Colada, Peach Daquiri, Screaming Orgasm to name a few.

(Q) What is the shelf life of the cocktails?

(A) The cocktails will last up to two weeks once they are in the KRUSH Refrigeration Unit, and up to three months in the 5 Litre containers. The cocktails can be frozen and thawed repeatedly without any damage being caused.

(Q) How big is a KRUSH Refrigeration Unit?

(A) Dimensions of Refrigeration Unit

Type	Capacity litres	Depth cm	Width cm	Height cm	Weight kg
Single Bowl	12	48	20	73	27
Double Bowl	24	48	40	84	51
Triple Bowl	36	48	60	84	65

CALL FOR A FREE DEMONSTRATION
TEL: 01246 855358

are also sold at 47.3 per cent. Do consider Beefeater and Bombay Sapphire Gins – both sold at 40 per cent, and Plymouth Gin at 41.2 per cent (its original 'standard' strength).

White rum has to be Bacardi (or at a pinch Dry Cane); you may also stock a specialist brand such as Wray & Nephew, but only the scruffiest shebeen would stock anything less.

Dark rums are an interesting area: Scottish pubs until a few years ago did a lively trade in value-for-money brands – but only a certain type of Scottish pub. Standard dark rums may not do much these days, except as a mixer; but the number of pubs stocking an overproof, especially Woods 100 or Pusser's, is increasing: is there scope for a Trafalgar Day promotion here?

With vodka, again, the action is in the upper reaches: Smirnoff Blue Label and Black Label, Absolut from Scandinavia, Stolichnaya and Moskovskaya from Russia and other authentic Eastern European brands – many of them flavoured with anything from bison grass to ginger and cloves – compete for space in the premium sector, while even in the standard sector newcomers such as Black Death from Iceland and Virgin Vodka are creating interest. The diversity is such that all sorts of promotions suggest themselves: do you know when Lenin's birthday is? The bottles should be kept cold if possible: one eye-catching way of serving them is straight in a shot glass, to be downed in one.

LIQUEURS AND SPECIALITIES

Very careful stock control is called for here. As far as traditional liqueurs are concerned, the range you really need to stock is dwindling: how many advocaats or Drambuies have you served in the last 12 months, for instance? And can you actually open your bottle of blue Curaçao, or is the lid stuck to the bottle?

There's little point wasting £6 or £8 a bottle on something that is really only held in reserve as a contingency: on the two or three occasions a year you're forced to say 'sorry, we don't stock yellow Chartreuse' the customer will probably settle quite happily for something else anyway.

Many of the bottles you see on the too-high-to-reach shelves are only stocked because there's a hangover from the 1960s that says the most aspirational bars are cocktail bars, and cocktail bars must stock Maraschino: but they aren't; and they mustn't; and why waste money on stock you can't sell?

On the other hand, if you specialise in cocktails you may need to keep a great number of different exotic spirits, and lay in additional specials from time to time to vary your cocktail list. The golden rule here is to find a supplier who will let you have mixed cases: this is an area where a temporary out-of-stock is less damaging than a permanent state of overstock.

If you want to specialise in cocktails but only to a limited extent – say for a particular crowd, or for special promotions – you may find that one of the many ranges of pre-mixes now available is actually more suitable than attempting to mix your own. Your staff will probably not have the expertise, the time or the space to shake up cocktails to order.

Modern speciality drinks are more problematical: when young people ask for a new drink such as Bezique or Archer's Peach County or Bailey's or Malibu, you have no way of knowing whether Bezique is going to sink like a stone while Bailey's and Malibu are going to become standards. Never order more than one case, on sale or return if you can, and don't order a second until the eleventh bottle of the first is finished. This applies even to growth drinks such as Tequila, which comes in both white and gold, both standard versions already well known in the UK and the latest top quality examples now appearing. That these are popular nationally does not mean that they will be popular with your clientele, so order cautiously. However persuasive the rep, however appealing the promotion, remember this: there are bottles of Bezique gathering dust on top shelves across the land, each representing hard-earned cash. In time they will become collectors' items, but until then they are unrecoverable outlay.

PRESENTATION

Spirits and speciality drinks benefit from correct presentation and service. For instance, a Scotch on the rocks has to be served in a clean tumbler with ice that doesn't float; there are correct glasses for Martini, for brandy, for liqueurs, and using them shows that you take pains.

British barstaff have never understood ice the way the punters do: the customer sees in his mind's eye a sparkling, broad-based tumbler with three or four big cubes of clean ice filling one-quarter to one-third of it and the spirit poured over, resting in the bottom of the glass. Barstaff seem to see a Paris goblet a quarter full of liquid, with two round-edged, sad little bits of ageing ice bumping about listlessly on top.

Part of retailing is seeing through the punter's eyes, and spirits service is one area where the visual aspect is both obvious and essential. (And while you're there – how about a clean white coaster like you get in New York?)

After all, going out is expensive these days, and when customers are liable to ask whether they're really getting their money's worth, the importance of keeping up appearances cannot be too strongly emphasised.

Legal Notes

Spirits must be served in multiples of 25ml or 35ml, and a notice to that effect must be displayed. This does not apply to cocktails – ie a mixture of three or more drinks – or where a customer asks for a specific quantity of spirit in a mixed drink.

CHAPTER SIX

GLASSWARE

Ted Bruning and Paul Cooper

Attractive and appropriate glassware is an important element in presentation. A drink served in the wrong glass does nothing to enhance the image of your pub, while attractive glassware will create an overall impression of stylishness. Customers will get more pleasure from drinking their g & t from your tall, slender, elegant glass than from the half-pint nonik that gets plonked down in front of them at the pub down the road.

Branded glasses can further enhance the presentation of products and act as a marketing device. Badged glasses differentiate products that would otherwise look the same. Another benefit is that they are often provided free of charge by the brand owner, saving you money! These benefits must be weighed against the disadvantage that your staff will spend time trying to find the appropriate glass and at busy times will inevitably use the wrong ones. Badged glasses are also irresistible to the 'collectors' among your customers, which is irritating even if they were supplied free.

Toughened glasses have the advantage of reducing the number of breakages, but you should consider whether this fully offsets the additional cost involved in buying them. The Brewers and Licensed Retailers Association (BLRA) recommends a switch to toughened glass in pubs instead of the more common annealed glass.

Toughened glasses have been on the market in this country for 40 years, but the method of toughening has raised a serious question about their safety and held back their progress in the licensed trade. The process used by French manufacturer JG Durand, involves plunging the glasses into cold water to chill them in seconds from 500°C to hand heat. The sudden cooling creates a super-tense surface which is almost impossible to break by impact.

Once the surface tension is compromised by repeated stacking, washing and scuffing, however, the glass can shatter at any minute, creating hundreds of small round shards which, while not as sharp as the long, sharp splinters yielded by annealed glassware, can still cause cuts and abrasions.

The relative virtues of toughened and annealed glassware have been an issue in the trade since the early 1980s, when violence in pubs, and in particular the increasing use of broken beer glasses as weapons, began to cause widespread alarm.

In the early 1990s the authorities slowly got behind toughened glasses. In 1991 the Health Education Authority and University of Wales researchers both recommended to the Home Office that toughened glasses should become the norm, while magistrates and police in many areas made their use a condition of the grant of licences. Amid the controversy, toughened glasses gained ground, and the BLRA estimated last year that one-third of British pubs and clubs now used them.

Supporters say that if anyone tries to break a toughened glass to use as a weapon, there are two possible outcomes: either the glass smashes into tiny pieces, or nothing happens at all. They also say that toughened glass is actually more durable than annealed glass, lasting up to 50 times longer in everyday use, and if they break during washing the rounded fragments will do a good deal less harm than the long, sharp splinters which come from annealed glasses. However, it is widely accepted that toughened glass must be replaced as soon as scuffing starts to appear.

Brewers and publicans also point out that toughened glasses have been used in enormous quantities for some years now, and the trade is not awash with anecdotes of exploding pints and bars full of shrapnel:

the case against them has, quite simply, been disproved by experience.

After years of scepticism, British manufacturers have at last come round to toughened glass, and there are now home-grown brands on the market for publicans to choose from.

But toughened glassware's hard-won acceptance is not the end of the story: there are already on the market plastic drinking vessels made of polycarbonate that look like glass, feel like glass, won't break for use as a weapon, and won't shatter if their surface is scratched or scuffed. At the moment it is three times as expensive as toughened glass, but it is claimed to last 20 times as long, and there are suppliers who believe it is the glassware of the future.

However, licensees should not rush into restocking with toughened glassware or polycarbonate without considering the likelihood of new weights and measures legislation and the requirement for lined, oversized glassware. For although the attempt to introduce such a requirement by Private Member's Bill failed, the government has promised legislation of its own, using secondary legislative powers if necessary, to effect the desired changes.

The BLRA is sedulously trying to keep the issues separate, but there is a very real danger that retailers who invest heavily in brim measure toughened glassware will be caught out when the requirement to restock with oversized glasses is enacted. For even though there will certainly be a phasing-in period, it will be intended to match the usual replacement cycle of annealed glassware, and publicans who have bought toughened brim measures will find themselves left with sizeable stocks of unbroken brim measures they can no longer use. If you are restocking, therefore, it may make sense to re-stock with oversized lined glasses.

Publicans worried about the 'extra' beer they will end up serving when the new requirements become law need not rush into installing metered dispense, either. When it seemed, some years ago, that Section 43 of the Weights and Measures Act would be enacted, some brands of lined, oversized glasses were redesigned to minimise overpour by making them taller and narrower, thus containing a smaller volume above the line.

The same fear of loss through overpour has tempted some publicans to use brim measure glasses for wine service. To wine drinkers this is heresy. Wine has to be allowed a very large headspace in which the vapours it gives off can collect, allowing the drinker to nose the wine properly. True wine buffs use huge glasses which they never fill more than one-third full, which may be a little extravagant for the average publican; but the glass should never be more than two-thirds full. This rule applies to white wine and red wine glasses (the elongated Burgundy goblet is a lot more attractive for red wine service than the round Paris goblet). Large glasses give the wine a greater surface area, which again allows the vapours to rise properly, enhancing the nose or bouquet.

A clean glass should be used for every drink. Re-filling a customer's glass is not good practice and has hygiene implications.

Whatever type of glassware you decide is right for your pub, it has to be truly clean. Glasses should

sparkle, and not be watermarked, smeary or covered in lipstick. The best way to achieve this is with a mechanical glasswasher.

There are many types available on the market, all of which vary slightly in the way they operate. However, they all wash your glasses and then coat them with a chemical called rinse aid that dries the glass by causing the water to sheet off.

The best way to ensure clean glasses is to have a clean glasswasher. Clean the filter and make sure the water jets are not blocked every day, and clean the inside of the wash tank at least twice a week to stop the build-up of dirt and bacteria.

You must also use good quality chemicals in the machine. The best cleaning fluids are non-caustic ones. Caustic cleaning fluids eat into the glass and cause etching after a couple of months which is detrimental to the appearance of your glasses (this is not so much of a problem in soft water areas).

A glasswasher should operate at a wash temperature of 45°C and a rinse temperature of 60–65°C. If your machine operates at lower or higher temperatures it will not clean efficiently. If your machine has a mechanical dosing unit for the detergent, this should be set by the company that supplied it. If you have to put the chemical in yourself, add two to three squirts of detergent, using a pelican pump, every four to five cycles.

Rinse aid is usually inserted by a mechanical pump built into the machine, often self-calibrated.

In hard water areas a water softener will improve the effectiveness of your glasswasher. If you have a water softener fitted to your machine you should ensure that you follow the instructions provided.

Lipstick appears to adhere to glass better than it does to lips, and even the best glasswashing machines will not remove a thick layer. Always wipe the rims of affected glasses before you put them in the machine.

There is always a tendency to dry glasses with a cloth when they come out of the machine. If your machine is working correctly, and your glasses are stored on glass-mats and not directly on a shelf, there should be no need to do this. In fact you could be making matters worse, as a residue of the detergent in which the cloth was washed can be left on the glass, preventing the rinse aid from working properly.

Some common problems that occur with glasswashers and solutions to these problems are listed below.

Fault: machine will not fill or rinse. **Check:** water supply. Action: Open stop tap fully.

Fault: machine not washing effectively. **Check:** filter, wash jets, detergent. **Action:** remove and clean blocked filters; unblock wash jets; use correct amount of detergent.

Fault: glasses not drying. **Check:** detergent, rinse aid. **Action:** ensure correct amount is being used.

Fault: condensation on glasses. **Check:** rinse aid, glass storage. **Action:** use correct amount of rinse aid, do not store glasses on a flat surface.

Fault: 'blooming' on glasses. **Check:** detergent. **Action:** use non-caustic detergents.

Fault: excessive foaming in wash. **Check:** rinse aid, tank water. **Action:** reduce amount of rinse aid being injected; ensure machine has not been cleaned with high foam detergent, eg washing-up liquid.

Health and Safety Notes

Hygiene is controlled by the Food Safety (General Food Hygiene) Regulations 1995, which set standards for the service of food and drinks. There is nothing in the regulations to prevent bar staff from serving a second or subsequent drink to a customer in the glass of their choice, including the glass in which they had their first drink should they so wish. However, it is probably better practice to use a fresh glass, unless the customer insists on using the same one.

Legal Notes

The sale of draught beer and cider must be made in measures of either one-third of a pint or a half-pint or multiples of half a pint.

These glasses must bear the official crown stamp, and where stamped glasses are not used the beer must be dispensed through an officially stamped meter. *This requirement applies to customer's own tankards.*

As the law stands at the time of going to press, where brim measure glasses are used a measure may consist of liquid and a reasonable head. The recommendation of the Brewers and Licensed Retailers Association is that the liquid content of beer and cider, once the head has collapsed, should not be less than 95 per cent of any of the permissible measures.

Weights and measures legislation also requires that the main spirits – whisky, gin, rum, and vodka – must be sold for consumption in measures of 25ml or 35ml, or multiples of these amounts. A notice must be displayed indicating the particular measure served in the pub. However, these measures do not apply when a customer asks for a particular quantity of spirit in a mixed drink, or when a drink includes one main spirit in a mixture of three or more liquids.

Wine when sold by the glass must be in quantities of 125ml or 175ml. Again, a statement must be displayed indicating the measures in use. It is acceptable to use both measures. Wine when sold in carafes must conform to either 25cl, 50cl, 75cl or one litre. All measures can be used in the same premises. Again a notice is required.

CHAPTER SEVEN

CATERING

Tony O'Reilly

TRENDS

What makes a great pub? Twenty years' ago you might have said, a scenic location with a warm and friendly atmosphere, a relaxing environment, cracking host and good beer, however, one important component would be missing – the food!

The pub trade is rapidly changing to accommodate customer's increasing expectations. Gone are the days when the publican could rely on 'wet sales' to solely sustain profit margins. These days good food is a key factor if the publican is to attract customers and realise required sales figures. Figures in recent surveys show that in a large percentage of cases, food to wet sales has reached a ratio of 60:40 in favour of food and, that a fair chunk of wet sales turnover is, in fact, attributed to sales of wine and beer purchased with meals.

Almost everyone offers food in one form or another is it the humble peanut to a three-course gourmet selection, what is paramount how-

ever, is that you realise your market and never over stretch yourself.

Having had extensive experience up and down the country, visiting over 500+ pubs in the past three years to dine at, I can honestly say that my numerous experiences have varied immensely.

Some pubs are producing fine food to rival any two- or three-star restaurant. However, there are still those that have not yet mastered the art of satisfying the culinary expectations of their customers.

The following advice is for those considering introducing a food operation to their establishment. It might also be helpful to those who have not, as yet, achieved their culinary vision.

TRAINING

The first question to ask yourself is: can you cook?

You don't need to be a master chef to run a pub kitchen, but you do need a sound understanding of food hygiene, basic culinary skills, a little experience, a pinch of imagination, a flair for presentation and the ability to cope under immense stress, which is an occupational hazard.

Certain people might be able to get by without any formal tutoring. However, anyone keen to understand the rudiments should seriously consider teaming up with either a local college or a nationally recognised training company to receive instruction and maybe gain a formal qualification.

Colleges and training providers won't be able to teach you everything, but they'll inform you of the fundamentals of cooking that will cover hygiene, food safety, cooking principles and proper service.

If you consider this to be at the right choice for you then the next step is to contact the Training and Enterprise Council (TEC), or a college for expert advice and guidance on the appropriate part-time National Vocational Programmes (NVQ) or SVQ (Scotland) they have to offer.

For part-time programmes, a training provider would probably expect you to be employed in an appropriate position within the trade, as NVQs and SVQs can only be taught and assessed in a realistic environment, i.e., your workplace. Alternatively, the college may run a public restaurant that meets the criteria of a realistic working environment.

Nowadays most breweries have in-house training programmes for employees and potential employees, and one or two of the major breweries offer basic City and Guilds Cookery Certificates aimed specifically at the pub trade, but these are not normally open to outsiders. A few run training programmes for would-be licensees, but cooking is usually only an element of the full programme.

However much you learn in a training environment, it will never prepare you for 50 hungry diners – you have to experience that at first hand!

Perhaps, circumstances allowing, you could try assisting in the kitchen of another eatery. That would help you gain the relevant experience and, give you a good practical grounding.

Alternatively, circumstance and finances permitting, you might employ the services of a reputable consultant. The consultant will visit your establishment to devise a suitable menu, based on customer profiles; assess staff and kitchen capabilities and organise appropriate training, gradually easing you and your staff into the new menu. Once this is established you and your staff should feel confident and comfortable enough to work on your own.

PLANNING

Before determining an appropriate style and level of catering, find out what your market wants. Once this is established, you can begin planning the scale and pitch of your catering operation.

The best way to go about establishing your intended market is simply to visit successful pubs and restaurants in the surrounding area to give you a clear indication of the potential clientele.

If you prefer a more scientific approach, you can try the market research technique known as the mosaic formula, which profiles an area by type of resident and postcode to give an indication of disposable income within a given radius. It then finds out how far people are prepared to travel for a meal to come up with your potential customer base.

Even then, constructing and pricing a menu can be a little hit and miss. Most establishments aim for an average of 50–60 per cent gross profit. However, this might not be applicable to all dishes on the menu – for instance, there are seasonal fluctuations in the prices of fresh commodities.

There are particular dishes that may only cost 15–20% of selling price and some, especially vegetarian dishes, where costs may only represent 10% of the actual selling price. That might incite you to sell that particular dish at a 'marked down' price, however, research has proven that many customers are generally 'put off' being offered suspiciously low priced meals, this also being the case when offered meals that are priced too high.

In most parts of the country a charge upwards of £7 may be an realistic average main course price, for no other reason than that is what people expect to pay.

I know of a particular company that takes the average local menu price as a basis then sticks 10 per cent on top, reasoning that as it is superior to other local establishments its customers will be happy to pay the extra. For the record, it does work in this instance!

THE DINING AREA

Having established a style and level of operation, the next step is to create a matching ambience.

The first thing to remember is that there should be no conflict between drinkers and diners. Clearly designate an area for diners, and ensure that everyone is aware of it. Should the occasional drinker stray into the wrong area then don't be shy – all you have to do is tell them politely. It can be extremely off putting for diners if drinkers have their elbows in their ears when they are entertaining.

When it comes to choosing suitable décor for the dining area there is no substitute for a professional interior designer, assuming you can afford one. Make sure you brief them clearly on your ideas – after all, it's your pub and it should reflect the standards you wish to convey. Don't let the designer bully you into something you don't want. Take their advice, but don't allow yourself to be swayed if you are not entirely happy with their suggestions.

If hiring a designer isn't an option, and you have to do it yourself, one frequent mistake to avoid is the false economy of buying cheap furnishings. They will fill the room, but how long will they last? Buy furnishings that are practical, of a high quality, and above all hard wearing.

STAFF

If, for any number of reasons, you will not be cooking yourself, you will need both a good chef and a competent team.

How much you can pay will, of course, be entirely dependent on your projected overheads and turnover, and only you will be able to decide what you can afford. My research concludes that an average salary for a good pub chef should generally be in the region of between £200–£250 a week with bonuses. I myself though have placed head chefs in leading pub restaurants with their salaries exceeding £500 per week. This salary, however, reflects a number of key factors including the quality and standard of the food produced, the number of covers per week and, the prices charged. It might be possible to employ a chef who will work for less, and good luck to you. But be warned that if you pay a low wage you can expect a high staff turnover, which does nothing to help establish your food business in its start-up phase and causes operational problems even at the best of times. Always be fair, and

remember: if you pay peanuts you get monkeys!

If you employ an experienced chef you will need a set a menu that will challenge them. If the chef is allowed to become complacent there is the risk that boredom will set in – which will eventually be reflected in the quality and presentation of the food.

LUNCH AND DINNER

Food service is usually broken down into two sittings with very different patterns: lunch and dinner. Lunch-time diners have little time and expect to be served quickly and efficiently, whereas evening diners are more leisurely.

Catering for all your needs

Viscount Catering Limited is a leading, long established manufacturer of light, medium and super heavy duty catering and refrigeration equipment.

Its brands are well known with four of them being established in the 1800s.

Products include cooking ranges, grills, griddles, fryers, steamers, ware washing, preparation, refrigeration and serveries to mention but a few.

The products are manufactured in the home of stainless steel namely Sheffield and our long established expertise always guarantees a high quality product.

The heavy investment which we have made in modern manufacturing equipment allows us to offer probably the most competitive prices in the trade and we operate from 130,000 sq. ft. factory close to the M1 motorway. We employ some 175 people many of whom have been with us between 25 to 40 years.

Planning is an essential part of our service and it is free to our clients. We use the latest release Autocad systems for design and when offering a turnkey package begin with an assessment of the client's needs working closely with him or her until the scheme is planned and specified precisely. The service covers planning, design, manufacturing, installation, commissioning and staff training.

The training may be carried out on the client's site or in our own training kitchen.

Visitors are always welcome as it is our pleasure to show people round our factory when they are able to judge at first hand our capabilities and commitment.

The brands which we own are Moorwood Vulcan, Sadia Refrigeration, Electroway, Jackson, Lef Bishop, Henry Nuttall and Advanced Counters & Serveries. Supplying equipment to almost all of the ships in the Royal Navy is one of our proud boasts and our customers include MOD, Royal Navy, Royal Airforce, Army, universities, schools, hotel groups, fast food outlets, industrial canteens, etc, etc.

Projects range in size from £1000 to £1M.

Contact us on: 0114 257 0100 and we will make arrangements for one of our well experienced sales managers to call upon you to discuss your requirements.

JUST PUT US TO THE TEST

Viscount Catering Limited,
Green Lane, Ecclesfield,
Sheffield, S35 9ZY
Tel: 0114 2570100
Fax: 0114 2570251

Email: sales@viscountcatering.demon.co.uk
Web: http://www.popltd.co.uk/vdpyork/viscount

As a rough estimate, a lunchtime diner will take eight to ten minutes to reach your establishment, where they will then have 40 minutes before they have to leave. You should therefore allow no more than seven minutes to serve their starter and 15 minutes for their main course.

There seems to be an internal clock ticking in waiting customers that rings after 15 minutes, whereupon the customer will start worrying about whether they will be served in time to eat and enjoy their meal, without having to wolf it down. You only get one chance with this type of customer, and if you fail the first time then I'm afraid they'll probably never dine with you again!

So you have got to get it right from the beginning, and if you do then they will most likely visit to dine in the evening as well.

Evening service is quite different to lunch. Diners have time to relax and socialise and usually expect to spend much longer dining. As a guideline allow fifteen minutes for the starter and another ten minutes after they have finished their starter before you serve the main course.

If you have a restaurant licence covering designated areas of the pub there's no need to hustle diners out along with the drinkers at 11.20pm. If they're having a 'substantial' meal, they can carry on buying drinks up to midnight Monday–Saturday and 11.30pm on Sunday, with the standard 20 minutes drinking-up time on top. From a staffing point of view, you will need one waiter or waitress for every 12 covers, plus an additional person to take care of the bills. That person might be you, so it will give you an opportunity to chat to

the customer to ascertain whether or not they enjoyed themselves and the meal.

Above all else make sure that all staff, both kitchen and front of house are familiar with every dish on the menu and that they can adequately explain each one to the customer should it be necessary.

KITCHEN CREATIVITY

It's great to have superb gastronomic ideas, but if they are not practical you are not doing yourself any favours or impressing your customers.

Work through all new ideas carefully before actually offering them to the public. I have worked with many a publican who would change their menu because I was in their kitchen, and would add new dishes as they went along.

On one occasion when working in a pub I found hollandaise and Béarnaise sauce – which I enjoy making – added to the menu. It never entered the licensee's head to make sure he had enough eggs!

Whenever you introduce a new item, have a dry run at it – if only to time it and see how long it takes.

FRESH VERSUS CONVENIENCE

The balance to be struck between fresh foods and prepared dishes is a fine one, which must take into account the standard and experience of your kitchen staff, what the clientele will expect, and whether you can charge enough to warrant buying fresh.

But how to define the term fresh? Meat is available pre-portioned and chilled in pouches; fish are sold gutted and skinned; potatoes can be bought ready peeled and cut for cooking. Are these fresh or not?

One important point is that the standard of pre-prepared dishes and ingredients has improved greatly in recent years. Gone are the days, I'm relieved to say, when the standard pub vegetables were frozen peas or tinned beans with chips, and when the best a vegetarian could expect was cauliflower cheese with chips and frozen peas.

Advantages of using frozen foods are that they are convenient and that the prices don't fluctuate in comparison to fresh foods. There are many frozen food companies producing good quality products, with some so good that they can't be distinguished from fresh. These products however, should never be used to 'con' customers – there are some unscrupulous publicans out there that continue to pass frozen dishes off as their own home cooking!

In fact, there are few advantages in buying frozen foods other than that they are convenient. I'm not knocking frozen foods, as there are many good quality products available, but they can usually be distinguished from fresh, and when people are entertaining or being entertained they expect more.

My advice would be, whatever you buy, whenever possible buy fresh vegetables. There is no excuse not to as they are so easy to prepare and cook – and so cheap.

One of the drawbacks to using only fresh food is their short shelf-life, which means you spend half your time shopping. Fresh meat, for instance, should be purchased two to three times a week, and vegetables and dairy products bought daily. Fish should be purchased fresh every day or as required. It makes no sense to buy fresh and then freeze it – you might as well have bought frozen in the first place!

In fact you will find that in most cases frozen fish is fresher, the reason being that it is frozen at sea immediately after it is caught.

Some products have to be purchased frozen either due to insufficient trade to warrant buying fresh or, they are not available fresh in this country, e.g. exotic meats and tropical fish. It is advisable in this case to get samples from various companies and compare prices to secure the best deal.

Frozen food needs to be correctly thawed before use, and a common problem is deciding how many portions to thaw. There are some which can be cooked from frozen, but unless you have enough – and adequately powerful – microwaves, you are limited in the number of frozen products you can cope with efficiently in a session.

Frozen dishes are increasingly being superseded by chilled foods and, with major advances in chilling technology, you can purchase most products chilled with a fridge-life of up to 14 days. It usually only needs 8–12 minutes in a water-bath to regenerate dishes ready to serve.

What benefits does the microwave offer?

Standard microwaves are great for reheating prepared dishes, but as far as cooking goes they have always been a non-starter with me.

I once worked in a West End restaurant that had 40 microwaves to cope with the volume of customers (about 1000 a night), and I'm sure the chefs used to glow in the dark as they left for home! But all they were used for was to bring the food up to correct service temperature – economically, not very wise.

If you must cook with a microwave, then your best bet is to buy a high-powered (not a domestic) combination microwave/conventional oven. They can bake potatoes in under ten minutes, roast a rack of lamb in under six minutes, grill a chicken breast in under four minutes, and bake an individual pie lid in under three minutes – quite impressive!

PROMOTIONS

Themed evenings and events are a great marketing initiative, and provided you do your costings properly they can be a lucrative earner, with the bonus of drawing new custom as well as refreshing the jaded palates of your regulars.

Always do your research thoroughly to find out what excites your regular customers; but remember, their saying they would love to come is not the same as buying a ticket!

To attract a broad spectrum of customers always publicise forthcoming special events well in advance and as broadly as possible. To get free publicity in the local media you might incorporate a charity fundraising element – that usually guarantees a few column inches.

The more outrageous and innovative your event is, the better. I heard of one publican who held a Caribbean evening and had two tons of sand delivered to the pub along with giant umbrellas, beach tables and beach towels – in January.

Curry nights are another excellent promotional idea in the winter months, although now they are widely referred to as Baltis – the 'nouveau' term used to refresh Indian cuisine.

Thai cuisine is the new Chinese and is another good idea for a themed evening. If you are not proficient in ethnic cuisine there are many companies producing good quality sauces that only have to be added to meat to create the perfect, authentic dish.

You might also consider trying a British regional promotion – you can always find genuine recipes if you look hard enough – but, whatever you decide to put on, make sure you don't overstretch yourself.

CATERING FOR VEGETARIANS AND VEGANS

Catering for vegetarians is a must these days, and can be financially rewarding, as the number of vegetarians is increasingly steadily.

Even so, it still may not always be practical to cook fresh dishes daily for vegetarians. You might have to 'batch cook', cool and freeze; or, alternatively, you might want to try convenience vegetarian foods, of which there are many now available.

One problem commonly encountered by vegetarians when eating out is lack of choice. They want variety just as much as anyone else, and what they tend to get is pasta smothered in a cheese or tomato-based sauce. This definitely doesn't go down too well with most vegetarians: I constantly hear them complain that if they're only going to be offered pasta, why bother going out for a meal in the first place?

They expect more – quite rightly so, when they're paying for a meal out – and they demand an imaginative dish that will set their taste-buds tingling. If you're short of inspiration, there are many good vegetarian recipe books on the market. My wife and daughters are vegetarians and I have, over the years, built up a vast repertoire of imaginative and colourful meatless dishes.

Many people do not understand the difference between vegetarians and vegans. While vegetarians will eat eggs and milk-derived products, and some will even eat fish, vegans will have nothing to do with any food product derived from animal exploitation: no dairy products, no eggs, and definitely no fish.

Fruit and vegetables, pulses and nuts, and cereals of one sort or another are all vegans will eat – they even put soya milk in their coffee! – and it's worth including one or two vegan-friendly dishes on your menu as less strict vegetarians can order them as well.

Here are some other tips useful in catering for vegetarians and vegans:

◆ Don't serve a vegetarian crumble or other main dish made from the same vegetables you're serving on the side.
◆ An excellent meat substitute is Quorn, derived from fungi; but beware: vegans won't eat it because at the moment it is bound with albumen, which is derived from egg white; and some vegetarians tend to take offense if offered meatless products that resembles a steak, chop or mince!
◆ Vegetarian portions should be larger than equivalent meat dishes in order to yield the same nutritional value.

SUNDAY

With the gradual relaxation of licensing law, Sunday lunches have become the ultimate earner – and they're so easy to do! But there are a few things to remember.

Roast the meat off the day before. I know there's nothing better than freshly roasted meat, but to maximise portions the meat needs to be cold before you carve it. Of course, you could always set the alarm for 5am so you can roast the meat on the day and still leave time for it to cool down to carving temperature – but I think not!

With a little planning and organisation it is possible to be completely prepared for Sunday lunch – with the soup simmering on the stove alongside the gravy, the cold starter and cold sweet in the refrigerator, the meat cooked and carved ready for service, the roast potatoes in the oven next to the hot pudding, and all the vegetables cooked in readiness so they only need to be reheated in the microwave – by the time you open the doors at noon.

Certain publicans suspend serving snack foods such as sandwiches and rolls on a Sunday lunch. If your kitchen is inundated with roast meals and you are short staffed it can be a dilemma whether or not to serve the usual weekday fayre as well as a roast.

When in doubt, fall back on the philosophy that whatever the customer wants you should give them. With planning and organisation there should be no problem serving sandwiches on a Sunday – and there is as much money to be made from a selection of sandwiches as there is from more substantial meals.

Still, if you really feel you have to discourage people from ordering sandwiches during the busy Sunday lunchtime session, don't just take them off the menu: try increasing the price instead.

FREE NIBBLES

If you've decided to put free nibbles on the bar, there's one golden rule to follow: disregard the cost!

Treating your customers will soon backfire if you let yourself appear to be mean. If it is done well, on the other hand, the returns can be highly satisfactory. A happy customer is the best possible messenger for your pub, far better than any advert on radio, in the newspaper, or even on TV!

Try something else other than the usual and boring crisps and nuts. Roast potato wedges with plenty of salt on them go down well with drinkers with the added bonus that it also encourages them to drink a little more.

BARBECUES

Pub barbecues are a growth area and are an excellent way to increase profits: as well as a full restaurant,

you can have a whole garden packed with diners.

This is especially true if your pub has lovely gardens or a picturesque location – for instance on a riverbank or lakeside, or even beside a canal.

Generally, barbecues do not detract from the ordinary restaurant trade: on the contrary, they can be a great boost to overall customer numbers.

Barbecue customers seek the relaxed atmosphere of eating 'alfresco', rather than the more formal restaurant experience, and while they may not be prepared to stand the expense of treating the whole family to a restaurant meal, they may be happy to part with less money and have a family barbecue.

But organising a barbecue involves more than just cooking out of doors. First, you should thoroughly assess your garden, asking yourself some hard questions, such as whether it's attractive enough, whether it's big enough, where the barbecue itself should stand, whether you have enough tables and chairs, where to store the food for the barbecue, whether you have adequate chill/cool facilities, how the servery should be arranged, how people should actually pay for their food – cash at point of sale or by prepaid ticket – and what fire precautions/first aid you need.

Next, buy the right barbecue. If you're not building one yourself (and if you are, build it bigger than you think you need), don't necessarily go for the cheapest type on the market: they usually don't last very long and will need replacing regularly.

Go for something robust which will see you through the barbecue season and beyond without falling

"Think I'll Go For The Fish!"

Eating out is one of life's greatest pleasures. The good news for you is that in the year up to February 1998, there has been a steady increase in the eating out market, with eating out in pubs becoming more and more popular!
Fish has always been a favourite on the pub menu; in fact, British pubs use approximately 26,000 tonnes of fish per year, which is about half a tonne of fish per pub! Publicans have obviously "hooked:" a few "fishy" customers already with the most popular species served being prawns, scampi, haddock and plaice. However, with over sixty varieties of fish and shellfish available in the UK, the menu choice may be increased considerably.

Benefits

A profitable business needs satisfied customers. Having an excellent product to offer is the best start. Fish is that product. No other food offers as wide a range of tastes to suit so many different customers. With considerable interest in ethnic cuisine such as Italian, Mexican and Thai, customers are prepared to be more adventurous with food, which in turn increases the business open to you. Whilst firm favourites such as fish and chips still remain on the menu of most pubs, the image of fish has changed radically in recent years and it is now seen as an exciting, modern and healthy product. This is confirmed by the fact that customers eating out are opting for lighter, healthier meals. Offer your customers the choice of fish and reap the benefits. In fact, communicating the "lighter" meal benefits of fish may encourage business lunches when the consequences of a heavy lunch can be somewhat negative. Remember, fish may be served in soups, salads, sandwiches, as starters and as main courses. The choice is endless for your customers, and for your kitchen staff it provides opportunities to experiment with ingredients and cooking methods. Boost your liquid profits, too, by recommending suitable drinks to complement your fish dishes! To summarise, it makes good sense to include fish on the menu because: **Fish**
-is extremely versatile;
-is available in many convenient forms which are easy to buy, prepare and cook;
-is ideal in every catering situation;
-provides value for money. Species such as whiting, coley and ling offer a great value and are just as tasty as more familiar lines;
-allows scope for creative cooking with different species available to suit every budget;
-provides healthy margins;
-is exciting to work with;
-responds well to a variety of cooking methods;
-is popular with customers;
-is light yet filling;
-is healthy, and;
-is an excellent source of protein, vitamins and minerals.

Versatility

No matter the size of the kitchen - fish is the ideal choice. Its versatility means that it may be combined with any number of ingredients and cooked using a variety of methods. Fish allows you, the publican, to provide a menu that customers will regard as more desirable than the ready meals available in the top supermarkets, yet if necessary, the kitchen staff can assemble the ingredients into meals using the minimum of skill and without special equipment. Fish, therefore, is ideal in every catering situation allowing scope for creative or simple but tasty cooking with different species available to suit every budget.

Cooking

Remember that fish is naturally tender and cooks quickly. It is important not to overcook fish, as prolonged cooking will result in the flesh becoming tough and dry in texture. There is no need to serve fish in complicated sauces to increase the menu selection, just offer the more unusual species cooked simply, allowing the flavour of each to be relished.

Quality

Consumers are demanding better quality foods, both when eating out and for cooking at home. It is vital, therefore, that caterers and retailers are able to satisfy this demand for quality fish products.

With this in mind the Sea Fish Industry Authority - a statutory body - operates internationally recognised Quality Award Schemes which assure just that. The schemes cover the complete range of products from fresh, chilled fish to frozen, value added lines. The principal aim of the Quality Award scheme is to provide buyers with the assurance that their suppliers have passed a very thorough, independent inspection.

Menu

It is so simple to include fish on the menu. The following is a small selection of recipes which can be easily prepared. (Recipes available from the Sea Fish Industry Authority).

Cullen Skink
Rich Seafood Chowder
Crab Mousse
Smoked Mackerel Pate
Tropical Salad
Prawn, Courgette and Pasta Salad
Smoked Mackerel Toasties
Smoked Fish Baguettes
Indonesian Fish Curry
Winter Waffle Bake

Cheers!

i. (Source: Taylor Nelson Mealtrak

ORIENTAL MACKEREL FILLETS

455g (1lb) mackerel fillets
Marinade:
4 x 15ml spoon (4 tablespoons)
fresh orange juice
2 x 15ml spoon (2 tablespoons) soy sauce
2 x 15ml spoon (2 tablespoons)
fresh chopped parsley
juice and rind of ½ lemon
1 clove garlic, crushed
1 x 5ml spoon (1 teaspoon) Garam Marsala
Preheat the grill

1. Place the mackerel fillets into a shallow dish. Mix the marinade
   ingredients together and pour over the fish.
2. Cover and chill for 20 minutes.
3. Cook the fillets on a lightly greased grill pan for 4-5 minutes,
   basting with any remaining marinade.
4. Serve with noodles and stir fried vegetables.

Serves 4

ROAST COD WITH DILL AND LIME SAUCE

4 x 170g (6oz) thick cod or haddock steaks,
fresh or defrosted
Dressing:
100ml (3½ floz) white wine vinegar
50ml (2 floz) olive oil
2 x 15ml spoon (2 tablespoons) lime pickle
2 x 15ml spoon (2 tablespoons)
fresh chopped dill
70g (2½oz) butter
salt and pepper
Preheat oven to 220ºC/425ºF, Gas Mark 7

1. Place the fish in a shallow bowl, pour over dill and lime dressing.
   Cover and marinate for 15 minutes.
2. Melt 30g (1oz) butter in a pan. Add the fish, skin side down and cook for 3-4 minutes
   until golden brown. Turn the fish over and cook for a further 2-3 minutes.
3. Transfer the fish into an ovenproof dish, and reserve any juices in the pan. Bake for
   5-8 minutes.
4. Add the marinade mixture to the pan. Add the remaining butter and whisk
   continuously until the sauce has thickened. Season. Place on a bed of spinach and
   serve with the sauce.

Serves 4

SOLE WITH CRANBERRY SAUCE

4 x 170g (6oz) lemon sole or megrim fillets,

fresh or defrosted, skinned

60ml (4 tablespoons) cranberry sauce

knob of butter

1 x 15ml (1tablespoon) cranberry juice or sherry

salt and pepper

Microwave Power: 800 Watt

1. Lay the fillets on a board, skinned side uppermost. Spread each fillet with 1 x 15ml (1 tablespoon) cranberry sauce.
2. Roll the fillets and cut in half lengthwise. Place in a suitable dish, dot with the butter and pour over the cranberry juice or sherry.
3. Cover and cook on HIGH for 3 minutes.
4. Remove the fish from the juice and add remaining cranberry sauce. Cook on HIGH for 30 seconds.
5. Pour the sauce over the fish, season and serve with a selection of vegetables.

Serves 4

MEXICAN FISH TACOS

455g (1lb) huss or cod fillets, fresh
or defrosted, skinned and cubed
1 x 10ml spoon (1 dessertspoon) sunflower oil
1 small onion, sliced
$^{1}/_{2}$ green pepper, deseeded and chopped
1 clove garlic, crushed
1 x 425g can chilli beans
3 x 15 ml spoon (3 tablespoons)
tacos sauce, mild or hot
1 x 15ml spoon (1 tablespoon) tomato puree

1. Heat the oil in a large pan and cook the onion, pepper and garlic until soft and transparent.
2. Stir in chilli beans, tacos sauce and tomato puree.
3. Add prepared fish, stir carefully, cover and simmer gently for 5-6 minutes until fish is cooked.
4. Serve in tacos shells with lettuce and a salsa.

Serves 4

MACKEREL FILLETS WITH NOODLES

455g (1lb) mackerel fillets

2 x 15ml spoon (2 tablespoons) sunflower oil

·1 small onion, finely chopped

2 cloves garlic, crushed or chopped

1 x 400g can chopped tomatoes with herbs

300ml (1/2 pint) red wine

salt and pepper

115g (4oz) egg noodles

toasted sesame seeds, to garnish

1. Heat the oil in a pan. Cook the onion and the garlic until soft.
   Add the tomatoes, red wine and seasoning.
2. Bring to the boil, reduce the heat and add the noodles, cover
   and simmer for 3-4 minutes until the noodles are half cooked.
3. Place the fillets on top of the noodles and spoon over the sauce.
   Cover and cook for 6-8 minutes.
4. Garnish with toasted sesame seeds and serve with a
   selection of roasted peppers or seasonal vegetables.

Serves 4

HOT PRAWN COCKTAIL

255g (8oz) cooked peeled prawns

1 x 15ml spoon (1 tablespoon) tomato puree

5 x 15ml spoon (5 tablespoons) mayonnaise

1 x 15ml spoon (1 tablespoon) chilli sauce

dash Worcestershire sauce

dash lime juice

1 x 15ml spoon (1 tablespoon) finely chopped chilli

1/2 lettuce, shredded

1. Mix together the prawns, tomato puree, mayonnaise, chilli sauce,
   Worcestershire sauce, lime juice and chilli.
2. Line individual dishes with shredded lettuce and spoon over the prawn sauce.
3. Serve with bread as a starter.

Serves 4.

FRENCH STYLE HADDOCK

455g (1lb) smoked haddock fillets,
skinned and halved

knob of butter

2 x 15ml spoon (2 tablespoons) milk

1x 250 ml creme fraiche

fresh chopped chives

black pepper

Preheat the oven 190ºC/375ºF, Gas Mark 5

1. Place the fish in a dish, add the butter, milk and creme fraiche. Season.
2. Cover the dish with foil, cook for 15 minutes, remove the foil and cook for a further 15 minutes.
3. Serve the haddock with sauce, potatoes and spinach.

Serves 4

PESTO MOULES

2kg (4ld 7oz) fresh mussels, washed and
scrubbed and debearded

30g (1oz) butter

2 shallots, finely chopped

300ml (½ pint) white wine

2 x 15ml spoon (2 table spoons) lime juice

2 x 15ml (2 tablespoons) pesto sauce

fresh chopped basil, to garnish

1. Melt the butter in a large saucepan and cook the shallots, until soft and transparent.
2. Add the wine, lime juice and pesto sauce, bring to the boil. Add the mussels all at once, cover and cook over high heat for 4-5 minutes, shaking the pan occasionally to ensure even cooking.
3. When all the mussels have opened (discard any that remain closed) transfer to a heated serving dish, reserving the liquid.
4. Reduce the liquid by boiling rapidly for 3-4 minutes.
5. Pour the liquid over the mussels, garnish and serve with French bread.

Serves 4

SCALLOPS A LA BORDELAISE

670-895g (1½-2lbs) queen scallops
shucked and shells reserved
1 x 10ml spoon (1 dessertspoon)
sunflower or olive oil
1 shallot, finely chopped
1 clove garlic, crushed
2 tomatoes, skinned, deseeded and chopped
1 x 15ml spoon (1 tablespoon)
fresh chopped parsley
lemon rind, to garnish
salt and pepper
125ml (4 floz) dry white wine
40g (1½oz) fresh breadcrumbs
30g (1oz) butter, melted
Preheat the grill

1. Heat the oil in a pan and add the shallot and garlic. Cook for 1-2 minutes.
2. Add tomatoes, parsley, lemon rind, seasoning, wine and scallops.
   Cook for 2 minutes, stirring occasionally.
3. Spoon each scallop back into a shell with the tomato mixture and place
   into a large heat proof dish. Sprinkle over the breadcrumbs.
4. Drizzle over the melted butter and place under a hot grill.
   Cook for 1-2 minutes until the breadcrumbs are golden brown.
5. Serve as a starter.

Serves 4

CURRIED KEDGEREE

455g (1lb) smoked haddock fillet, fresh or
defrosted, skinned and cubed
170g (6oz) long grain rice
30-55g (1-2oz) butter or margarine
1 x 15ml spoon (1 tablespoon) curry powder
2 eggs, hard-boiled and chopped
1 x 15ml spoon (1 tablespoon) lemon juice
salt and black pepper
2 x 15ml spoon (2 tablespoon)
fresh chopped parsley

1. Cook the rice in plenty of boiling, salted water for 12-15 minutes.
   Drain well and keep hot.
2. Meanwhile, melt the butter in a large pan, add the curry powder and fish.
   Cook for 5-8 minutes. Stir in the cooked rice and half the chopped egg.
3. Stir in the lemon juice and season to taste. Garnish with the
   remaining egg and parsley.

Serves 4

BAKED SWORDFISH
WITH MUSTARD

4 x 170g (6oz) swordfish or shark
steaks, fresh or frozen
salt and pepper
2 x 15ml spoon (2 tablespoons)
wholegrain or French mustard
30g (1oz) butter, melted
30-55g (1-2oz) fresh breadcrumbs
mixed with 1-2 x 15ml spoon
(1-2 tablespoons) fresh chopped parsley
Preheat oven to 180°C/350°F, Gas Mark 4

1. Place the steaks into a lightly greased ovenproof dish and season.
2. Brush with the mustard and pour over half the melted butter.
3. Bake for 10-15 minutes (20-25 minutes, if frozen).
4. Add the remaining butter to the breadcrumb mixture and sprinkle over the steaks. Cook under a moderate grill for 5 minutes until crispy.
5. Serve with potato salad and sliced tomatoes.

Serves 4

PLAICE WITH SALSA

455g (1lb) plaice or lemon sole fillets, fresh or
defrosted, skinned
2 x 15ml spoon (2 tablespoons) plain flour
1 x 15ml spoon (1 tablespoon) sesame seeds
fresh chopped parsley
salt and pepper
2 x 15-30ml (1-2 tablespoons) olive oil
Salsa Sauce
1 red pepper, 1 yellow pepper
1 large tomato, chopped
1 x 5ml spoon (1 teaspoon) sesame seeds
1/2 red onion, finely chopped
pinch caster sugar
Preheat the grill

1 Prepare the salsa: Grill the peppers turning occasionally until blackened. Leave to cool and remove the skin. Cut in half, remove the seeds, core and finely chop.
2. Mix the remaining salsa ingredients together and set aside.
3. Combine the flour, sesame seeds, parsley and seasoning together. Lay the fillets in a board, skinned side uppermost and roll up. Coat the each fish roll in the flour mixture.
4. Heat the oil in a shallow non stick pan and cook the fish roll for 4-5 minutes, turning occasionally.
5. Serve with mashed potatoes and the salsa.

Serves 4

apart. In fact buy two: one for cooking on, and the other for keeping the food warm once it is cooked. Gas-fired barbecues are ideal as they heat up far more quickly than all-charcoal models.

Finally, you might also teach yourself how to cook properly on a barbecue and maybe have a practice run before trying it out on the customers. When you've got a hungry and expectant crowd you don't want them having to wait while the barbecue slowly heats up; nor do you want to find that the barbecue simply isn't big enough and a backlog of orders is building up.

And the last thing you want is to find yourself panicking and serving insufficiently cooked food – which at best will be brought back by your distinctly unimpressed customers and at worst will poison them. (A good tip is to part-cook some of the food in the main kitchen and then transfer it to the barbecue for finishing off.)

If you are holding a special barbecue event and anticipate more customers than your equipment can cope with you might consider hiring specialist equipment for the occasion. There are also quite a few companies offering the right equipment and advice for special occasions such as ox or pig roasts.

Finally, a tip: always use disposable crockery and cutlery, as the good stuff has a tendency to vanish outdoors.

Cooking for the public is unquestionably a different ball game to cooking for family or friends, but they share the same basic philosophy – whoever you cook for, you are undoubtedly out to impress!

My personal outlook is: 'You are what you put on a plate. If it looks good, then you look good. If it's rubbish . . .!'

THE PREMISES

Before you begin a food operation it is paramount that your premise complies with current legislation. That includes general cleanliness and state of repair; layout, design, construction and size; the provision of suitably located hand basins; adequate lighting and ventilation; appropriate drainage; the availability of toilets (ventilated and not opening directly to rooms where food is handled); and the provision of changing facilities for staff where necessary.

In areas where food preparation/cooking takes place there are additional, more specific requirements regarding the nature of surfaces to be used (to enable effective cleaning), the provision of appropriate facilities for washing equipment and food, and the provision of fly screening to openable windows where necessary.

Despite rumours about what is or is not permitted, the Regulations do not specify particular products. There is not, for example, a requirement to use stainless steel: it just happens to be a suitable and durable product. There are, inevitably, different ways of complying with the legislation depending on the budget available

and the hygiene standard appropriate for the use.

If you have any doubts about whether your pub complies, especially where the kitchen either has not previously been used for trade or if you intend to expand the food side, you can get advice from the EHO.

Obvious though it may seem, if you are making changes because you believe the law requires it of you it's worth checking that this is so – many people don't, and end up doing unnecessary work, or doing necessary work wrongly. Similarly, if you are making changes because you want to, it may be advisable to check beforehand that when you've finished the alterations will comply. In either event, doing so may save time and money.

THE PRACTICES

The fundamental requirement of the legislation is the need for a formal assessment in which potential food safety hazards are identified and methods of controlling them are specified.

Hazards include contamination by micro-organisms (in particular food-poisoning bacteria) or chemical or physical contaminants. Chemical contamination (eg the contamination of beer with line cleaner) is readily avoidable by the appropriate use and storage of cleaning products. Physical contamination (ie contamination by flakes of paint, insects and insect remnants and all other 'foreign bodies') can be avoided by good housekeeping and protection of food.

The biggest issue is avoiding the opportunity for food-poisoning

CINDERS BARBECUES
CATERING SYSTEMS

Barbecues
designed for the
Professionals

British made using high quality stainless steel and carrying a two year warranty, these units are the ultimate profit generating barbecues.

All units are quick and easy to use, clean and transport - folding for storage and with a model to suit any occasion, place or time.

For further information please telephone:
015242 62900
Fax: 015242 62955

• THE HOTELIER •

Total Grill Area - 1134 sq ins (7312 sq cms);
Total Heat Input - 65,000 Btu/Hr (20kw)
Weight - 137lbs (37 Kgs)

• THE CLUBMAN •

Total Grill Area -
567 sq ins
(3656 sq cms);
Total Heat Input -
34,000 Btu/Hr (10kw)
Weight -
83lbs (37 Kgs)

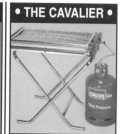

• THE CAVALIER •

Total Grill Area -
567 sq ins
(3656 sq cms);
Total Heat Input -
34,000 Btu/Hr (10kw)
Weight -
57lbs (26 Kgs)

• THE CATERER •

Total Grill Area - 1134 sq ins (7312 sq cms);
Total Heat Input - 68,000 Btu/Hr (20kw)
Weight - 103lbs (47 Kgs)

CALOR
CERTIFIED
For Safety & Performance

REGISTERED FIRM
FM 30695

ASSOCIATE MEMBER
HIRE
ASSOCIATION EUROPE
MEMBER

Cinders Barbecues Limited

By Carol Millar, Sales & Administration Manager (UK)

Carol Millar has been with Cinders Barbecues Limited for eight years and has seen a substantial rise in the use of barbecues in Pubs and Hotels, especially over the last 3-4 years. Many Publicans are now looking on 'barbecues' as an important part of the service to their customers and are choosing their barbecue equipment and menus accordingly.

At first many Publicans were wary of using barbecues making comments such as 'they take a long time to get going and then there is all that cleaning up afterwards'. Unfortunately many tried (in the name of economy) to use domestic barbecues to cater for, sometimes, hundreds of people, and although there was probably nothing wrong with the units they were not designed for catering volumes. We have seen a huge increase in eating out', together with a higher focus on Food Hygiene and Safety, over the past few years. Publicans are now looking at the barbecuing side of their establishments more seriously, and on a longer term basis. Extra revenue opportunities for Pubs and Hotels with space in garden or on patio have never been easier and are only limited to the imagination of the user. Using the correct equipment in the right location can create a taste of the great outdoors within minutes, combining high profit with all round entertainment, ensuring customers will return for more.

Barbecuing is not a new method of cooking. The word refers to the Haitian word barbacoa which means a grid of green twigs suspended on sticks over a fire. The South American Indians used this as their main method of cooking and they were not alone in this. The same method was developed and used many hundreds of years ago in the near East, in South East Asia and in the islands of the Pacific. Not surprisingly with a way of cooking that has been around for so long, there is very little which cannot be cooked on a barbecue.

One of the joys of barbecuing is its flexibility. Provided that it is not actually raining or blowing a gale, barbecuing is an all year round activity, and appeals to all ages. If you are thinking of introducing barbecues to your premises here are some tips to help you get the most from them.

● Spend considerable time, and discuss with all concerned, deciding where you are going to place the unit. This factor may influence the type of unit you are to purchase - gas, charcoal, wood or electric. Built in barbecues are also a possibility but first try several areas with a portable unit to detect any unforeseen hazards or problems. Once you have decided, consider building a frame for a unit to be 'slid in' rather than 'built in'. This means the whole of the barbecue and its surrounding areas can be thoroughly cleaned and serviced. Also the unit can be stored indoors - if not used in winter - thereby prolonging its life span. If you purchase a gas unit make sure you purchase a unit that is CE approved for use in the UK and all units should be specifically designed and approved for professional catering purposes.

● Charcoal, Wood, or Gas? What type of unit do you want? Electric units need an outside outlet and can be expensive to run. They are usually small and not really suitable for quantity catering purposes.

All barbecues cook by constant radiant heat and the barbecue flavour is produced by food juices falling down onto a hot surface and then rising and caramelizing around the food. The effect can be enhanced by using herbs and seasonings. All barbecues have a cool spot and this can be used as a holding area but the aim is to cook and serve food immediately.

● Charcoal is heated until it glows.
● Wood is burned until all that is left is a pile of glowing embers.

Both these traditional barbecues have a steady source of heat which cannot be turned up or down, and there may be an uneven heat if there are windy conditions. Can be messy to fill and sometimes difficult to light. The quality of charcoal and wood used can vary enormously. For catering conditions they can be inconvenient. But, they do still have a following.

•Gas heats up lava rock, ceramics or heat-exchangers. Gas can be either Natural - but this means the barbecue has to be static - or liquefied petroleum gas (LPG for short) in the propane (RED bottle) variety. LPG fuelled means the barbecue can be portable. These barbecues are easier to control, quicker to light and easier to cope with. Portable also means you can move them about to get the best advantage according to the time of day or year you are barbecuing. Gas fired can also be economical. Dependent on use, lava rock should be replaced about once a year, ceramics need to be replaced if they crack. Heat exchangers tend to last the longest.

NOTE: Butane (BLUE bottle) is usually used only for small domestic barbecues.

● Safety and Hygiene are extremely important and a little help from your local Health Officer before you begin could be advantageous. Know all the laws and use common sense. Quality foods, careful cooking and customer welfare really do pay dividends.

● The staff you choose should have an outgoing and responsible nature which will ensure the barbecue function has a lively atmosphere. More importantly, staff should be well trained on safety and hygiene and should know about the type of fuel he/she is using.

● Your menu should be well prepared in advance. Make sure you keep the fat content of the food to a minimum. Fat causes flares and smoke - the last thing you need at any function. Try not to barbecue food straight from the fridge and never barbecue frozen food. Experiment with your menu and have a good supply of accompaniments.

● Organise your function well. Decide if tickets are to be sold prior to the function or if food is to be purchased on the day. Is food to be served to the table or will guests queue at the unit? Will food only be served during a specific time or be available for the duration of the function. If you are having a theme night make sure the theme is carried through to drink, music, decoration etc. The setting is as important as the barbecue - nobody wants to be sitting in a weed filled garden or rubbish filled patio.

● Use your local newspaper to advertise and in-house notices will attract customers who may not have visited your establishment previously. Small flyers are cheap to produce but you need someone to deliver them. Don't forget the most valuable free advertising is 'word of mouth'.

Barbecues can be at any time of the year and with thorough planning can be very rewarding both financially and personally. Along with your everyday barbecues on balmy evenings you could advertise special menus for Wedding Day Evenings, 18th and 21st Birthdays, Retirement, Works or Beach Parties. Do not forget those special days in the year like Halloween and Bonfire Night, St. Valentines Day, Easter and May Day. There are theme nights such as Caribbean, Wild West and Spanish. What better way to end a Rally or Treasure Trail than with a barbecue?

Carrying themes through to the drinks (trying out some of those exotic mixers for instance) and music (a chance here for some of those live bands and groups) can usually guarantee a different type of person to each barbecue. In this way they don't become the same old boring weekly barbecue for everyone.

Fancy dress may be an idea. Remember, there are lots of accessories available to help your barbecue party go with a bang such as balloons, bunting, party poppers, streamers, garden torches, sparklers, fairy lights/disco lights. Let your imagination run wild or even have a competition for the best idea for a barbecue theme.

Quick - no fuss barbecues are excellent as very profitable fundraisers for clubs, charities, PTA's and scout groups! There are also many Patio Heaters' on the market today, which means outside eating can be considered for more occasions.

TIPS.
• Prepare menu in advance
• Organise and advertise your function thoroughly.
• Soak wooden skewers for 30 minutes to prevent burning.
• Metal skewers are stronger than wooden ones.
• Brush cold grill with oil to prevent sticking.
• Trim excess fat from meat to prevent flare-ups.
• Keep a spray bottle of water handy to extinguish flare-ups.
• Keep barbecue away from dry grass or other hazard,
• Never allow children near a barbecue without adult supervision.
• Never leave a lit barbecue unattended.
• Assemble all equipment before you start.
• Use only competent staff at the barbecue.
• Check food often when cooking.
• Use heavy fireproof oven gloves.
• Always follow manufacturers instructions.

There are numerous recipe books for barbecues on the market today and many bodies like the Scottish Salmon Information Service, Meat Marketing Board, British Potatoes and so on, are always willing to give advice and recipes. Many breweries are also producing their own books which give advice and recipes for barbecues. Some Manufacturers also provide books.

Here are a few of my favourite recipe ideas you may like to try:

Bacon and Potato Kebabs

• **Ingredients:** *Tinned jacket baby potatoes, *strips of bacon, *small tomatoes and *whole small mushrooms

Use metal skewers as they take the weight better.

Method: Wrap a strip of bacon around each potato. Place three wrapped potatoes onto skewer with a tomato or mushroom at either end. Place in centre of barbecue and cook for 8 - 10 minutes turning frequently. Serve on a bed of salad or rice as starter or with steaks or gammon as main dish.

Fruity Scottish Salmon Kebabs

(serves 4)

• **Ingredients:** *450g (1lb.) Scottish salmon fillet, cubed, *1 pineapple, peeled and cubed, *8 cherry tomatoes, *4 shallots, quartered, *10 mls (1 dstsp) sunflower oil, *juice of 1 lemon, *Pinch of dill seeds (optional), *salt & pepper and *8 pre-soaked wooden skewers

Method: Alternate cubes of Scottish salmon on wooden skewers with diced pineapple, shallots and cherry tomatoes. In a bowl combine oil, juice, salt and pepper, dill and soy sauce. Brush over kebabs. Cook for approximately 5 minutes, depending on thickness of kebabs on a hot barbecue. Serve with crusty bread and salad.

Yams

To prepare the yams, which should be smooth skinned with no dark spots, scrub the skins, but do not peel. Trim off both ends. Slice the yams lengthwise into 1/2 inch thick slices. Rub with oil and cook on open grill for approximately 8 minutes per side until tender. A good accompaniment to all vegetable and meat dishes.

Rum Banana

(one for the sweet toothed amongst you)

• **Ingredients:** *Large ripe, firm, banana, *half a lemon, *1 teaspoon rum, *1 small 'Mars Bar' or similar , *whipped cream or Ice cream, *25cm x 15cm piece heavy duty foil for each

Method: Peel the banana and place in centre of the piece of heavy-duty foil. Cut down the length of the banana but do not cut through. Squeeze the juice from the lemon over the banana. Pour the rum into the cut down the middle. Cut the chocolate into 1/2 inch slices and ease into the middle of the banana along its length. Crush the foil together along its length leaving a small air space. Crush the ends together and fold up to form a boat shape. Refrigerate until required if not cooking straight away. Cook on open grill in the foil for approximately 10 minutes. Check after about 8 minutes and do not overcook. Serve with the cream or ice cream.

bacteria to be introduced into food, to survive in food, and/or to multiply in food.

If you are new to the food business and are not familiar with the conditions that food-poisoning bacteria thrive on and the practices that control them, training courses in basic food hygiene are widely available.

To assess the food safety hazards you need to consider all stages from the purchase of supplies to the serving of the food. At each stage there are things that can go wrong and ways of preventing them from doing so.

There are a number of points at which controls are essential to prevent food safety hazards arising, for example thorough cooking, correct handling and storage after cooking, thorough reheating, and the prevention of cross-contamination. It is these controls that you need to monitor by, for example, carrying out temperature checks.

(If you have barbecues these need to be included in your consideration of food safety hazards with particular reference to the potential for undercooking of meat and for cross-contamination. It may be advisable to cook the food in the kitchen first to ensure that it is cooked through thoroughly and then, without delay, finish the dishes on the barbecue to give them the desired flavour. However you tackle it, barbecuing is a form of cooking that requires particular care.)

The requirement for a proper assessment did not exist in previous hygiene legislation. In addition to the advice in the *Industry Guide*, general guidance on how to make sure you have complied with this require-ment is available from your local EHO, as is information on 'Assured Safe Catering', one way of approaching the task. Another approach is SAFE (the Systematic Assessment of Food Environment), available from the British Hospitality Association (0171 404 7744).

Temperature control legislation in relation to the bar and the display of food is detailed in the footnotes of Chapter 10. The Regulations generally require that food that might otherwise give rise to a health risk must be kept at appropriate temperatures.

For the most part this means refrigerated at 8°C or below or kept hot at 63°C or above. Certain exemptions for one-off display have been mentioned. In addition, food that is cooked and then chilled awaiting use must be cooled as quickly as possible following the final heat processing stage. Quick cooling (eg through spreading food out, dividing into portions, etc) is good practice in any event in order to avoid risks from those bacteria that can survive cooking and subsequently cause illness if food is left at room temperature for too long. As a guide, it is advisable to cool food within 90 minutes.

There are also requirements relating to the condition of raw materials/ingredients accepted by the business, the protection of food from contamination, and arrangements for refuse.

PEOPLE

There is a requirement for all food handlers to maintain a high degree of personal cleanliness, and to wear appropriate, clean clothing.

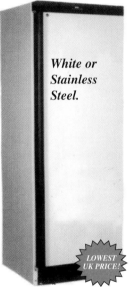

Delta Catering Equipment

How can you have over 6000 Watts of heating for the running costs of 1300 Watts, plus FREE air conditioning!?

Simple... let DELTA install a heat pump system to your bar or restaurant for the special price of £1295 for a room of 20′ x 20′. You and your customers will have year round cooling or heating as required for a more comfortable environment.

These systems are very economical to run and offer the most efficient controllable heating available. There aren't any electric elements in these systems, they work by reverse refrigeration and are becoming the standard way to heat larger commercial buildings because of their low running costs and competitive installation costs (often cheaper than other systems) All have an infra red remote control for setting of the fans, temperature, timer, etc. They are also virtually silent in operation and very discreet in appearance. The indoor units are placed at high level on the wall and so unlike radiators do not interfere with placing furniture. DELTA only install quality equipment such as Mitsubishi and Corona and therefore reliability is first class. In addition to outright purchase DELTA can offer leasing and rental schemes to suit almost everyone. For example, the room above would cost around the price of a pint per day over three years.

For further information a quote or demonstration please contact DELTA on 01485 533 777.

CELLAR COOLING is essential for keeping kegs at the correct temperature to allow the beer to be pulled and be in the right condition to avoid costly wastage. Modern systems have been designed for solely cooling cellars. They are therefore very efficient and unlike equipment of 15 years ago very reliable. The modem cooler has very few parts to go wrong and the latest compressors are whisper quiet and energy efficient, saving you money all round. Equivalent systems can cost around 30% less in power consumption.

Some hotels and pubs have to switch off their cooling system at night due to the droning noise that guests and neighbours complain about to the landlord. There have been a number of instances where DELTA have been asked to replace old equipment just for this reason. DELTA are now the only company to offer a 14 day money back scheme on the cellar cooler. If for any reason you are not satisfied with the new equipment, they will remove it and offer a full refund. This is in addition to guaranteeing the lowest installed price Nationwide.

ICE MACHINES are often neglected by the user and cursed when they fail. Most machines require weekly cleaning if only to satisfy health regulations. However, in our experience these machines are rarely serviced by a refrigeration engineer who will not only check and clean the refrigeration system, but also remove scale and sludge that often builds up in the pipes and jets of the water pipes. A service might seem a waste of money if the machines working okay but could save the replacement cost of a compressor that is overheating due to a choked condenser, perhaps costing £250. A regularly serviced machine will also run more efficiently and save running costs. If you are considering buying a new machine, a make worth considering is Profi*Ice. The only British machine and one that is proven to cost less to run than its competitors, saving at least £100 per year in combined water and electricity costs. This machine also has no thermostats to fail or water pump and does not use hot gas defrost therefore saving a vast amount of power used by running the compressor for this purpose. The compressor is under great strain from hot gas defrost and so by not using it for this its life could be doubled. The Profl*Ice has no water pump or jets and therefore will not suffer the usual problems caused by scale and hard water. The condenser is sited at the front and can be reached by lifting out the grille for cleaning by the operator. So this machine requires little maintenance, no water filters, has very few parts to fall and the really good news is its competitively priced and comes with a three year parts and labour warranty. Be wary of makes only offering extended parts only warranties, the labour charges could make up for it!

BACK BAR BOTTLE coolers are your silent salesperson. It is proven that they will help sell more bottled beer than just shelves often by around 30%. This excellent sales aid needs to be cared for though. Follow these simple guidelines for efficient operation.

• Bottles should be loaded at closing time to give the cooler time to cool the bottles.
• Rotate stock so cold bottles are at the front.
• Store bottles in the cellar if possible before loading, they are then already cold.
• Keep sliding door track clean at all times and lubricate with furniture polish or WD40.
• Have the refrigeration system checked every six months for efficient operation and longer life.
• Keep doors shut except when removing a bottle.
• Switch off the light when your business is closed.

Many people complain about their coolers not being cold enough, this can often be sorted by correct operation as above. However, many coolers aren't quite capable of coping with busy periods. If you are looking for a new cooler, there are many to choose from but only one mainstream model offers truly cold temperatures and rapid cool down as well as being of the highest quality, this is Gamko. Made in Holland this cooler has high quality sliding doors with durable handles.

For further information Contact:
Delta Catering Equipment
Bergen Way
King's Lynn
PE20 2JG
Tel: 01485 533 777
Fax:01485 535 444

In addition, no person who has a condition (or is a carrier of a disease) that could put food at risk may work in any food handling area in any way which might contaminate the food with harmful micro-organisms. Anyone who thinks or knows that they have this type of infection must report it to the proprietor. The EHO can advise on what action to take if this situation arises.

Finally, anyone working in the food business must be supervised and instructed and/or trained in food hygiene to a level appropriate to the work they do. The nature of the supervision, instruction or training is not specified, but those involved in catering activities need to have a level of awareness that matches the risk involved with the food they handle. Many local authorities and colleges run short courses that provide an understanding of food hygiene issues and good practice.

THE FOOD SAFETY ACT 1990

It is this Act that provides local authority EHOs with the powers they need to take action when necessary. It is also this Act that specifies the standards that food for sale is expected to meet. The Act also, for some offences, provides a defence in law (a recognised excuse) if it can be established by a food business that all reasonable steps have been taken to prevent the offence occurring, and due diligence has been shown.

It is worth seriously considering whether, if someone did fall ill after a meal at your pub, you could be really confident that thanks to the procedures you have in place you

could rely on this defence. There are various practices that are not specifically required by law but that do help to show that due diligence is being shown, and that the food safety risks identified are being monitored, eg the daily recording of refrigerator temperatures and/or the date marking of food cooked on site to assist with stock control.

HEALTH AND SAFETY RISKS

Particular risks may be posed by items of catering equipment such as slicing machines. Here the provision and use of appropriate guards and the training of those who use and clean machines is essential. A safe system of work for both using and cleaning machinery is also important.

If you have staff under the age of 18 they may not clean machinery where in doing so they are exposed to risk. Also the positioning of dangerous equipment needs to be considered to ensure that users are not likely to be distracted or knocked by others working nearby.

Other safety issues include the safety of gas appliances, electrical safety issues and the type and condition of the floor to avoid slips and trips. If a dumb waiter is provided the testing requirements referred to in Chapter 3 for cellar lifts/hoists apply.

Finally, the Control of Substances Hazardous to Health Regulations discussed in relation to beer-line cleaner and carbon dioxide (again see Chapter 3) applies equally to hazardous substances cleaning chemicals such as oven cleaner.

NUISANCE

Nuisance complaints relating to food businesses usually relate to noise, smells or refuse.

Noise is usually associated with music and/or the noise of customers (eg using beer gardens), although occasionally the noise of an extractor system may become an issue.

Complaints about refuse are usually easy to avoid by ensuring adequate bin provision and emptying arrangements.

Cooking odours are occasionally the subject of complaint, the likelihood of course depends on the type of cooking undertaken and the position of the extract or in relation to other premises. When carrying out any alterations, such as the provision of a new extractor system (for which planning permission may be needed), it may be worth considering the potential for nuisance and, where it seems likely, pre-empting this in terms of the type of system installed.

If complaints are made and the local authority is satisfied that a statutory nuisance exists, a notice requiring the abatement of the nuisance within a specified time can be served. Non-compliance may lead to prosecution in the Magistrates Court. It is a defence to show that the 'best practicable means' are being employed to avoid or counteract the effects of a nuisance. In attempting to establish this the technical and financial implications can, along with other factors, be taken into consideration. A right of appeal against a notice exists. (For more on nuisance see Chapter 11).

GENERAL

Finally, all food businesses are required to be registered with the local authority under the Food Premises (Registrations) Regulations 1991. If you are not certain if you are registered the EHO will advise and provide you with a form if necessary. There is no fee.

Health and Safety Notes

Requirements relating to hygiene are contained mainly in the Food Safety (General Food Hygiene) Regulations 1995. These are concerned with the conditions of the premises, the practices employed and the personnel involved. As far as practices are concerned, the general regulations are supplemented by the Food Safety (Temperature Control) Regulations 1995.

Guidance on all aspects of the Regulations is available from environmental health at your local council. There is also a book, the *Industry Guide to Good Hygiene Practices: Catering Guide* published by HMSO (ISBN 0113218990) giving guidance on complying with all aspects of the Regulations. In enforcing the legislation environmental health officers (EHOs) will have regard to that guidance.

Legal Notes

Registration with the local authority of premises used for food business is required by law. If a food business is run for five or more days in any five consecutive weeks, the local authority has to be informed.

If a new food business is to be started, then 28 days notice should be given to the local authority.

If vehicles are used in connection with the business, the local authority should also be informed, as they should if there is a change of proprietor or if the business changes.

It is important to ensure that best practice is exercised in relation to food handling and that you are aware of current legislative requirements for food safety, hygiene, composition and quality and that you take adequate steps to inform and train staff and carry out regular refresher courses.

SUPPER HOUR CERTIFICATES

The usual permitted hours for licensed premises cease at 11pm weekdays and 10.30pm on Sunday, Good Friday and Christmas Day, with a 20-minute drinking-up time. However, in a restaurant or an area of a public house set aside for dining it is possible to extend the terminal hour by one additional hour subject to the sale or supply of alcohol being ancillary to a meal.

A Supper Hour Certificate is obtained by application to the Licensing Justices at any Transfer Sessions upon no less than seven days' notice. The fee is £25. The court will usually require a plan of your premises and the detailing of the area to which the Certificate is to apply. Once granted, there is a requirement that you display a notice in the part of the premises explaining the effect of the Certificate.

Where a Supper Hour Certificate applies there is a 30-minute drinking-up period. No new drinks can be supplied during the drinking-up period.

PART THREE
PERSONNEL

CHAPTER EIGHT

STAFF TRAINING AND RECRUITMENT

Andrew Palmer and Ted Bruning

Traditionally, self-employed licensees have only rarely extended formal training to their staff. The small tenancy or free house has had neither the resources nor the need for formal training: casual and part-time staff either learnt the ropes or they didn't last, while those who showed an aptitude for the trade learnt all they needed from watching the landlord and landlady at work and picking it up as they went along.

Three developments have rendered this kind of practice out of date.

1. The advent of the long lease has given tenants more security and a business environment in which to train their children as assistant managers and possible successors in the business.

2. Both customer expectations and the rules and regulations have made food service a far more complicated business than in the past. Food service at a compara-tively sophisticated level is now a *sine qua non* for most pubs, and qualified staff are needed to pro-vide it properly.

3. It is now legal for 16 year olds to work behind the bar. Again, this makes it worthwhile for tenants, lessees and free traders to give their older children a formal grounding in the trade.

These changes occur against a back-ground of ever-rising customer expec-tations. Customers have different expectations of the *type* of service offered by big town-centre managed houses and country free houses; but they expect the same *level* of service in both. Only trained staff will deliver their expectations.

A great benefit that arises from having trained, experienced and trustworthy staff is that the licensees can take holidays or go sick without incurring the expense and anxiety of hiring relief managers.

NATIONAL VOCATIONAL QUALIFICATIONS

One of the common qualifications taken by experienced licensees as well as new staff are National Vocational Qualifications (NVQS) or, north of the border, Scottish Vocational Qualifications (SVQs). These are qualifications you can get simply by proving you perform your everyday tasks to nationally recognised standards, whether you are an experienced licensee or new part-time barstaff.

NVQs in Catering and Hospitality operate on four levels of increasing responsibility. However, you do not have to complete Level 1 to achieve Level 2 and so on; you do whichever Level you feel is suitable for you.

NVQ Level 1 Food and Drink (Bar) is quite basic, but its benefit is that it standardises good procedures in serving. It is suitable for new and junior part-time staff. Most staff easily achieve Level 1, making them enthusiastic about progressing further.

Level 2 Serving Food and Drink (Bar) covers the increased responsibility and technical skills needed by experienced bar staff who can work unsupervised. It is an excellent motivator for confident bar staff.

Level 3 On-licensed Premises Supervision Management is suitable for senior staff and is mostly used by assistant managers and licensees who are likely to be responsible for the day-to-day running and supervision of the pub. It covers staff training and supervision, contributions to policy, managing drink service and cellar operations, security, stock control, health and safety, and maintenance.

Level 4 On-licensed Premises Management is the highest level of NVQ available at the moment specifically for running pubs. It is suitable for those with total responsibility for maintaining and expanding the business, and covers financial control, staff recruitment, training and retention, establishing and updating policy and procedures relating to customer service, health and safety and employment legislation, managing all aspects of drink service and cellar storage and evaluation, and maintenance of the pub and all equipment.

An NVQ Level 5 is in development and it is expected to cover responsibility for profitability of the business, and the planning and performance of your own and others' work.

Traditional qualifications often involve attending a course and sitting a formal exam. Candidates work for their NVQs literally as they do their everyday jobs, coached and assessed by their employers or training providers. NVQs confirm that they can do their job. They are ideal for people who hate exams, as the qualification is confirmed by assessment, not a make-or-break exam.

NVQs are also ideal for people who cannot take time out to attend formal courses and study for traditional exams. They fit in with the normal work routine and are particularly suitable for staff because they allow the licensee to train and assess practically and with immediate benefit to the business.

You can take them at any age, and you take as long as you want. It may take a year to gain a whole

NVQ. You gain an NVQ by completing a number of units which make up the total qualification for the particular level you want. Your work programme will include enough background study to ensure you have the 'underpinning knowledge' which is usually checked during the routine assessments.

MODERN APPRENTICESHIPS

Modern Apprenticeships are a training route that takes young employees (aged below 26) up to Level 3 NVQ. They are run jointly by a recognised training provider (brewer or college) and the licensee.

FUNDING AND IMPLEMENTING NVQS

There are four ways to implement NVQs.

1. Licensees can form a small consortium to pool their resources and experience. Members of the British Institute of Innkeeping (BII) who are not part of large pub groups have cooperated on pilot schemes, notably in the southwest, Hampshire, Kent and Herts and Beds sections. Licensees host feedback sessions where problems and best practices are shared. This method suits the small pub best as training is usually only given when 10–12 people commit themselves to an NVQ programme.
2. Larger businesses undertake every aspect of the NVQ programme themselves in-house.
3. It is possible to bring in external help for certain parts of the pro-

cess, such as pinpointing business requirements.
4. A Modern Apprentice who will be supported by an external trainer and assessor.

Funding is usually available to licensees for NVQ training through local Training and Enterprise Councils (TECs); see your local phone book. All TECs have a list of training providers.

To find out more, contact:

◆ your local Business Link (0800 50020), which will advise on funding and support, or
◆ the British Institute of Innkeeping, Park House, 22–24 Park Street, Camberley, Surrey GU15 3PL; tel 01276 291003
◆ the Hospitality Training Foundation for more information on Modern Apprenticeships and NVQs; HTF, 3rd Floor, International House, High Street, Ealing, London, W5 5DB; tel 0181 579 2400

As far as recruiting staff is concerned, self-employed licensees will continue to find value in the traditional methods of word of mouth and local advertisements. But in the age of virtual reality, the launch of a national careers promotion initiative will interest many publicans.

This initiative, Leisure Careers UK (LCUK), has been established by the BII with powerful backing by the government as well as the industry, to communicate the genuinely worthwhile career opportunities in this colourful sector for all levels of ability.

The LCUK national careers promotion encourages closer liaison between industry and young people, as well as their career advisers. Its interactive website, www.barzone. co.uk – which has been commended in an international survey – gives a wealth of information and details drawn from life of the reality of working in the industry. It includes:

◆ **BarZone:** you can enter a music, sports or food bar and participate in music and pub quizzes, or access profiles of real people working in these venues detailing job responsibilities; music is linked live to Capital Radio and the Pepsi Network Chart website

◆ **WorkZone:** company work experience programmes and placements; background information to industry; material aimed at careers advisers and teachers

◆ **CareerZone:** career finder service allowing people to determine their ideal career within the industry. Career seekers can register their CVs, allowing employers to search for new recruits on the website. There's also a guide to industry qualifications and illustrations of structured career pathways, and case studies of young people building successful long-term careers within the licensed leisure industry.

◆ **PyschoZone:** a light-hearted psychometric test to analyse users' best-suited job within the industry.

◆ **PrizeZone:** surfers register and win BarZone mega bi-monthly prizes – which have in the past included tickets for Spice Girls concerts.

Hypertext links have been created with other youth-oriented websites like YouthNet, Careers Mosaic, Peoplebank, Careersoft, Wolverhampton University and Lifestyle UK.

The Brewers and Licensed Retailers Association reports 20,000 hits a week on the new careers section of its website, www.blra.co.uk

The LCUK website www.barzone. co.uk has scored more than 300,000 hits in its first seven months. Three new 'zones' have been added to the initial five. They are:

◆ **PressZone:** shows the excellent media coverage about LCUK and includes latest press releases.

◆ **IndustryZone:** updates you on LCUK progress. You can request presentation materials for education visits and search the National Register of Students currently working in the industry.

◆ **EducationZone:** Aimed at teachers and advisers and describes availability of structured work experience templates and support materials (including teacher guides and parent/student guides), teacher placements within the industry and lists useful organisations. It aims to feature on-line register and contacts details of industry speakers prepared to present locally to schools, colleges and universities.

HIRING AND FIRING

Christine Bradley

Every day, and without necessarily realising it, publicans are applying one or other of the current employment laws in their dealings with staff.

Employment law is complex these days, and while many publicans will have a reasonable working knowledge of it, this chapter will act as a reminder of the more important aspects that readers will encounter. Many problems can be avoided with a little forethought and pre-planning.

What follows is designed to serve as a reminder, and should not be taken as a comprehensive guide. There can be no substitute for recognising the potential exposure under unfair dismissal and other legislation, and if needs be checking with a solicitor for confirmation that the steps about to be taken do not hold any hidden dangers.

THE CONTRACT OF EMPLOYMENT

There is a statutory obligation to provide a set of written minimum terms and conditions of employment to each member of staff, no matter how few hours he may work.

Properly drafted employment documentation can also be of great benefit to the employer. Once in place it will quickly become a valuable part of daily record-keeping, not just a burden of paperwork. Drafting even the most basic list of terms and conditions, generally framed, is good practice, even if it is only designed to comply with the minimum set out in the Employment Rights Act 1996 – date of commencement; dates of continuous employment; details of pay, hours of work, place of work, holidays, pensions and sick pay; notice provisions; any collective agreements; disciplinary rules and grievance procedures.

Doing more than the bare minimum is recommended, however. The more comprehensively the terms are set out the better, because reference back to the written contract will assist an employer in addressing staff problems as they crop up. In addition, detailed consideration of the clauses to be included at the outset of the relationship will enable you to be confident that you are operating sensible and proper systems so as to ensure full compliance with the law.

RECRUITMENT

When recruiting, remember that you need to ensure that you do not fall foul of anti-discrimination legislation, which now includes the Disability Discrimination Act 1995 that came into force in December 1996.

The basic rule is to be careful not to treat any individual less favourably than another on grounds of sex, marital status, age, ethnic or national origin, or disability. All candidates must be assessed solely on their qualifications, relevant knowledge, experience and personal qualities. Equally, all candidates should be assessed on the basis of the same job-related criteria, regardless of marital status and/or assumed domestic responsibilities.

Job descriptions and recruitment literature should be drawn up to reflect accurately the requirements and duties of the job and should be referred to consistently throughout the recruitment process. Any explicit or implicit bias in the way a job is described and the duties outlined must be avoided, so any job description or advertisement should be gender free, ideally stating that you are an equal opportunities employer (and that you therefore have a written equal opportunities policy).

In short-listing candidates, all applicants should be treated in the same manner, and the interview list should be drawn up with reference to a clear job description based on qualification requirements, skills, experience and so on. It is vital

that special care is used to avoid setting conditions relating to physical strength or appearance unless these are essential to the nature of the job – eg where it could be argued that only one sex is physically capable of doing a particular job. Setting conditions is fraught with danger, as these can give rise to an inference of indirect discrimination, as can selection based on qualifications or dexterity or a preferred age range.

When rejecting applications for interview, ideally a note of the reason for the rejection should be kept on file as evidence of the fairness of selection should your decision ever be challenged.

It is wise to arrange for applicants to be interviewed by more than one person so as to avoid any inference of personal preference or prejudice. Where this is not possible (and even if it is), careful notes of the interview should be kept. It is of paramount importance that interviewers are careful to avoid asking questions from which discrimination could be inferred, particularly in relation to child care responsibilities; for example, it should not be assumed that a married female applicant will be unable to work during evening hours. For the same reason, questions should not be raised as regards an applicant's marital status and whether they have children, or in relation to an employee's religious beliefs. As these questions do not generally relate to the requirements of the job, interviewers are laying themselves open to unnecessary criticism by even raising them.

If it really is necessary to assess whether the performance of the job would be affected by the applicant's personal circumstances, this should be discussed without any detailed questions based on assumptions about marital status, children and domestic responsibilities. If it is necessary for the jobholder to be flexible, the requirements of the job should be explained in detail to all applicants and all applicants should be asked if they feel able to fulfil those requirements.

Once interviews have taken place you should record your reasons why applicants were or were not appointed as objectively as possible. This may prove vital evidence should a claim of unlawful discrimination be brought.

Disabled applicants have the right not to be discriminated against for a reason relating to their disability unless you can show that the discriminatory treatment in question was justified. Disability discrimination is in its infancy in the UK, and the application of the Act to any particular situation is far too detailed to go into here. Suffice it to say that to justify discriminatory treatment on the ground of disability, you have to show that your reasons were settled upon only after you had considered your duty to make adjustments to working practices and to the working environment to accommodate the requirements of individual disabled candidates (or for that matter existing employees).

EQUAL OPPORTUNITIES POLICY

To minimise your exposure to discrimination claims generally, you should have a written equal opportunities policy, particularly as these days

industrial tribunals have the power to grant unlimited compensation.

An equal opportunities policy should provide a framework for ensuring that individuals are treated equally and fairly and that decisions on recruitment, selection, training, promotion and career management are based solely on objective job-related criteria.

A written equal opportunities policy can also provide a defence if you are faced with complaints of discrimination, particularly sexual or racial harassment, suffered at the hands of other employees or even of a third party – for example if the stand-up comic booked to do a spot on your premises starts picking on members of staff on grounds of race or sex, or if a guest at a private party makes unwanted advances to your bar staff.

Given your liability for discrimination and harassment by third parties, you should be able to show that you took reasonable measures to warn of the need to treat employees and colleagues equally and avoid discrimination and harassment. This will include setting up a procedure for dealing with complaints of harassment, implementing the policy through staff training and education, and even where necessary displaying notices warning third parties against behaving in a way that could be construed as discrimination or harassment.

EMPLOYING ILLEGAL WORKERS – A CRIMINAL OFFENCE

Since January 1997 it has been a criminal offence to employ someone who does not have permission to live and work in this country. If convicted, you can face a fine of up to £5000 per offence.

It is up to you to check the status of new employees before they start work. To protect yourself, you should insist on having sight of the original of one of a number of documents listed in the Regulations – a passport, a P45, a national insurance card and so on. Having seen the original document, take a copy of it for the personnel file, and you have a complete defence under the Act.

However, in complying with the Act, you need to be sure that you do not act in a way that could constitute, or be interpreted as, racial discrimination. The only way of avoiding this is to ensure that you ask *all* employees for this information, no matter how unlikely it may be that there are any problems about their right to work, since to act otherwise might be seen as treating a particular group less favourably on the grounds of their race, which would be discrimination. Essentially you should not make assumptions about an applicant's right to work or their immigration status based on their race or their national origin.

WAGES

Publicans need to know whether they can dock the wages of staff they suspect of pilfering or otherwise causing stock shortages.

Provisions for making deductions to recover staff loans, cover damage to uniforms, etc should be set out in the contract of employment; if they are not, written agreements should be made before staff loans are made or uniforms handed over.

Other restrictions are set out in Part II of the Employment Rights Act 1996, which requires that in cases of cash deficiencies or stock shortages no more than 10 per cent of the employee's gross salary for that payment period can be deducted in any one payment period. Deductions in respect of cash shortages or stock deficiencies that occurred more than a year before are also restricted. Breach of this statute can lead to a claim against you at an industrial tribunal and could result in your being ordered to repay the sums deducted. It is only sensible therefore to ensure that there are internal procedures in place to enable the provisions of the Employment Rights Act, better known by its old name – the Wages Act – to be adhered to.

WORKING HOURS

In the licensed trade, more so than in many other businesses, it is prudent to build flexibility into working hours. The right to vary each employee's hours according to the needs of the business must be specifically reserved in the contract of employment.

However, even though you should retain some power to vary your staff's working hours/days, you must not exercise it in an arbitrary, capricious or inequitable way, nor apply it excessively or oppressively, as to do so might breach your obligation of good faith which underlies any employment relationship. You should also be wary of insisting that an employee work longer hours than specified in the contract, and equally careful when seeking to reduce an employee's normal working hours, particularly if it means a reduction in the employee's normal earnings.

Considerations relating to the duty to provide a safe system of working and avoiding liability for stress-related illnesses should be borne in mind when drafting flexibility clauses. In addition, the impact of the Working Time Directive will have to be accommodated in the near future. Regulations in relation to this came into force on 1st October 1998 and provide for daily rest of at least 11 hours, weekly rests of at least 24 hours, a minimum annual paid leave of three weeks (rising to four weeks in 1999 and to be pro rata for part timers), breaks for employees who work more than six hours a day, a maximum working week of 48 hours including overtime, and a restriction on night workers working more than eight hours at a stretch. Employees will be able to agree to work for more than 48 hours in a week, but this will be subject to restrictions. When drafting contracts for new employees it makes sense to ensure that your arrangements in relation to working hours take into account the provisions of the Working Time Regulations 1998 on the one hand, as well as reserve flexibility so as to assist you in dealing with the demands of your particular business.

TRANSFER OF UNDERTAKINGS (PROTECTION OF EMPLOYMENT) REGULATIONS

Care should be exercised when taking over a pub that is trading as a going concern. The Transfer of Undertakings (Protection of Employment) Regulations entitle employees transferring from one employer to another to carry on under the same terms and conditions as before (with the exception of pensions), and if any dismissals are required, extra care should be taken to avoid exposure to claims of unfair dismissal.

The Regulations apply to all employees, including part timers, and dismissals of employees with more than two years continuous service which can be shown to be connected with the transfer will be regarded as automatically unfair. The new owner will succeed in persuading an industrial tribunal that dismissals of this nature were not automatically unfair if he can show that they happened for an economic, technical or organisational reason entailing changes in the workforce.

An economic reason could be where the profitability of a business cannot be sustained unless at less than current staffing levels. A technical reason could be where an employer wishes to introduce new technology and the existing employees do not have the necessary skills. An organisational reason could be where the new employer wishes to operate at a different location and it is not practical to relocate the staff.

If one of these reasons exists, provided the dismissals are carried out fairly, they would most likely be found to be fair, thus avoiding liability for compensation. However, such dismissals may well fall within the definition of redundancy, so a redundancy payment would have to be made.

A prudent employer taking over a going concern will obtain the fullest information about its employees and seek the advice of an employment law specialist before embarking on any dismissals. As a minimum, information as to the employees' length of service, contracts of employment and the like are vital to avoid exposure in this area.

PART-TIME WORKERS

It is a common misapprehension that part-time employees can be treated in a different, even an inferior, way to full-time staff. In fact, part-time workers have the same rights as full-time workers in the same category and in particular, after they have accrued two years' continuous service, they acquire protection against unfair dismissal and entitlement to redundancy payments.

In addition, to avoid discrimination claims, you need to ensure that part timers have equal rights to any benefits, such as pensions and maternity leave, that are afforded to full-time employees.

Part-time employees, even temporary or maybe casual workers, now have access to the same employment protection laws as their full-time counterparts, and it is imperative that terms and conditions of employment are pro rata with the full timers. Care must taken to avoid discrimination, for example in relation to equal pay.

DISMISSAL

To state the rule at its most simple, if after a period of two years' continuous service an employee is dismissed, he or she may have a claim of unfair dismissal. Protection against unfair dismissal is governed by statute, and you need to be able to demonstrate

one of the five potentially fair reasons for dismissal, which are:

1. misconduct
2. redundancy
3. lack of capability
4. work which would otherwise contravene a duty restriction which has been imposed by statute
5. some other substantial reason.

In addition when dismissing, it is important that the employer acts reasonably. You must follow a fair procedure when carrying out a dismissal, and this usually involves a process of warnings, investigations and consultation. Only in particular circumstances will an employer be able to dismiss an employee without warning (a summary dismissal). This normally arises in circumstances involving a serious breach of contract such as gross misconduct (conduct involving breach of disciplinary rules and the like).

It is also important to bear in mind that for all employees – no matter how short their period of service or how few their number of hours worked – when dismissing (save for cases of summary dismissal) there are minimum statutory notice periods that must be complied with, as follows:

◆ service of less than a month – no minimum notice required
◆ service of more than a month but less than two years – one week
◆ service of over two years – one week for each completed year of service up to a maximum of 12 weeks after 12 years' completed service.

When dismissing, employers need to be sure that they have given the

S E R V I C E S   L T D

"1974 - 1997, 23 years service to The Licensed trade"

THE COMPANY

- Established in 1974
- Specialising in providing relief management for public houses and licensed catering establishments
- Professional and experienced staff
- Operating throughout Great Britain
- Serving the major national and regional breweries and leisure companies

THE OBJECT

- Supply relief management of the highest calibre
- Allocating management contracts to match the experience, suitability and background of the relief management team to the particular assignment
- Short term holiday relief and longer term holding operations

THE RELIEF MANAGER

- Carefully selected following a lengthy assessment and reference cross-checking
- Required to have a minimum of three years experience in the managed house trade
- Required to maintain a security deposit of £1,000
- All relief managers are required to pay a daily premium to the company to indemnify clients against losses not arising from defalcation up to £1,000 over and above the security deposit

NEED A RELIEF?

Whatever the reason: holiday, sickness, dismissal, we can provide you with professional management.

01332 348228

PERMANENT SERVICES

"Selecting and placing quality managers for over 20 years"

Inn Relief Services carry out an in-depth study of all establishments which register a recruitment need, to identify the specific skills and personal attributes, which the correct candidate will need to possess in order to successfully undertake the position.

MAKE IT PERMANENT

In the strive to continually improve our service, in order to remain at the forefront of the recruitment services sector, we now select and place managers in permanent positions.

ENSURING SUCCESS

One of the most valuable asset any establishment can acquire in order to ensure success, is the right team or person in management.

Inn Relief Services knows the importance of securing the right people. The services we offer are designed to ensure that the candidates selected, are specifically matched to your individual requirements, hence, reducing the risk of inappropriate management recruitments.

SERVICES AVAILABLE

- Immediate Relief Assistance
- Large Database Of Professional Managers
- Effective Advertising Of Vacancies In Appropriate Trade Press

- CV Scanning & Evaluation
- In-depth Interviewing
- Candidate Testing
- Final Interviews

"YOUR SPECIFIC NEED"

We will provide assistance in any individual or combination of areas within the recruitment process, right through to the total management of all your managerial recruitment needs.

01332 348228

"Essential assistance to the license trade"

1. STOCKTAKING SERVICE

The Stock Report provides an evaluation of:

- Cost value of sales in any period
- Retail value of each stock line
- Gross profit achieved on each stock line

- Stock value held for each stock line
- Number of days stock held, based on the correct periods sales

SAME DAY RESULTS

2. FINANCIAL REPORT SERVICE

This service produces a Financial Report, similar in form to the Annual Accounts but with a greater emphasis on the analysis of the houses income and direct costs, with overheads being grouped into key controllable or fixed cost areas.

The Financial Reports are usually produced to the same accounting period to which the stock reports are produced. They provide a snap-shot indication of how the business is fairing. They provide essential information to enable the client to manage their business.

3. PAYROLL SERVICES

Whatever your payroll needs, we can help!

- fast and reliable processing
- strict confidentiality
- hourly or fixed rate payrolls
- weekly, monthly, periodically paid employees
- payments made direct to employee bank accounts via BACS

- summarised/detailed payroll reports and ledger journals prepared
- client specific pay slips designed, or detailed security ones

01332 348228

appropriate period of notice or they will be exposed to an action for breach of contract, in which case the remedy is damages for the period of notice that should have been given.

Where an employee is able to claim that he has been unfairly dismissed, the financial implications can be quite significant. Unfair dismissal compensation is commonly awarded under two heads:

◆ a basic award of up to £6,600 (at September 1998), calculated on age, length of service and salary
◆ a compensatory award up to a maximum of £12,000 (at September 1998), subject to the employee's obligation to mitigate his loss by getting another job.

Conduct dismissals are probably the most common types of dismissal, and while small employers do not need to have disciplinary rules in place, the benefits of drawing them up will be well worth the trouble for even the smallest employer when the time comes for disciplinary measures.

An important part of any employer's day-to-day relationship with employees is governed by the disciplinary rules, such that time spent in drawing them up will stand the prudent employer in good stead in the long run.

The following might be considered for inclusion by employers in the licensed trade: the right to search, rules on the consumption of alcohol at work, a no smoking policy, adherence to a dress code, rules as to compliance with security procedures and rules as to compliance with the laws relating to the operation of public houses.

Dismissal on grounds of ill health is an area which can be fraught with difficulties. Employers need to balance the competing pressures of their own need to get the job done against the employee's right to sufficient time to recover and receive fair treatment. Employees who are frequently absent over a period due to minor ailments may find that their dismissal is by reason of conduct rather than capability, but to ensure that you take the correct line on ill health dismissals; you must always take care to discover the full facts of each case and then follow the relevant procedure to the letter. Once again the prudent employer will have taken the trouble to set up a policy on sick pay at the outset.

Whatever the reason for dismissing an employee, there is quite a high exposure to compensation claims and many pitfalls to trap the unwary, so seek advice from a specialist employment lawyer in the early stages.

CONCLUSION

Employment law, more than many other areas of law, is constantly changing, and no guidance notes will hold good indefinitely. The best advice is to recognise the complexities of this legislation by taking steps to prepare for problems that might arise, thus ensuring a solid footing based on laid-down terms and conditions, policies and procedures.

Above all, you need to recognise that you must proceed cautiously when dealing with problems that will inevitably crop up from time to time. As in many cases, licensees are responsible for the acts or omissions of their employees; it is essential to have in place a proper system of education and training so as to minimise your exposure. Careful record-keeping, access to a basic source book on employment law and liaison with employment law experienced professionals for detailed advice should stand you in good stead to guide you through the minefield which is employment law.

Health and Safety Notes

If you have not previously been an employer and are not familiar with health and safety legislation it is advisable to seek advice from your local environmental health officer (EHO). He will be able to provide you with guidance and information on relevant requirements and explain how they apply in practice to your situation.

Even if you do not envisage employing anyone at the outset it is still advisable to do this, as much of the legislation applies to self-employed people in respect of their own health and safety and, of course, there is a duty to safeguard the health and safety of non-employees such as customers and contractors.

(NB: unless otherwise stated leaflets referred to below are available from environmental health at your local council.)

As far as obligations towards employees are concerned, the Health and Safety at Work Act 1974 requires employers to safeguard their health, safety and welfare. The Act also specifically requires that where there are five or more employees a written health and safety policy be provided. This comprises a general statement of responsibility and commitment, details of the organisation in place (key individuals, etc) and the relevant arrangements (specific procedures, safe systems of work, training, etc). Guidance can be obtained from your local EHO; alternatively a booklet which you complete to create a policy can be purchased from HSE Books (01787 881165 – *Our Health and Safety Policy Statement – Guide to preparing a safety policy statement for a small business*).

The obligations placed on employers by the Health and Safety at Work Act are wide in their application and general in nature. More specific and detailed requirements are included in various sets of Regulations. To assist you in identifying and addressing the specific health and safety issues associated with your business, the Management of Health and Safety at Work Regulations 1992 require that you undertake a 'risk assessment'.

This means simply identifying health and safety hazards associated with your business, assessing the risks posed and dealing with these risks as appropriate. A practical approach may be to consider aspects of the premises itself (eg awkward cellar access) and aspects of the activities that take place (such as different people's jobs, delivery procedures, entertainment events, etc).

In doing your risk assessment it is helpful to be clear about the difference between 'hazards' (the potential for harm) and 'risks' (the likelihood that harm will happen). It may be, for example, that while the risk is very low the hazard is so serious that preventive measures are appropriate. Also, it is useful to involve employees when making the assessment as they may have identified problems in practice that you have not appreciated. If you have five or more employees you must keep a written record of the main findings. The assessment needs to be reviewed periodically, particularly where change introduces new hazards.

A guidance booklet, *Five Steps to Risk Assessment – A step-by-step guide to a safer and healthier workplace*, is available. This helps you to carry out the assessment and provides a means of keeping a record.

During any health and safety inspection you may be asked about risk assessment and (where applicable) be asked to produce your safety policy. Certain accidents are reportable to your local environmental health office in accordance with the Reporting of Injuries, Diseases and Dangerous Occurrences Regulations 1995 (RIDDOR). In any accident investigation the relevance of the risk assessment (and, where applicable, the safety

policy) to the accident in question is likely to be considered. (A leaflet is available that explains which accidents are reportable accidents and includes a form to use.) With regard to accidents there is also a requirement to keep a record of all staff accidents in an accident book.

Other legislation to be aware of includes:

◆ the **Manual Handling Operations Regulations 1992**; see the notes on these in Chapter 3.

◆ the **Electricity at Work Regulations 1989**, which include requirements relating to all aspects of electrical safety including the maintenance of the electrical installation so that no electrical danger arises (this includes electrical appliances as well as the fixed wiring). Periodic checks should be made to ensure that this is so. Various appliances are liable to greater wear and tear and therefore warrant more frequent examination. Also, anyone doing any electrical work must be competent for the job in question.

◆ the **Control of Substances Hazardous to Health Regulations 1994 (COSHH)** as amended by the COSHH (Amendment) Regulations 1996; see the reference to these with regard to hazardous substances in the cellar in Chapter 3.

◆ the **Personal Protective Equipment at Work Regulations 1992**; these require, for example, that appropriate personal protective equipment including gloves, eye protection, etc be provided where there are risks to health that cannot otherwise be controlled.

♦ the **First Aid at Work Regulations 1981**; these are concerned with the arrangements for and provision of first aid.

♦ the **Provision and Use of Work Equipment Regulations 1992**; which include requirements relating to the suitability and maintenance of work equipment, the guarding of dangerous parts of machinery, and training.

♦ the **Workplace Health Safety and Welfare Regulations 1992**; which are concerned with aspects of the workplace itself, eg the condition of the floors, the provision of handrails to staircases, the use of safety glazing where necessary, etc.

♦ the **Gas Safety (Installation and Use) Regulations 1994**; which are concerned with the safety of gas installations/gas appliances and work done on them.

♦ the **Employer's Liability (Compulsory Insurance) Regulations 1969**; these require the provision of appropriate employer's liability insurance.

♦ the **Health and Safety (Information for Employees) Regulations 1989**; these require specific information to be brought to the attention of employees. The poster (or leaflets) required is available from HSE Books on 01787 881165. There is also a requirement to

consult with employees, either directly or through a representative, under the Health and Safety (Consultation with Employees) Regulations 1996. A requirement also exists under the Safety Representatives and Safety Committee Regulations 1977 to consult with trade union representatives where applicable.

♦ the **Health and Safety (Young Persons) Regulations 1997**; these relate to the Management of Health and Safety at Work Regulations and the risk assessment required under that legislation. The risks that might arise because of the lack of experience, lack of awareness and immaturity of persons under 18 need to be specifically considered and addressed. Information about risks and controls needs to be provided to parents of children under school-leaving age. (You should note that there is already a requirement under the Offices, Shops, and Railway Premises Act 1963 for young persons not to clean dangerous machinery if doing so exposes them to risk from moving parts.)

The above gives a brief summary of some of the health and safety issues to be aware of. The named leaflets, and others that explain the various requirements in detail and help you apply them, can be obtained through your local environmental health department or from HSE Books. A number of leaflets have recently been introduced specifically to assist small businesses.

The requirements may seem numerous and complicated but, in general, compliance is straightforward; if in doubt as to what is expected of you, seek advice. A thorough health and safety risk assessment will enable you to identify the risks that require attention and help you to prioritise them. Don't do this in isolation: involve staff, keep them informed and ensure that training needs are addressed.

Legal Notes

In many instances licensees are responsible for the acts or omissions of their employees. It is essential therefore that a proper system of educating and training staff is in place to ensure full compliance with the law relating to the sale of intoxicating drinks and the operation of public houses.

Ensure that you have a contract of employment. Simple forms of contract are available. Be aware of the necessity to have a disciplinary procedure and ensure it is implemented. Keep records carefully of any verbal warning, written warning, final warning or dismissal.

Pay As You Earn (PAYE): Obtain the appropriate booklet on PAYE from your local tax office.

Employers' National Insurance Contribution: learn and understand the requirements.

PART FOUR
OPERATIONS
MANAGEMENT

CHAPTER TEN

BAR DESIGN AND MERCHANDISING

Paul Cooper

This chapter deals with the servery itself – its design, layout, equipment, and how to make it work for you. This is probably your most dramatic personal statement in the pub and is certainly your greatest sales aid. It can send many messages to customers about you and your pub. The question that must be considered is, is it saying what you want it to say?

WHAT TO STOCK

In the first instance, you need to establish the range of goods that you are going to sell. You should consider the full range of products available: beers, ciders, minerals, spirits, wines, snacks, tobacco, confectionery. Determining your drinks range is dealt with in Chapters 3, 4 and 5, but I will deal with the other products here.

There are three options available when considering tobacco products. You can choose not to stock the products, sell them from behind the bar, or sell them from a cigarette machine, with other products such as matches and cigars behind the bar. The first option is not one you should consider seriously unless your pub is to be completely non-smoking, in which case you will doubtless be marketing it heavily as such. Although the margins are small, tobacco sales can provide additional income and incremental profit with no extra effort on your part. Selling tobacco products also provides an additional – and indeed essential – service to, on average, over 30 per cent of your customers. The remaining choice is whether or not to have a cigarette machine. Machines can be bought outright, rented or supplied and maintained by a company that pays commission based on sales. If you buy a machine you will have to pay for its maintenance. If your machine is rented, or supplied on a commission basis, most owners will maintain them as part of the service. The choice is a matter of personal preference, but most people opt for the latter as it creates fewer problems for them.

If you decide to stock cigarettes behind the bar, you must consider security – cigarettes tend to be the most pilfered stock lines in a pub.

Depending on your customer profile, additional tobacco products such as rolling tobacco and papers, cigars and pipe tobacco should be considered. If there are potential sales to be made you should stock the products; they provide both additional income and a service to your customers. Some publicans prefer not to stock rolling papers as they feel it encourages drug use.

It is more or less an essential that you stock matches. Providing them on the counter top in the frog of a brick on which to strike them could be a nice touch.

Most pubs stock bag snacks, and some also stock confectionery. You must decide whether or not these products will appeal to your customer profile. If you run a family pub there will probably be a demand for confectionery and standard bag snacks. A town-centre young persons' pub will probably have little demand for sweets, but stocking an adult premium range of bag snacks, eg tortilla chips, Brannigan's crisps, Pringles, etc (and of course charging premium prices) will generate sales.

Other impulse lines may be worth stocking but you should consider whether they will generate sales, eg hot nuts, jellybean machines, Peperami, etc. There are always new products on the market that may work in your pub.

DESIGN

Although the bar has to be essentially functional, it should still be considered within the overall design of the pub. When designing the bar, ensure that it will match the pub and does not clash with the rest of the décor. It must appear an integral part of the premises and not look as though it was plonked in as an afterthought. If you are running a trendy wine bar you may want to have your bar built in bright colours with chrome fittings – which would look somewhat out of place in a thatched fifteenth-century inn.

Similarly, what is already there may not suit your needs or the character of the outlet. In the 1960s many beautiful traditional pubs were lovingly refurbished and fitted with the then obligatory melamine-topped bar. I have yet to see one of these design wonders that still looks as trendy and tasteful as when it was fitted. Depending on the cash available, though, it may not be possible to rip out your bar and start again. It may simply be a case of replacing or re-covering the top and front.

The position of the servery within the pub is equally important. You must ensure that it is prominent and easily accessible from all areas of the bar and that it does not create bottlenecks. Customers standing at the bar will be in the way if it is positioned next to toilets, entrances, etc. The size of the bar also needs consideration. If it is too small it will be impossible to serve customers within an acceptable time. If it is too large you are wasting drinking space and reducing the number of customers you can fit into the pub. In either instance the outcome will be the same: lost sales.

The amount of space behind the bar should be considered in the same light: too little and staff cannot work efficiently, too much and you are wasting space.

It is a personal choice whether you have bar trays, beer-mats, bar towels, serviettes or nothing on the counter to stand drinks on. The most important thing to ensure is that it remains clean, dry and free from spills. Wet or dirty items should be replaced as often as required and not left until they are sodden and disintegrating, and ashtrays should be emptied into a metal receptacle and cleaned regularly.

THE BAR-BACK AND COUNTER-TOP

The bar-back or back fitting is the greatest sales aid you have; it is where your customers look to find out what range of products you sell. Yet few pubs maximise the potential of the back fitting to ensure that customers know exactly what products they provide.

The design and layout of the back fitting should be determined by the products, your sales mix and the type of pub. But before examining the back fitting in detail, we will look at the counter-top and how best to display your products.

Draught products form the majority of items displayed on any counter-top, and although generally declining in sales still account for well over 50 per cent of sales. Considering they generate such a huge proportion of sales it is amazing how little time is put into planning their positioning on the counter.

You will soon find that customers tend to head for a particular part of the bar when they enter the pub. This position has the greatest selling potential and will usually be the busiest point. Place your best-selling products at this point and don't clutter it with items that detract, eg a glass washer or glass collection point.

Also consider the most convenient positioning of products in relation to each other – that is, store the tonic near the gin! Minimise the distance that staff need to walk from any part of the bar to a particular product; it may help to divide a large bar into several stations, with the whole product range available at each one. Tills should be positioned with care, because ease of access to them will affect service speed.

The golden rule is to group all products of a similar kind together, enabling customers to see the full range all at once. Cask ale drinkers will head straight for the handpulls, so lining up all the handpulls side by side allows them to choose from your full range. If you have a couple of handpulls at one end of the bar and a couple at the other end with different ales on them, the customer may think you only stock two ales when in fact you stock four. In addition, a bank of four handpulls has a much greater visual impact than two sets of twins.

If you have more than one bar, make sure you have the full range on display in each bar. If volumes do not warrant having more than one pump for each product line, then simply use the pumps on one bar as dummies so the customer knows what's available, even though it may mean staff occasionally having to slip into the other bar to complete an order.

The same principles apply to keg products: position products of the same kind next to each other. There are two ways of displaying keg products: T-bars or individual branded fonts. T-bars enable the full range of products to be displayed next to each other but may not be in keeping with your type of outlet. Branded fonts may be more suitable but they can look cramped and cluttered. The choice is a personal one.

Another item that warrants consideration in the layout of the counter is glass collection. Designated collection points are essential in a busy pub to ensure that you don't run out of glasses, and thus jeopardise the speed of service, but don't clutter up the counter-top either. Collection points should be positioned to avoid key selling points but where they are easily accessible from all areas of the pub.

DISPLAYING

Premium bottled drinks

Premium packaged lagers have seen a huge growth in popularity over the past ten years. Starting from a very low base, they now account for 10 per cent or more of liquor sales in pubs that offer a full range of products, and for a much higher proportion of sales where the product range does not include cask or keg products.

Alcopops and ready-to-drink spirit mixes have been a major growth area over recent years. Traditionally, these would all have been displayed in fridges below the back-bar shelf. But if they are big sellers in your pub – and generally they are now the second-biggest selling product group – they warrant more prominent display. The best way to exhibit them is to install eye-level chillers, a fancy name for high-level, glass-fronted fridges. These display the products in the way customers want to drink them: cold. To be effective, though, they have to be designed into the back fitting. A bar cooler plonked on the back-bar counter-top looks exactly that, and has a negative effect on the display you are trying to enhance.

If you don't have the money to invest in eye-level chillers, or if they are not in line with the décor and style of the pub, an alternative is to create displays of bottled products. These should be neat, clean, uncluttered and make use of any point of sale material you can get. Once you have created a display, it is important to keep it neat and clean – and intact. Staff have a tendency to sell bottles from displays, which leaves them looking tatty; and a dusty display tells the customer that the product doesn't sell. Displays must be backed up with a stock of cold bottles in your under-counter fridges.

There is a tendency to fill fridges with a single row of each product you sell. The most effective use of fridge space is to have blocks of product, with a maximum of two products per shelf. The appearance and sales impact can be further enhanced by vertical stacking, ie having the same product on two or more shelves in a vertical line.

If you are unable to achieve this presentation due to lack of fridge space you should examine your product range and establish whether you really need to stock all the products, whether they all need to be in the fridges (it is preferable to serve chilled soft drinks but not essential as ice can be added), or whether you have room for additional refrigeration.

Having just mentioned point of sale (PoS), now is a good time for a quick note. PoS kits usually contain enough material to redecorate your entire pub. But use it sparingly. A small amount, well placed and well selected, will look much more effective than plastering the pub with PoS until it looks like a discount store. Keep the leftovers, though: it's

important to replace your displays every four weeks at least, or they'll lose all impact. Another point: those Christmas-tree lights that many publicans feel necessary to drape around the over-counter shelf all year round. I was once told that they use these lights when they are serving after time – being less bright than the normal lighting they're less likely to attract police attention. Don't do it: it looks tacky.

Minerals

Consumption of minerals is increasing, for three reasons: public intolerance of drink-driving; increasing awareness of the health risks of alcohol; and a growing number of teetotallers (including under-18s) using pubs. With this increase in

New cellar lifting and storage system

A new system that will lift and position casks and kegs in cellars, in many cases more than doubling the cellars capacity, has been introduced by brewery engineers Chadburns Ltd.

The system comprises a overhead hoist, which doesn't use any valuable floor space, and a stillage system that will enable casks to be stored in two tiers. Also incorporated is an automatic tilt that will gradually tilt the cask as it is emptied.

The introduction follows the publication of the Health and Safety at Work guidelines which does not allow even a 9 gall cask to be fitted manually. This means that in due course all cellars will have to be fit-ted with a mechanical lifting device, which is far from easy in most cellars with restricted floor space and head room.

The new system lifts and positions casks of various sizes on a two tier stillage systems. The control is by a simple to operate push button which enables the casks to be positioned accurately in the stillage. The optional automatic tilt mechanism ensures that the minimum amount of ullage is wasted, increasing the beer output by around two pints per cask.

Details of the cellar system is available from Chadburns Ltd, Park Lane Bootle, Merseyside L30 4UP. Telephone 0151 525 4155.

consumption comes a demand for more exciting adult-oriented soft drinks such as flavoured mineral waters. The latest growth products in the younger market are high energy soft drinks, eg Red Bull.

There is little to be gained from displaying standard soft drinks prominently, as everyone expects them to be there. But adult-oriented soft drinks are not available in many pubs, and therefore can create a point of difference. To make your customers aware of these products and promote them they should be displayed in the same way as premium packaged lagers.

The same could be said of the many branded soft drinks such as Tango, Lilt and Fanta that have hitherto been more the province of the non-licensed retail trade.

With the growth in family dining, it makes sense to be able to offer under-14s the same brands of soft drinks they drink at home – and if you do, make sure they're aware of it.

Spirits

The normal way of displaying spirits is on optic, and a traditional back fitting would have an optic rail running its full length at eye level.

But, in the context of declining spirit sales, you need to think about whether this is right for your pub. The eye level of any back fitting is the best sales area available. Is it advisable to devote the whole of this area to products that are in decline? You may gain a greater advantage from turning part of this area over to displaying higher volume products, growing products or new products

on display shelves or having eye-level fridges.

On the other hand optics provide a quick and easy method of dispensing spirits, and reducing their numbers can lead to reduced speed of service. One alternative is to have two Optic rails in the same place, one slightly lower and behind the other. Or you may decide that your style of operation is better suited to free-pour spirits and thimble measures.

Whichever method of dispense you choose, there are a number of details to take into account when deciding the layout of your spirits.

The best presentation is achieved by grouping spirits into white spirits and dark spirits, with sub groups of like products, eg whiskies, vodkas, etc. Market research has also shown that sales may be increased, oddly enough, if you place two or more bottles of the same brand next to each other.

Wine

Wine is probably the most difficult product to display effectively.

A combination of ice-buckets, wine racking and display shelves will send your customers the message that you stock a range of wines. This should be backed up with a wine list, either on paper, card or chalkboard, giving information about the wine to assist customers in their choice – country of origin, percentage alcohol by volume, taste style, etc. If, due to your customer profile, you stock only a basic range of wine, it may be enough to display it in an ice bucket or fridge and train staff to provide other information should anyone ask.

Impulse Purchases

Some products, including bag snacks and hot beverages, are impulse purchases. Customers do not come to your pub to buy a packet of crisps, but may purchase them to accompany other products.

You can increase sales of impulse products by ensuring they are displayed prominently. Customers are more likely to make a purchase if they have seen the product. The ideal ways to display impulse products are at eye level or to devote a blackboard to advertising them. You could put crisps in baskets on the back bar or even have special shelves built to display them. Hot beverages can be promoted by positioning a coffee machine behind the bar in full view of the customers.

New products

New products need prominent positioning. Position your displays and point of sale in the hotspots of the bar – the places where customers' eyes are drawn. These are different in every outlet but are typically prominent corners and above till positions.

Making space

A number of other considerations should be taken into account when analysing a back fitting. Tills are often put here but it's a good idea, where possible, to move them to the counter front. This reduces the number of times staff need to turn their backs on the customers and also frees space on the back fitting for displaying products – you are not in business to sell tills! Nor do you sell glasses,

so don't use the back fitting to display them. There is no advantage or sales building potential in doing this – it just wastes valuable space.

Gravity dispense

Serving real ales direct from the cask and making a feature out of the casks on the back fitting creates the image of the traditional pub serving traditional products.

There are disadvantages, though. In order to maintain the beer in peak condition you need to provide some kind of cooling system, which takes up space. As it is not easy to get a head on beer drawn straight from the cask you risk impairing the presentation of the beer. And unless there is a large amount of space it is not practical to rack barrels to allow them to condition.

However, if you wish to display one or two guest beers in this way the problems are somewhat reduced.

Chalkboards

Chalkboards are often part of the bar area or back fitting, and using them to best advantage is important. They can convey innumerable messages to customers – promotions, forthcoming events, food specials, menu, new products, wine list, cask ale list and so on.

Chalkboards (and posters) will only work as a sales aid if they are well written. This is a skill that not everyone possesses, so be honest with yourself about your talents. A badly written or incorrectly spelt board will give a negative message to customers. If you are not good at writing chalkboards, it is worth trying to find a good chalkboarder among your staff and delegating the job. In some areas there are professional chalkboarders who will create wonderful boards that really do the job of communication well.

Bar stools

Bar stools are a feature common to nearly all pubs, and in many outlets they are beneficial. People like to stand or sit at the bar, particularly if they are on their own, and bar stools give out the friendly message that it is all right to stand or sit around the servery and maybe chat to the staff.

Busy outlets, on the other hand, often need to encourage customers to move away from the bar once they have bought their drinks. If you have to keep the bar clear all the time or nearly all the time for customers waiting to be served, then don't provide stools at the bar.

But the same bar stools which are impractical during busy sessions provide a welcome facility for customers at other times. If this is the case, they can be stored out of the bar area during busy sessions.

Health and Safety Notes

The Food Safety (General Food Hygiene) Regulations 1995 require a 'high degree of personal cleanliness' from persons who work in a food handling area, which includes bars, as the legal definition of 'food' includes drink.

Staff should not smoke behind the bar because smoking involves hand-to-mouth contact. This does not prevent staff smoking elsewhere provided they wash their hands before serving again. Bar staff therefore need access to a 'suitably located' hand basin with hot water, soap and hand-drying facilities. Depending on where the nearest alternative is, a facility is commonly provided at the bar itself.

Where food is being served from the bar there are particular food safety issues to consider in addition to the hand-washing facility. In particular, do you intend to have food on display and, if so, for how long?

The Food Safety (Temperature Control) Regulations 1995 apply to foods that may support food-poisoning organisms. The Regulations allow for the one-off display of food outside the prescribed temperatures for specific periods (up to four hours for cold food and up to two hours for hot food). However, it is good practice generally (and a specific requirement where the exemptions do not apply) for hot food to be kept at or above 63°C and for cold food to be kept at or below 8°C.

You also need to consider how you intend to protect open food while it is on display. If you have domestic pets they are a potential source of contamination and their access to food handling areas needs to be appropriately controlled.

Finally, care needs to be taken with regard to ice production. 'Potable' water should be used, and ice machines and freezers need to be kept clean. The use of trays to make ice may result in an undesirable level of handling, as does allowing customers to help themselves. Ice-buckets should be kept clean and covered and emptied regularly. Scoop handles should not come into contact with the ice.

As part of the health and safety risk assessment required of everyone in business (see Chapter 9), issues to consider with reference to the bar area and people working in it include glass breakage; the condition of the floor (in terms of slipping and tripping); how to reduce the potential for violence to staff; measures to reduce their exposure to tobacco smoke and the potential effects of passive smoking; and, where applicable, access to the cellar. If a cellar hatch is located behind the bar it is vital that a safe system of working, incorporating appropriate protection to the opening, is provided. The protection (eg chains or bars) needs to be sufficiently far from the opening to provide an effective barrier before anyone could lose their footing.

Legal Notes

The bar includes any place exclusively or mainly used for the sale and consumption of intoxicating liquor. So if a place in licensed premises is not so used, or the main use is not for the sale and consumption of intoxicating liquor (eg a room mainly used for dining), then the place will not be a bar.

Details of notices that must be displayed in on-licensed premises are given in Appendix V.

Food hygiene is controlled by the Food Safety (General Food Hygiene) Regulations 1995, which set standards for the service of food and drinks. There is nothing in the Regulations to prevent bar staff from serving a second or subsequent drink to a customer in the glass of their choice, including the glass in which they had their first drink, should they so wish. However, it is probably better practice to use a fresh glass, unless the customer insists on using the same one.

CHAPTER ELEVEN

MARKETING, PUBLICITY AND PROMOTION

Danny Blyth

Publicity is the key to successful marketing of your pub. It brings your business to the attention of a bigger audience, generating extra trade you otherwise might take years to build up.

But you needn't be Max Clifford to make the media work for you. Nor do you need to spend much of your hard-earned turnover. What successful publicity calls for is some understanding of the media and its needs, a little imagination, and the commitment to spend the time required.

The publicans with the healthiest businesses are often the very same who enjoy regular doses of good publicity. From an early stage in the trade they realised that time spent on being 'media friendly' was very well worth it. This chapter explains some of the basic techniques you need to achieve the same.

GETTING YOUR TERMS RIGHT

The first step to understanding the media is getting your terms right.

Public relations (PR) is activity put into getting your pub editorial coverage. This ranges from calling the local paper to tell them about your big charity night to nominating your house for an award. It results in 'editorial' — an independent third party writing, then printing or broadcasting, a message about you over which you haven't the final say. Though PR involves time and expense it is not paid for.

Advertising is bought. You decide what is said about you and you pay the price. Then there is advertorial, a paid-for advert produced to look like editorial and usually headed 'Advertisement feature' at the top of the page.

We shall concentrate on editorial — what you don't have to pay for but is most prized, as more people are likely to see it and take note.

To be a successful publicist you must understand what is newsworthy, or of interest to the media. Most newsworthy is the unusual: 'Dog bites man' isn't a great story, but 'Man bites dog' is. And so, while your putting on a new guest ale might be newsworthy among your regulars, it isn't front-page news outside.

In all your PR and publicity work, therefore, focus on your main events, like big-scale fundraisers, quirky anniversaries you celebrate at the pub or some praiseworthy community involvement. And keep things unusual.

PLANNING AND TARGETING

Planning and targeting are crucial to good publicity, which rarely falls into your lap. Start by looking at your local media and get to know them well. Read, watch and listen with the dual purpose of spotting PR opportunities and gaining an understanding of what your local media considers newsworthy.

Develop a good relationship with the local papers and radio, letting them know that you are prepared to talk. Target individual journalists and ask them down to your pub – they don't receive many invitations. Meeting journalists will also help you understand what they consider newsworthy, and how to spot those off-beat stories they most enjoy. They will also impress on you the importance of having a good photo opportunity at whatever event you are trying to publicise.

Maintain a file of all media relevant to you – papers, magazines, radio and TV, including as many personal contacts as possible, with address and telephone details. It should record each contact's deadlines for receipt of information: all

media run to rigid deadlines, and too often good stories aren't covered because the information arrives too late.

Take some time to call all contacts on your list and ask how they prefer information and photographs to be sent – fax, e-mail, letter, colour print, transparency – and to whom to send them.

Identify the key areas of your business you most need to publicise, such as increasing restaurant trade or functions room hire, and focus efforts towards them. The good publicist knows what he's about – and why.

Once you have your list of priorities and your media list it is often a good idea to take time to map out a media plan of action for the year and detail any costs (such as the odd advert). A separate plan for each event is also useful. If, say, you have a beer festival each August, effective planning will allow you to get the story into the local Campaign for Real Ale (CAMRA) newsletter for the start of the month, the two local papers in the week before the event and radio the night before. Knowing and responding to the separate deadlines for each will maximise your chances.

CONTACTING THE MEDIA

There are two ways of letting journalists know what story you have to tell: telephone contact and news release.

Telephone contact is best reserved for fast-breaking events of great importance, or if you have already cultivated a good contact. If you really must call journalists:

◆ call between 10.30am (after the morning editorial meeting) and 1pm (after which field trips are made)
◆ always ask for the 'news desk' in the first instance
◆ prepare a concise outline of what you have to say
◆ be ready to note any request for further information they need (and get back quickly with the details if required).

The more common way of supplying information is by news release. A news release is a brief outline of what is going to happen, the bare bones of a story for consideration by a news editor. PR pros have perfected this to an art, but you can often do just as well – if you follow the golden rules.

◆ Use plain white (white because the whole release can then be scanned into the newspaper's system) A4 paper, headed in capitals, 'NEWS RELEASE'.
◆ Type or laser print your details, using good black ink (also for scanning purposes!) double spacing and wide margins.
◆ Keep it tight, use only one sheet of paper.
◆ Be accurate with all details like times and name spellings.
◆ End with a 'person to contact' for further information and include a telephone number.
◆ Address to 'the News Editor' and mail in good time to meet the deadline.

WRITING A NEWS RELEASE

The keyword is brevity: get to the point and stick to it – don't ramble.

Start with a headline and keep it short, something like 'Soap stars wanted at local pub'.

The first sentence or introduction is crucial, and should always stand alone as your first paragraph; for example: 'The King's Head, Main Street, is looking for TV soap star lookalikes as part of its fundraising drive for Main Street Primary School.'

The news editor looks for five keys in a news release: Who? Where? What? Why? and When? Give these keys a separate paragraph each. The intro grabbed the interest and now needs to be followed up with the necessary detail. A paragraph on Why? will show that you are planning a fundraising night for the local school's computer fund. What? will show that you intend to have a soap opera quiz plus a soap star lookalike competition with prizes. Carry on with the other questions, then revise by looking through your release again, asking all five key questions.

Remember: a well-written release that can go straight into the editorial system – either via e-mail or the scanner (see above) – may even be published unaltered.

A good photo opportunity improves your chance of getting coverage no end: design opportunities into your plans. For instance, if you are organising a fundraising disco, why not make it a Spicy Spin Disco, inviting girls to come dressed as Spice Girls with the best-dressed winning prizes? A raunchy photo opportunity like this would be highly likely to get you on to the front page of most local papers.

A good licensee would be able to fill the pub with his disco alone. The PR-minded licensee would get free local paper coverage before and after the event as well. The really seasoned, PR-minded licensee would get all this, arrange some sponsorship from a supplier like Bacardi Spice, and land himself some coverage on radio and in the trade press as well. You must think big and spend time on the telephone and writing press releases if the coverage is to start rolling in.

Having said that, don't be put off by lack of success. Your release might have arrived the day a royal made a surprise visit to the area. By calling (calmly!) to find out why, you may find there was a good reason for the story not being used, and they might offer to do something with your pub later. Never assume that you've a right to press coverage.

PRO-ACTIVE PUBLICITY

Once armed with all this know-how, you are finally ready to get pro-active and set things moving. There are three distinct stages to your development as your own press officer.

1 The core business

Remember that you are, and must remain, primarily a publican and not a publicist. Good publicity might be successful in getting people to try out your pub for the first time, but the pub has to live up to the promise if they're to come back. Don't let stardom get in the way of standards at the pub: the best PR of all is always word of mouth.

The first pro-active move, therefore, must be to achieve high standards and develop unique features that might enable you to win awards.

Awards are perhaps the best form of publicity: they invariably earn column inches, and the story is how great your pub is. There are award schemes run by pub companies, trade suppliers, tourist authorities, CAMRA and a host of other organisations, covering everything from floral displays to children's facilities. You can sometimes nominate yourself for many schemes and, if not, you can normally persuade a friendly third party to enter you.

If you do win, or are even shortlisted, work it as hard as you can for as long as you can (most awards are current for a year). Make sure the organisers have the local press briefed, and then tell them yourself as well, just to be sure. After the initial splash, display your cuttings, use A-boards outside, hang your certificate over the fireplace where everyone can see it. Some businesses even print their awards on all their letterheads, compliments slips, price lists, brochures, press ads, everything. In short, tell everyone. Your publicity machine is up and running – and running on the basis of solid pub business instead of hype.

Second, treat guidebooks with the same energy as awards schemes. There are a plethora of guidebooks published today, and being listed in any can only benefit trade. But never pay to get into a guidebook. Paid-for listings have no clout; and all too often an approach for a paid-for listing is a con. You send your cheque, but no book ever appears or, if it does, it's a grubby A5 photocopied leaflet. Instead, spend an hour browsing in W H Smith, and jot down the details of guidebooks you'd like to appear in. For the most prestigious guidebooks – the *Good Beer Guide*, for instance – nominations are entirely independent and often secret, but there are others that welcome applications. Call the publishers for details on how listings are made (again you can sometimes arrange nomination) and get cracking.

2 Free opportunities

Look at what opportunities are going begging. Often there is free publicity to be had that on its own might only bring one or two extra people out per night, but as part of the overall package that is the image of your pub it can add up to something significant.

For instance, if you have regular music or entertainments nights, look to getting them included, free, in the listings sections of local papers and in 'What's On' magazines. Phone the person who puts that section together and ask how they like to receive details and when. Some licensees have devised their own form which they fill in and fax to the appropriate editor every week.

Local radio stations often have a variety of guests from all walks of life on sundry talk slots or to review the papers on air. Why not call the producer in charge of such a show and volunteer? Frequently they're short of candidates, and if they're not the most they can do is turn you down.

There are also opportunities to be a guest writer in all sorts of titles, from local papers through to publications like *What's Brewing*. Use them to get your pub's name spread more widely. But do send a topical and lively contribution and not a whinge. Be positive about your business.

3 Making your own news

After getting your pub in the frame for awards, and going on to exploit what free opportunities exist for you, you will begin to become 'media wise'. You will now be ready and able to be more ambitious and get out to create the news, speaking to the media in advance of your big events, such as charity fundraisers or special celebrations for big dates like Hallowe'en.

You might like to create a special newsworthy event for yourself by celebrating an unusual anniversary. The stranger it is, the more

BHMA Limited has been changing the face of pub retailing for the past seven years. Based in Cambridgeshire, BHMA's directors Patrick and Joanne and their valued team have been driving the standards of in-pub merchandising and the presentation of chalkboards with relentless aggression. They started trading as a company offering training in these subjects only. Since then the company has grown swiftly.

BHMA now manufacture many products to assist publicans to communicate their messages to prospective customers. The product list offered seems endless, and includes such items as Chalkboards, Signs, Banners, Fascier Boards, Amenity Boards, Table Furniture, Chalkboard Stencils and even their own trademarked brand of pens for chalkboards, called quite simply: Pens4Chalkboards™. To acquire a brochure of the products available customers only have to call 01353 776305. E-mail BHMA@aol.com.

BHMA is a Greek word pronounced VEE-MAR which means to step ahead, the name fits the company perfectly, if you are existing customer you will know that already of course.

BHMA Limited has been changing the face of pub retailing for the past seven years. Based in Cambridgeshire, BHMA's directors Patrick and Joanne and their valued team have been driving the standards of in-pub merchandising and the presentation of chalkboards with relentless aggression. Success has come from quality training courses for both of these subjects. The courses are a one day event covering, Space management, Human behavioural patterns, Hot spots, Impulse and Demand product requirements, Communication requirements of effective chalkboards, Chalkboard art and more. The course results are amazing, delegates from any background can achieve high levels of competence and confidence in a very short space of time. Pubs that are visited after the course usually show a sales uplift on targeted products and a substantial improvement in chalkboard presentation. Training can be taken to any part of the country, saving travelling costs for the twelve to sixteen delegates the course can cater for. Information packs are sent out on request by phoning 01353 776305.

Director, Patrick Huggins says, BHMA have worked with most of the licensed retailers in the country in some way or other, and are continuing to do so, because of the popularity of both the training and the product quality they offer. More information on BHMA products can be found under Bar Design & Merchandising.

newsworthy; be sure to stress this while talking to the press (as well as telling them what a good picture your event will make). Choose a good, fun theme, but choose so you can run the event well (events should always be for customers first and media second). Always try to get your suppliers to contribute to funding, pointing out you expect good PR. They're liable to be more helpful with the possibility of added publicity. As for inspiration, pick up on your pub's geographical or historical connections. Or you could have a core of regulars with an unusual hobby. Make things topical by relating your event to something in the public eye.

If, for instance, gardening is big in your area, why not hold an 'Alternative Chelsea' during the Chelsea Flower Show. You could offer prizes for the weediest weed, most miserable houseplant and least appetising vegetables. Silly? Yes, but also quirky and newsworthy — and worth a picture. But whatever you decide, proper planning and targeting, involving pre-event liaison with the media, will make or break the event.

What will also help greatly is involving your staff in your plans: properly briefing them about a publicity-driven event, taking on board their views and suggestions, and making sure they are entering into the spirit of the thing. The last thing you need is a microphone thrust in front of a member of staff who feels uncomfortable in fancy dress, resentful at being made to make a fool of himself, and uncertain as to what it's all about.

ADVERTISING

As a licensee you'll be regularly plagued by requests for advertising – and indeed there will be times when you actually want to advertise. Here's a quick guide to making the most of however much, or little, you choose to spend.

Press advertisements take two main forms: display and classified. Display ads are interspersed through the editorial pages of the paper and are described by size: a full page, half, quarter, or a smaller size delineated by its depth in centimetres and width in columns (eg 14×2, 25×3). Classifieds are the smaller ads grouped under headings (classifications) such as Goods Wanted, Accommodation to Let etc, printed in a standard format, and charged by the line or word. 'Semi-displays' are in fact glorified classifieds that use a different format to stand out from the rest.

The golden rule when buying print ads is never to let yourself be rushed into anything, even at that 'once-only bargain price' or as part of a special feature on the area's pubs. Consider the publication the offer is coming from and ask yourself if it is read by your target customers. Get the advertising salesman to supply details of its readership and circulation. Also query what the offer is in terms of position and design. Does it mean your pub being listed among a host of others, perhaps giving just the pub name and address set in a small pint pot illustration? There's little point in just being one of the pack: the point of advertising is to attract attention!

That doesn't mean you shouldn't take part in special promotional features: it means you should do so in a way that suits your business aims. The reason why businesses advertise is because advertising works: if you've got a product, you need to shout about it. But the medium and the message both need to be chosen very carefully.

Where to place your ad

The key to successful advertising is getting the right ad in the right media at the right time. Choose the time and place that's going to mean the most to you. For instance, if your pub is an alehouse with six cask beers you might choose to advertise in a local CAMRA newsletter, which will not only be read by CAMRA members but will be distributed through pubs and off-licences in the area to thousands of people who have one thing in common: they like real ale. If it's your food trade you want to boost, on the other hand, you might like to go for a 'What's On' publication and the 'Eating Out' section of the local paper, whereas your accommodation trade might be better boosted by an ad in a tourist guide.

Whatever your choice of medium, tailor the message to suit a particular target market. Keep the wording brief and to the point – the chances are that there isn't a brilliant copy-writer inside you.

Design

Then comes the design stage. An advert is either 'made up' for you by the publication, or you can have it originated by a pro such as a graphic designer. No matter which route you take, insist they make the design simple and in keeping with your pub's desired image.

Try to incorporate either an illustration or a photograph – these really do grab the readers' attention. But ensure they are good quality – a poor illustration might even lose you business, so it is worth paying a little bit more to get better quality. You can use different typefaces as well as devices such as bold or italic print, or 'reverse print' (black on white). But use them sparingly for proper effect: too busy or cluttered an advertisement looks dreadful and says nothing. The same applies to colour, either full colour (which can be expensive) or 'spot colour' (a single colour in addition to black type).

The chances are that you won't be entirely satisfied by your first efforts. So, to maximise your chances, always ask the publication or your own designer to supply a 'rough' (an outline design) for your prior approval. Inspect this carefully, check whether they've followed your design specifications and look carefully for setting errors that might appear in the text – especially details on things like opening hours and telephone numbers. Mistakes here can be crucial. Apply the same checking procedure to the proof. And always insist that everything is as you want it: you're paying, and advertising isn't cheap!

If, however, the publication messes things up for you by poor reproduction (like fuzzy pictures and poor print quality), get on the telephone to the advertising manager (not any executive you might have dealt with) and demand recompense. There's no need to go overboard: the paper wants your repeat business and isn't going to argue if it has genuinely made a mistake.

There is one other kind of advert that can present you with a real problem, and that's advertising in the literature – yearbooks, programmes and so on – which often supports community events and organisations. This sort of advertising can't be proved to help your business, but it's hard to turn away, and if you do turn it away you can end up getting a bad name in your community. Why not turn the situation to your advantage by appearing to offer more than you've been asked for? Take the ad, yes, but use it to offer a cut-price dinner for two for the first three or five brought back to the pub; or perhaps offer to donate 10p to the community group concerned and 10p off a pint for every copy of the ad traded in at the pub.

Is it working?

One thing's for sure, there are an awful lot of ads in the average newspaper. How can you be sure yours is having an impact? Even if trade goes up immediately following the insertion of an ad, it doesn't necessarily follow that the ad was responsible. A coincidental refurbishment or a change of landlord at a neighbouring pub is just as likely to lead to a temporary boost in your trade as those among its regulars who liked things as they were vote with their feet.

All businesses need to track the response to their advertising to be sure they're not wasting money. The usual way is to ask new customers to state with their order where they saw the goods or services advertised, but that's not a good option for a pub: 'Three pints of lager and a packet of crisps, and by the way, I'm here because I saw your ad in the *Gazette*' – it doesn't work, does it?

One old trick that both increases the drawing power of the ad and helps you monitor its success is to include a low-value coupon in the artwork – a few quid off a meal for two, 50p off a pint of lager, that sort of thing. Not only is a money-off offer an attraction in its own right, you can tell precisely from the number of vouchers returned how successful your ad has been and whether it's worth repeating.

This sort of lure can also be used in leaflets stuck under windscreen wipers in the municipal car-park or handed out outside the railway station in the evening rush hour. It's also useful as a way of building special kinds of business: half-price pink champagne with every dinner for two will fill the restaurant on St Valentine's Day, for instance; while a free bottle of house wine with every three-course dinner for two taken between 6pm and 8pm Monday–Thursday will help boost an otherwise quiet period.

COSTS

Finally, a word on costs. Always look at the whole cost picture, both when you are called by a rep and when you are actively knocking on their door. Get them to quote for a range of sizes and for use of spot and full

Pictorial signs, Main house facias, Amenity signs, Antiqued interior signs, Interior and exterior chalkboards. Themed wall painted murals. Exterior lighting

Health advertising is a family business involved in the design, production and installation of high quality pub signs.

Our wide-range of finishes (gold leaf, painted lettering or vinyl) enable us to tailor signs to our client's exact needs and budget. Signs can be designed specifically to suit the architecture of individual premises and we will incorporate our client's own ideas if desired. We are also able to incorporate the standard 'in-house' design require-ments of individual breweries.

Signs may be constructed either with timber/aluminium or GRP, Pictorials are hand-painted and lettered and supplied on a timber or aluminium face edged in hardwood.

Specialist iron work can be supplied or signs may be fitted to existing structures if required. Sign lighting can also be installed by qualified electricians. Costing is carried out on an individual job basis.

A full portfolio of our work is available or we will send you a brochure upon request.

Interior and exterior painting and decorating.

Interior special effects and finishes.

Established 30 years or more in the sign business and specialising in well designed, high quality pub signs and pictorials for free house, brewery and pub chains.

We research produce and fix - oh, we also put on the extra lights if needed. The traditional aspect of pub sign work appeals to the signwriter, this is where his skills are, by the way we all appreciate the added advantage of our computers for helping out with the donkeywork, but they can't stand by a little country inn and decide the colours for the walls and signs and how the picture should be displayed (well not quite yet) so, if you have a signwriter who can paint pictures, is a long distance traveller who can climb ladders then its not a bad way to make a living.

We like to research our pictorials, after all if you have an unusual pub name, you need to know the history etc. to provide a good pictorial, whether it be heraldic or some local traditional you can be sure that some old timer who has his own seat in the corner and his own mug on the backshelf, knows better. Do not be put off when we say all our signs are aluminium faced and have aluminium or hardwood edges, are pre finished in two pack paint and are all lettered in 23 carat gold lettering, they are good value and very competitive in price, don't forget they can be refinished several times over many years.

How about a nice interior wall mural or even the whole place themed in some classical or period style, no problem to us, we can paint the cherubs, marble the pillars and paint you a Rubens on the ceiling.

If you need to talk about replacement signs on your pub, club or hotel then why not give us a call either myself or one of my two sons will advise you to the best of our knowledge, and should we get to a point where we agree in principle on ideas and costings then one of us will visit and survey the work to be done, don't worry we are always looking for ways to cut your costs and make a profit for ourselves at the same time.

All the best,

John Haden

colour, and to detail any additional costs in making up your advert and supplying proofs. Make it clear that you aren't going to pay any 'hidden extras' that mysteriously turn up later.

If you are going ahead with an advert, always negotiate on price. Every publication and radio station is open to negotiation on the full list price that appears on its 'rate card', and that's apart from the series dis-count where there is a percentage knocked off for taking space in a certain number of issues.

Be especially tough when trying a publication out for the first time. Dangle the carrot of further business if, first, you get a good introductory price and, second, the response is good. With ad people you are dealing with some of the thickest-skinned operators in the commercial world. Fight like with like.

CHAPTER TWELVE

MAXIMISING MACHINE INCOME

Ian Chuter

Amusement machines are an essential part of the pub business. Like them or loathe them, they make a highly significant contribution to the profitability of most licensed businesses, and good management can boost machine income by up to 30 per cent. The secret to quite how much you profit from amusement machines lies in the relationship you have with your chosen operator.

But all operators are the same – aren't they?

Yes, in the same way that all cars are the same, all restaurants are the same, and Accrington Stanley's latest signing is as potent as Alan Shearer. Certainly at the most basic level they fulfil the same function, but in reality some provide an awful lot more, consisting of a wide range of business services.

I'M NOT INTERESTED IN FANCY SERVICES, ALL I WANT TO DO IS MAXIMISE MY MACHINE INCOME

That's exactly what operators are there to do. All of their services are geared to increasing your profit from machines. Operating amusement machines is a highly skilled business. Products popular in city-centre locations might not have the same appeal in community pubs. Not only should your operator be able to select the right machines for your business, he can also tell you what price of play to operate at, and with amusement with prize machines (AWPs) what percentage payout setting will get the best return.

An agreement between the industry and the Gaming Board of Great Britain states that the percentage payout on fruit machines will not fall below 70 per cent. Clearly this does not mean that for every £1 staked the player receives a minimum of 70p back. The percentage payout level is an aggregate figure established over 10,000 plays. Percentage payout represents a variable whereby the licensee – in partnership and consultation with his chosen operator – can influence the level of machine income. And it doesn't follow that the lower the

percentage the higher the income generated, either. For example, in community pubs where there is a strong regular clientele, a machine will perform best on a higher percentage setting, typically up to 84 per cent. In premises with a more transient trade the optimum percentage may be 78–80 per cent. And in extreme cases, such as on AWPs sited on or near railway stations where the customer is killing time, a lower percentage of approximately 74 per cent can be successfully operated.

Although the price of play is limited to a 25p stake, this is a ceiling figure. It is possible to set machines on a 5p stake (20 plays for £1), 10p stake (10 plays for £1), 20p (five plays for £1) or 25p (four plays for £1).

SURELY CHOOSING AN OPERATOR LOCAL TO ME MAKES SENSE?

The national operating companies provide exactly that – nationwide cover – so in practice they can offer a localised service but with the added attraction of knowing the national picture. Many customers have found that they are better off using an operator with experience gained from working on a national stage and across all sectors of the machine industry.

BUT SHOULDN'T I GO FOR THE BEST RENTAL PRICE?

The best price certainly doesn't mean the cheapest. Opt for the cheapest, and you could end up with an outdated machine that breaks down regularly, isn't repaired on time and

doesn't take any money. If you take this route while the competition opts for the latest launch, which is regularly and promptly serviced, frequently collected, with the latest income protection measures against fraud, the likelihood is that you'll not only lose machine income, you could also lose some of your net sales trade as well. Although it's a cliché, there is a difference between price and value for money, and it is a difference that should be addressed.

WHAT'S THE BENEFIT OF CHANGING MACHINES REGULARLY – ISN'T IT JUST UNNECESSARY HASSLE?

Machines are changed only for business reasons: that is, to maximise your income. AWPs follow fashions, and having an older machine when your competitors – either pubs or betting shops – have the latest models will result in a drop in income. (Incidentally, it's important to recognise the competition posed by betting shops. Under the terms of the 1996 deregulation they were allowed for the first time to site a maximum of two AWPs. There is a strong cross-over of betting shop and pub customers, and the siting of machines represents an extra tier of competition to the on-trade.)

The art to changing machines is in the timing – that is, identifying when a certain product has peaked and bringing in a newer model before the income begins to drop. There is no set formula for this. Although typical machines will sustain income for up to 12 or 14 weeks, it may be that after the initial player learning curve income will

Ensure that what you have overhead... is not an
Overhead!

MAINTENANCE FREE

When you choose a conservatory style extension to your business START AT THE TOP.

No Compromise to Weatherproofing

Without doubt one of the commonest sources of customer complaint for conservatory installers is leaking, creaking or draughty roofs.

This is because it is quite a common practice in this market to rely on the installer to repair the inadequacies of a poorly designed roofing system whilst it is being erected.

For example, many glazed roofing systems need to be fixed by using large amounts of silicone to prevent leaks along the bars and stuffing the spider cap (the curved cap that covers the joining point of all the hip beams at the end of an Edwardian or Victorian style high pitched roof) with foam to prevent draughts.

Many suppliers, who market themselves as the manufacturers of conservatories, only manufacture, or assemble, UPVC windows and buy in the bar lengths for the construction of roofs. They therefore do not have in-house expertise in the design and installation of roofs and are dependent on third parties to advise them. These third parties want to sell their roofing systems to them and so the circle of poor performance is somewhat difficult to break.

Specialist Glazed Roofing Manufacture

Newdawn & Sun is a specialist glazed roofing engineering company that has pursued an aggressive programme of technical development. They have eliminated each annoying installation and performance issue that has become the market norm' for the erection and installation of aluminium and timber supported conservatory roofs and have taken their Glazed Roofing Systems to the forefront of both the Commercial and Domestic installation markets.

The technical innovations made by Newdawn in recent years are beginning to be copied but not improved upon. For example one of the jealously guarded trademarks of the company is **Snaptyte**™.

The Hole Story

The **Snaptyte**™ closure system provides a more secure and weatherproof means of controlling the polycarbonate sheeting on a timber conservatory (very popular in the licensed trade in which publicans are looking for the economy of a conservatory extension with the visual appeal that comes from exposed timber beams).

The **Snaptyte**™ system has been imitated by a few roofing companies who continue to drill screw holes to fix the bars to the rafters in positions that will let in water. In doing so they demonstrate their lack of understanding of the excellence of the design principles at work in the **Snaptyte**™ system.

Only the Newdawn **Snaptyte**™ product positions the necessary screw holes in places that are completely enclosed when the roof is finished making it impossible for water to get into however hard the wind might blow.

Strength & Security

In the self supporting market (i.e. where the aluminium bars that control the polycarbonate sheets provide the structure that holds the roof up) some manufacturers provide their installers with a special tool that enables them to snap in or snap out the polycarbonate roofing sheets conveniently from the bars in the roof.

These tools are not difficult to come by and any enterprising burglar armed with such a tool can easily pop out the polycarbonate panels from this style of roof absolutely silently and then basically step over any window locks that might have been fitted.

This is inconvenient enough when it is a domestic burglary but in an establishment that keeps in stock thousands of pounds worth of wines, spirits and foodstuffs we don't think that this is good e nough.

The Newdawn glazed roofing system makes a break-in of this type almost impossible. Thieves would actually have to make a lot of noise smashing the roof panels to gain entry this way. Noise is something that burglars are not keen on and we do not know of a case where a Newdawn roof has been broken into this way.

Service & Style

So if you are looking for a superbly efficient and good looking roof to cover your new restaurant extension or children's room, what does Newdawn offer you?

Firstly, they will provide you with a 'roof down', FREE consultative service that will give you the most cost-effective design to suit your needs no matter how complex your plans. This would include a free site visit to your business to discuss your actual requirements.

If your plans are to build a very large glazed building that requires a portal frame this will be evaluated on site and a bespoke manufactur-

ing service will be provided.

Looking at the overall design of your pub will determine the best style of extension to suit your needs. Newdawn not only provide the full range of Edwardian, Victorian or Lean-to styles but also offer a comprehensive range of accessories to finish the building work in style. From box gutters that will fit even the most complex shapes to electronically operated roof vents that can be opened and shut at the touch of a button.

Choice of Finishes

A choice of finishes is also available to match your decor including White, Brown and superb Mahogany and Golden Oak Woodgrain finishes. Where woodgrain finishes are required these are always laminated onto a colour matched substrate so that you are not left with annoying little white edges on either the inside or outside of the building.

All coloured components are made from materials that have been tested to withstand the extremes of temperature experienced in the UK and their excellent performance has resulted in their being exported to world markets as far away as Australia.

It is the consistent attention to detail of this sort throughout the product range that has set Newdawn apart from the rest in our view.

For further information, please contact:
Mike Newey
Managing Director
Newdawn & Sun Ltd
Tel: 01789 764 444
Fax:01789 400 164
E-mail:
sales@newdawn.sun.co.uk

begin to drop after six weeks. Conversely, a machine that your customers have learned to play and enjoy can last up to 20 weeks. It's certainly not welcome news for our colleagues in the manufacturing side of the industry, but we have sites where the same machine has generated excellent revenue for 18 months. However, I must stress that this is the exception.

The decision to change machines is a mixture of science and experience. As a national operator working across a spectrum of leisure sectors we have a wealth of data relating to the performance and product life cycles of machines. Combine this with an intimate knowledge of the amusement sector and a close relationship with all of the manufacturers, and you have the best possible credentials to make what is a crucial decision.

HOW BIG AN ISSUE IS SECURITY?

Machines, because they carry cash – particularly club jackpot machines that may have a float of £300 – are susceptible to crime. If a machine is physically broken into the loss is not just restricted to the cash box, but also relates to damage to the equipment and the resultant period of downtime. Fraud, or clever machine crime, is a separate issue that is sometimes harder to prevent. While it is impossible to claim that any machine is crime proof, we can make life an awful lot harder for the criminally inclined.

To start with, machines should not be sited near exit/entrance doors. There have been examples of gangs simply lifting the machine

and making off in a van. Machines can be supplied with alarm systems with tilt switches that will activate the alarm if the machine is tilted by more than a 45° angle. Security bars can be fitted in extreme cases.

Electronic Data Capture (EDC), which provides a wealth of information to assist in the identification of fraud, should be fitted. In straightforward terms, EDC is the machine equivalent of an aeronautical black box, in that it provides us with detailed and valuable information. It can tell us what amount of money should be in the machine, when the machine was switched on and off, and how many times it has been played every hour of the day and night. By using EDC it is possible to identify the time of a fraud, allowing us to narrow down the list of potential suspects.

Front-line staff, including collectors, should be trained to identify signs of machine tampering that would be unnoticed by laymen. Telltale signs include groups crowding around the machine, the winning of multiple jackpots, and multiple credits appearing on the machine. A significant proportion of machine crime is committed by organised gangs that move around the country. This being the case, it is vital that the authorities gather as much information as possible on their activities and methods. If you see a group of people who you believe may have targeted your machines, get descriptions and if possible a car registration number. The police are now beginning to take this type of organised crime extremely seriously.

In some cases customers will simply try it on. The most common approach is to claim that a machine has failed to pay out and demand money from bar staff. Our recommendation is to deal with this issue in the same way you would when people claim that they've been short-changed. Just as a check on the till balance can be made, so an engineer is able to determine how much any player has really won. In all cases the bywords are communication with your operator and vigilance.

WHAT ABOUT NON-GAMBLING MACHINES?

It may be that the location is big enough and has the right portfolio of customers to accommodate a video simulator – many of which are now available in mini-versions designed specifically for pubs. However, despite the appeal of hi-tech simulators, they come at a cost equivalent to five brand-new, state-of-the-art AWPs. As a consequence, you have to be certain that they are right for your business.

On video games it's possible for licensees to run a highest score or fastest time competition, thereby increasing repeat plays and attracting new custom. Furthermore, many of the manufacturers are including novelty features commonly known as 'cheats', whereby the experienced player can access an attention-seeking feature. A current example can be found on TT Manx, where 'the player in the know' can swap his 750cc Kawasaki for a thoroughbred sheep conversant with the highways and byways of the Isle of Man!

With reference to pool, we encourage our customers to participate in leagues and to stage in-house compe-

titions. We currently run 11 different pool promotions that are available to Rank Leisure Machine Services' customers. The objective is to assist in developing and sustaining trade, particularly on the traditionally quieter days.

AMUSEMENT MACHINES ARE JUST A PERIPHERAL PART OF THE BUSINESS, AREN'T THEY?

The latest figures produced by BACTA, the trade association for the domestic amusement machine industry, show that AWPs and club jackpot machines pay out an annual sum in prize money totalling £7.2 billion. Put into context, that's £19.7 million a day – the equivalent of a National Lottery roll-over jackpot 365 days a year.

Of the 240,000 AWPs and club jackpot machines in the UK, some 40 per cent are in licensed premises. Clearly, what we are dealing with is a significant element in the leisure industry, and one that plays an important part in the economic and commercial fabric of pubs and clubs. With the introduction of the £10 all-cash jackpot in June 1996, extensive research has shown that the on-trade takings have increased by 30 per cent where £10 all-cash jackpots have been combined with 25p play.

WHAT ARE THE LEGAL REQUIREMENTS OF SITING MACHINES?

Knowing your legal responsibilities is essential. The two main requirements relate to permits and Customs and Excise. Licensees require what is known as a Section 34 permit before they can site AWPs, and a Part III for club jackpot machines. The application and renewal procedure can be looked after by the operator, and most professional operators will do this as a matter of course. Permits are granted by the local magistrates and are not required for skill with prize machines (SWPs), pool, video, table football or pinball. Amusement Machine Licence Duty (AMLD) is a much more complex issue, and my advice is to get the most up-to-date information from your operator.

WHAT PRACTICAL MEASURES CAN I TAKE AS A LICENSEE TO IMPROVE MACHINE INCOME?

Advances in technology have made sound an important element of the entertainment value provided by an AWP, and manufacturers are investing considerable sums in sampled sound technology. Industry research has shown that sound represents 5 per cent of the total cost of developing a new AWP. Academic research has shown that players are encouraged by the noise and thrill of a machine paying out. A compromise needs to be struck between the sound

level generated by an AWP and the requirements of the public bar of a community pub. Too many licensees adopt a blanket ban on sound by requesting that speakers are disconnected altogether, when the volume can be adjusted by the operator's engineers.

Our experience clearly demonstrates that the best income figures are achieved on sites where the staff have a knowledge of their machines. As a company we encourage customers to appoint a machine champion – a member, or indeed members of staff who take an interest in the products on site; people who know the features of a new machine, who ensure that the glasses are cleaned every day, and who will report even the smallest of faults. We can help in this process by providing demonstrations, printed player guides, and promotional material.

Other simple measures that can be taken include ensuring that staff give out as many coins in change as possible. Five £1 coins instead of a £5 note given in change at the bar often results in extra machine plays. The simple recommendation is, if not love your machines then certainly respect them for their tremendous income-generating potential.

Legal Notes

Gaming by means of machines with a limited payout – skill with prize machines (SWPs) and amusement with prize machines (AWPs) – may be available on licensed premises subject to the grant of a permit from the Licensing Justices under Section 34 of the Gaming Act 1968. Usually a permit for up to two machines will be available. The licensing committee may require a plan of your premises indicating where the machines are to be located. Any more than two machines will usually require a separate special application.

Any other gaming on licensed premises is unlawful, although dominoes and cribbage and other specially authorised games may be played for prizes or stakes.

CHAPTER THIRTEEN

THE FAMILY TRADE

Ted Bruning

Only a few years ago catering for families with children was hardly an issue in the licensed trade. Pubs and hotels with separate dining rooms got a few families in; some soft-hearted landlords risked their licences by allowing children in with their parents; and an opportunistic and unscrupulous hard core served teen-agers with varying degrees of subter-fuge. The rest of us were left to fend for ourselves in the car park with a bag of crisps and a bottle of pop.

The pressure that led to the intro-duction in 1995 of Children's Cert-ificates built up slowly in the 1980s and 1990s and was part of the pub trade's growing importance in the eating-out market. Families on holi-day or *en route* didn't necessarily like the offering available at Little Chef or Happy Eater, and saw it as an injustice that the mere fact of having had children excluded them from pubs without separate family rooms; while the family rooms where they could legally sit were all too often cheerless afterthoughts, cut off from the bar and everything that makes a pub a pub.

Hours' reform in 1988, especially the extra hour on the Sunday mid-day session, added to the pressure. Going out for Sunday lunch became a majority occupation, but too many pubs could not legally cater to the new market and saw chain-owned food pubs such as Beefeater, with their larger premises and limitless capital resources, running away with the business.

The time before Children's Certifi-cates finally came in was one of adjustment. Police who used to prosecute if a door was left open between family room and bar began to turn a blind eye to well-run family pubs. Lawyers ruled it acceptable for children to dine in any area set aside for the purpose provided there was some token barrier – a change of level, or a low balustrade – dividing it from the bar. And play equipment sprouted outside pubs the length and breadth of the land.

When Children's Certificates fin-ally arrived they proved to be a damp squib. The Home Office left it to local benches to decide what made a pub suitable for children;

and the direst warnings of sceptics all came true. Too many benches ruled that a Certificate would only be granted where there were separate children's toilets with low-level WCs, where there were no gaming machines, where all drinks were served in plastic glasses, where there were nappy-changing facilities in both ladies' and gents' toilets and so on. One bench even tried to rule that Children's Certificates should not apply to any part of the premises where alcohol was for sale, which rather defeated the object.

This arbitrary approach has continued, despite warnings from both the Home Office and even the Magistrates' Association that the conditions attached to the award of a Children's Certificate should not materially alter the nature of the pub – or, in the words of one cynic, create a licensed Macdonald's. As a result, fewer than 5 per cent of pubs have bothered applying for a Certificate, and those that have applied have mainly been big managed houses – especially those designed with children in mind such as Allied Domecq's Wacky Warehouses – which can easily meet the most restrictive of magisterial criteria.

Still, the majority of pubs have not turned their backs on the family trade. In the years of waiting for Children's Certificates to be introduced they were sublegally discovering and meeting the challenges of the family trade, with the tacit cooperation of police forces that were largely sympathetic and had no appetite whatever for creating new and unjustifiable demands on their slender resources. This unsatisfactory state of affairs has continued since

the trade's disappointment at the form Children's Certificates eventually took. It means that very many pubs are deriving an indispensable part of their business from a trade that is on paper illegal and which 15 years ago would have resulted in lost licences.

Publicans should therefore bear in mind that in our culture there is still a consensus that children and alcohol do not really mix. What this means in practical terms is that happy families having lunch together in a well-run pub are unlikely to attract the attention of the law; but visiting constables will be concerned at encountering pale, pinched kids who ought to have been in bed an hour ago but are instead confined disconsolately to a corner under a giant TV screen. And if the said children are so much as sniffing alcohol, the offending landlord will find that a modern, *laissez-faire* attitude only goes so far.

IS THE FAMILY TRADE FOR YOU?

There can be no doubt that family custom has become essential to the pub trade as a whole – not just for the revenue it brings in, but because it corrects an impression built up in the 1970s and 1980s of pubs in general as exclusive, largely male, and all too often unsavory or even violent.

Having said that, the family trade does not suit every outlet. There is still a large minority opinion that pubs are places where grown-ups can escape the responsibilities of family life and be themselves as they used to be before the kids came along. This is a valuable market, especially after 8pm. If children are likely to upset your regular clientele – and indeed if your regular clientele are likely to upset children – stick with the market you know.

The key to the family trade is food service. The grant of a Children's Certificate is conditional upon it, and most families who want to use pubs will either be in transit or enjoying a meal out together. The main beneficiaries of the family trade are Beefeater-type steakhouses, pubs in tourist areas, and big road-houses on busy through routes. But not all pubs with a large food trade will be suitable for families. Pubs in busy commercial centres – next to an industrial estate, for instance, or on the high street – with a mainly business lunch trade and a younger, destination-bound evening trade are perhaps not places that ought to welcome children. It's unlikely that many families would choose such pubs anyway, and it may well be that the presence of children would make the regulars feel uncomfortable.

On the other hand, it's not only the touristy pubs or the big chain-owned carveries that can exploit the family trade. Pubs in or near shopping malls, for instance, might want to take on the mainly unlicensed cafeteria-style competition by aiming their catering at shoppers (which often implies children): staying open all day; serving tea, coffee and cakes; and offering value-for-money light lunches.

Community pubs, especially big housing estate pubs with plenty of space and a diverse local population, probably already doing well out of family Sunday lunches, might also seek to make more of the potential offered by young families. Why not build a whole new tea-time trade on the basis of cheap eating out for families who, for one reason or another, don't want to cook that evening? How about, as a variant on the happy hour, a promotionally priced family fun fry-up from 4pm–6.30pm?

MEETING THE SPECIAL NEEDS OF CHILDREN

Catering properly for the family trade is not merely a question of letting families through the door. Once they're in you have to understand their needs. For not only will you have to change the profile of your business to accommodate children, you will also have to alter your mindset to a degree. On the one hand, children running around freely are only a nuisance if you think they are; on the other, what seems to you like a well-behaved child sitting quietly with Mum and Dad is probably actually a little volcano who is bored, frustrated, barely restrained while in the pub and storing up a magnificent eruption for later. It's up to you to adapt to meet both extremes.

Feeding children, as you will know if you are a parent, is very different from feeding adults. The overflowing trencher of food that might appeal to the adult is just as likely to frighten a child and make him too anxious even to pick up a spoon.

Child psychology is different from adult psychology in other ways too: for example, an adult kept waiting for a meal gets hungrier, while a child kept waiting gets bored and becomes fractious, and by the time the food actually arrives is on too high a nervous plane to eat it.

Here are a few practical tips for feeding children from a parent who loves pubs in theory and would love to love more in practice.

Most children like 'brown' food – burgers, sausages, chips, fish fingers, croquettes and other fried items – and 'soft' food – pasta in sauce, beans, fried eggs. These form the basis of most children's menus. But many parents disapprove of this kind of food, and many older children don't care for it either. So in addition to special children's menus of brown and soft foods, offer half portions of the regular menu. Even if you don't sell a single one, you won't lose a penny. (Incidentally, filled pancakes are the ideal children's food. Children see them as both brown and soft, while parents see them as cosmopolitan and grown-up, especially if they contain spinach. They also cost next to nothing and are easy to cook.)

If you serve children hot food, they will burn their mouths. But all your food has to emerge from the oven piping hot for reasons of hygiene. So serve it on cold plates, and between dishing up and arriving at table it should have cooled enough to avoid those burnt tongues. Also, avoid menu items that remain hot for a long time after serving: closed-in fruit pies are a particular offender here.

Serve children quickly. A few minutes after ordering, they lose interest and become fractious, and when the food does arrive they won't eat it. Given children's predilection for brown and soft foods, this is ideal microwave territory. And it's good if the children's burgers and chips arrive before the grown-ups' *gigot navarin:* it gives the adults a chance to get the kids settled to their meals before their own food arrives.

Provide free amusements. A colouring book and crayon set can cost under 50p and earn the undying gratitude (and repeat business) of the grown-ups by keeping the kids absorbed and giving them a little peace.

Providing a high chair for younger children is only half the battle. Why not earn a parent's undying gratitude (and repeat business) by also offering plastic bibs and moist wipes? You could also keep a few jars of different baby foods in stock. These items costs very little (you could even charge!) but again earn the undying gratitude and repeat business of less well-prepared parents – and those who are normally very well prepared but just got caught out this time.

Drinks and snacks for kids

The traditional pub range of soft drinks is based on mixers and fruit juices. These are second-best for children and teenagers, who are used to a whole world of brands that traditionally have no presence in the pub trade.

The various guises of Coke and Pepsi have their followings, as do more traditional British brands such as Vimto and Irn-Bru. Then there are more exotic fruit carbonate brands, especially Lilt and Sprite, and heavily branded versions of old favourites, especially Fanta and Tango.

Sports drinks command the allegiance of health-conscious teenagers: important are Lucozade and Red Bull, but there is a host of other brands to choose from.

Then there are milk-based drinks. The post-mix shakes of the 1960s, which demanded special equipment and a lot of shelf space, have been superseded by pre-mix brands such as Frijj, which you can buy in very small quantities to test the level of demand without too much outlay.

Most of these brand-names will be entirely new to most publicans: but rather than believing everything the reps tell you, try asking your own children what they prefer themselves; or, if you have no children, try hanging (inconspicuously!) around the nearest CTN at school chucking-out time and see what the kids themselves choose to spend their pocket-money on.

Exactly the same is true of bag snacks. Trends in the pub trade have been towards more adult snacks: cashews; pistacchios; dry-roast, honey-roast, and even curried peanuts; scratchings; designer crisps such as Brannigans; hot nuts with special dispensers; Peperami; even (mercifully briefly) beef jerky.

Exactly the opposite is true if you really want to please an audience of children. They want the kind of cheap snacks – Nick Nacks, Monster Munches, Cheesy Wotsits and so on – that have never before had a pub trade presence. If you use a cash and carry there should be a rep who will tell you what sells to kids in the CTN trade.

Confectionery is something else the complete family pub will have to stock, albeit not in quite such profusion as a CTN: a range of eight to ten leading brands – Twix, Mars, Milky Way, Kitkat and so on – should be more than adequate.

But it isn't just kids who have a sweet tooth: a bar of Cadbury's Dairy Milk does down very well with a pint of Guinness, and 20p-a-shot jellybean machines are appearing everywhere. Children and adults alike will welcome a small display unit of selected confectionery lines located eye-catchingly near the till, and pub customers are not nearly as price conscious as CTN customers. In fact, they often don't even look at the prices of individual lines, only of overall rounds.

Play equipment

Children like to spend a lot of the time their parents spend in the pub outside it, making use of the climbing frame and other facilities you have thoughtfully provided for them. So what are the basic requirements?

Obviously, safety is the first consideration; and not just safety, but parental confidence in your standards of safety. Children might feel fine with the safety of whatever equipment you provide, but anxious parents – and your insurers – also need to be made to feel comfortable and secure.

It is a good idea to make sure any play equipment you buy is up to the requisite British Standard – look for the kitemark and the number BS5696. While you can't reasonably ensure that children are supervised by a responsible adult while playing outside it's sensible to erect signs recommending it, and to show you mean it by siting chairs and tables where parents can sit in comfort and still see what junior is up to.

Play equipment need not be too complicated: children will make up their own games, and equipment with finite possibilities may even limit their imaginative play. Space to run around and let off steam safely is just as important as fancy equipment, so plan your play area with the following three basic rules firmly in mind.

1. Fence the play area off completely from moving traffic, in the car-park as well as the road, with a gate a toddler can't open.
2. Provide a soft landing under each piece of play equipment. Wetpour – a pit filled with rubber granules bonded by quick-setting resin – is very highly recommended. It's expensive to install but very effective and almost maintenance free. Bark chip is just as effective and cheaper to lay, but takes some looking after: it needs to be raked back into position every day and not be allowed to scatter all over the countryside.
3. Separate toddlers from older children, who in their natural exuberance can cause distress and even injury without meaning the slightest harm. Fence the toddlers' play area off, and provide play equipment that is suitable for different age-groups: a 15ft slide is a death-trap for toddlers, while a three-foot slide won't do much for an eight year old.

Toilets

There is no real need for low-level urinals and WCs, although if you can provide them so much the better. But there are points to watch nonetheless.

◆ Parents with small children are much more anxious about cleanliness than unaccompanied adults, so pay special attention to regular checking, recleaning and replenishment.
◆ Turn down the thermostat! Children burn much more easily than adults, so make sure the hot water is not much more than lukewarm. (This will also save you money).
◆ Nappy-changing facilities at their most basic comprise a high table or shelf big enough to accommodate a baby, with enough clearance at the foot end for the adult doing the ministrations to stand. A handbasin, a hook for the nappy bag, and a pedal bin are also essential; more deluxe pubs might run to a free supply of baby wipes and nappies in a coin-slot dispenser.

These facilities, where provided, are almost always in the ladies' loo. This is a bit unfair, and if you can locate them in the gents as well, or in a neutral cubby-hole, or even in the disabled loo if you have one, so much the better.

Breast-feeding

If you cater to the family trade you will inevitably encounter a conflict between mothers who find it perfectly natural to breast-feed in public, and other, often older, customers who find it embarrassing or even revolting.

Most mothers who breast-feed are very adept at doing so discreetly, and those who don't care for the sight can always look away. But to avoid upsetting anyone it's best to have somewhere private available for the purpose – a facility many nursing mothers will actually welcome. Just because they breast-feed doesn't mean they want an audience. Your own private lounge might be the best place, subject to the usual security considerations.

Never, ever try to banish breast-feeders to the ladies. Would you want to have to eat your dinner in a toilet? But as not all mothers breast-feed, why not offer facilities for making up feeding bottles?

CONCLUSION

If all this seems too involved and too expensive, don't lose heart. The family trade can be extremely lucrative, especially if good summers are to become the norm, and catering for it is really no more involved than catering for any other market. And there are few sights more gratifying on a fine day than to look into the bars and the garden and see them filled with well-cared for customers, young and old, having a splendid time.

Health and Safety Notes

Ensure that in promoting the family trade you have considered the relevant issues as part of the health and safety risk assessment.

The children's play area is a particular source of concern. Steps need to be taken to ensure the safety of the equipment and the area in which it is located. Issues to consider include regular checking of equipment, eg for damage caused by wear and tear, misuse or vandalism, and the avoidance of broken glass in the play area. If you have any particular safety-related conditions, such as an age limit, this should be made clear.

Guidance on outdoor play areas exists in British Standards, and child safety organisations such as RoSPA can provide advice.

Certain items of play equipment such as bouncy castles necessitate a greater degree of control by the business, eg to ensure that the fixings remain sound and that it is used appropriately. The supplier of the bouncy castle should provide you with the necessary information on its safe use. Electrical risks associated with the compressor arrangement also need to be addressed.

Legal Notes

Much of the law relating to young persons is confusing and misunderstood. The basic rule is that (except in certain circumstances) children under 14 are not allowed in the bar.

Difficulties arise with what is meant by a bar. It is defined in the Act as 'any place exclusively or mainly used for the sale and consumption of intoxicating liquor'. From this it can be seen that if there is a bar counter in a room where drink is sold and consumed, under 14s will be excluded. However, should the room contain an area set apart – as, say, a dining area separated by a rope or a screen of pot-plants – and that area is used for a different purpose, it may not be a bar to which the legislation applies.

The exceptions to children being excluded from a bar are when the child is:

◆ the licensee's
◆ a resident in the pub but not employed there
◆ simply passing through the bar from one part of the pub to another (eg on the way to the toilet, if there is no other convenient way)
◆ there by virtue of a Children's Certificate.

Licensing Justices may grant a Children's Certificate allowing under 14s to remain in the bar if they are satisfied that the environment is suitable and meals and beverages other than intoxicating liquor are available. Many licensing committees have been criticised for being too stringent in their requirements for the grant of a Children's Certificate – it is essential to obtain the local policy document if an application is contemplated.

Although 14 to 18 year olds are permitted in a bar at the licensee's discretion, it is not permissible:

1. to sell intoxicating liquor to under 18s or permit them to consume alcohol in the bar
2. for a person under 18 to buy or attempt to buy intoxicating liquor or to consume it in the bar
3. for anyone to buy or attempt to buy any intoxicating liquor for consumption by a person under 18 years in the bar.

NB: a pub landlord may not sell intoxicating liquor to any person under 18 for consumption away from the pub, or allow any other person to buy liquor for a person under 18 for consumption away from the pub.

By historical anomaly, this does not apply to off-licences. Nor does it apply where a pub has an area set aside for the service of meals, where an adult may buy intoxicating liquor for a child as young as five years old. However, if you sold intoxicating liquor to an adult knowing it was intended for a young child who was a customer in your dining area, and that child consequently became intoxicated and possibly ill, you would have to consider (a) whether the magistrates would still consider you a fit and proper person to hold a licence, and (b) what your civil liability might be.

By another historical anomaly, persons aged 16 may buy beer and cider to drink with a meal in an area set aside for meals. In theory, this allows you to serve unaccompanied teenagers drinks with restaurant meals – but before you start imagining the potential for, say, a St Valentine's Night promotion aimed at flash young lads out to impress, bear in mind the possible consequences to yourself if anything went wrong.

CHAPTER FOURTEEN

ADDING VALUE

Paul Cooper

This chapter deals with ways to add value to your business in two areas: ways in which you can make all the areas of your pub work for you, and additional services you can offer.

It is essential that you make as much use as you can of your capital and fixed costs – the pub and its land. This will enable you to make the greatest profit. Small details can make a big difference in making your pub special and worth visiting, but there are many practical issues to consider when you are seeking to add value to your pub.

The ideas discussed here will not make money for all publicans, but will work in certain types of pub in certain locations. It is impossible to recommend which you should or should not deploy in your pub. It is up to you to decide which are appropriate, where your skills lie, what money you have available and what will give you the best returns on your money and time. It is unlikely that your pub will be suited to all of the ideas, and even if it is, it is unlikely that there are enough hours in the day to do them all. However,

you should endeavour to do as much as reasonably practicable to generate incremental income – as long as it leads to additional profit.

The point of all of the suggestions is additional income, so I will concentrate on the considerations needed before you make a commitment.

FUNCTIONS ROOM

Do you already have a functions room, or enough unused space to create one? And is there demand for one? Is there one at a nearby pub, and if there is, what niche does it fill? Is it posh, so you can offer a value-for-money alternative? Or is it basic, leaving the market for more up-market events open to you?

If you already have a functions room, you should consider whether it could or should be extended. You should also consider whether to keep it at all – whether you should in fact find a more profitable use for the space. If you don't have one, it is worth considering converting any unused space you may have – a disused first-floor room, or an old barn

Carling Premier. So smooth, it's effortless.

Always a top performer, Carling Premier has developed a reputation for bringing your customers something a little different:

- Its patented smoothchill system delivers a perfect pint every time
- A tight, creamy head that lasts until the bottom of the glass
- The coolest lager on the bar, served at a refreshingly chilled 2°C
- Innovative in its association with music, both through sponsorship and its memorable TV and press advertising.

COMMITMENT

Carling Premier has confirmed a five year sponsorship deal with IPC's NME - the UK's leading weekly music paper. The agreement gives Carling Premier title ownership of the event formerly known as the NME Brat Awards and continues to develop the brand's strong links with music.

The newly titled **NME Premier Awards** will continue to celebrate British music at its best, kicking off in January 1999 with a raft of events across the UK.

The 5 year sponsorship deal represents a long term commitment to delivering increasing support and success to Carling Premier's customer base.

Extensive media coverage, both locally and nationally, of the NME Premier Awards and the surrounding NME Premier events will raise the profile of the brand putting it in the forefront of consumers' minds.

Additionally, Carling Premier will be able to offer the trade exclusive and innovative promotions building on the association with new and exciting music.

Carling Premier - the automatic choice for people wanting something different to classic lager

FOR A LAGER TO SUIT YOUR CUSTOMERS EVERY NEED AND OCCASION - JOIN THE CARLING FAMILY
Contact customer services on 0345 700701

or outhouse. But, even if the space is lying idle and can be converted at a reasonable cost, you still have to evaluate demand for the room.

Assuming you have decided to enter the functions market, bear in mind your functions room's purpose and the facilities you will be providing. If the room is to be used solely for pool or major sporting events on big-screen TV it is pointless lashing out on expensive, high quality décor. But it is just as pointless fitting out a room intended for wedding receptions with lino floors, woodchip wallpaper and plastic chairs.

There are many potential uses for your functions room and each one needs careful consideration before you commit to it.

A functions room could be the ideal place to put your pool tables, provided there is a market for pool and the clientele is one you want to cater for. You will need to consider the supervision of this room. Unless you are going to open a servery in the room and pay for the additional staff you will not know exactly what is going on in there. You must also consider the difficulty of using the room for anything else if it means moving and storing the pool tables first.

If the room is relatively small it may only be possible to use it for conferences and meetings (although a large room could also be used as a private meetings room or conference facility). A meetings room will only work if you have a catchment area that includes businesses and social/voluntary organisations. Research the facilities already offered in nearby pubs and hotels. Find out what they offer and how much they charge.

You will probably be able to under-cut the large hotels and offer an equivalent service.

Create a tariff of charges for the different facilities you can offer, which should include:

◆ a day delegate rate to include room hire, paper and a pencil for each person, mineral water, cordials, mints, morning coffee and biscuits, buffet lunch and afternoon tea and biscuits.

◆ an equipment hire service. Initially, the most cost-effective way to do this is to hire the equipment from a local company and pass the cost on to your customers. Equipment that may be requested includes a flip chart (don't forget to provide pens), overhead projector and screen, slide projector and screen, and television and video.

◆ cost scales for additional services, eg alternative lunch menus and room hire (remember 20 people in your functions room creates costs for you in staff, time and cleaning).

The conference market takes a lot of building up and continuous marketing. Can you generate repeat business by hosting regular events in your functions room? Are there local voluntary organisations, sports clubs or societies that have regular meetings and could use your facilities? Alternatively, you could use the room for entertainment. If you have a large-screen TV to show sporting events, why not make use of the functions room for this? This has the advantage of ensuring that vocal supporters will not upset other customers. You may be able to create a reputation for your pub for live bands, comedy nights or even less frequent events such as magicians or palm reading. If there is a local demand, arrange a monthly senior citizens tea dance or Saturday night dinner dance.

An obvious use for a functions room is for private parties. These can be good moneyspinners. Again, you need to assess the facilities you can offer. Prepare a package containing information on different buffets and sit-down meals you can offer, room hire charges and any other services available, eg tie up with a good local DJ so you can offer the music for the party. (A cautionary note on 18th birthday parties – some of the guests will be under 18.)

Weddings can be a good source of income but they take a great deal of time and organisation. If you decide to cater for wedding receptions, you have to be prepared to commit the time needed to organise them. A wedding is one of the most important events in someone's life and if you make one mistake, no matter how small, it may ruin the whole day.

The easiest way to deal with enquiries for wedding receptions is to have information prepared and readily available. Think about all the services that someone expects at a wedding reception – bar, wine, full three-course meal, buffet for the evening. To offer more than your competition, team up with other local businesses and offer a complete wedding service. If you can get an agreement between yourself, a photographer, a cake maker, a car hire service, a wedding-gown maker and hirer, gentleman's suit hire, etc,

you could all offer the complete service, each recommending the others. But remember, your reputation will be affected by the service offered by companies that you have recommended.

Another use for your functions room may be as an occasional restaurant, possibly to cater for your Christmas meals and parties.

No matter what services you offer, the most important thing is to coordinate with the organiser of the event on every detail, in particular the required layout of the room. Do not assume anything, ask the question. When you think all the arrangements are agreed, confirm them in writing, then telephone to check the arrangements a week before the event.

It should go without saying that you should keep a large, page-a-day diary specifically for your functions room and write every event in, whether or not it is confirmed (You do not want an unexpected wedding party turning up.) Allocate the job of taking bookings to one person, so there can be no confusion as to who is responsible for organising events and there can be no double bookings. Chase up provisional bookings for confirmation. Do not assume that because a provisional booking has not been confirmed after two months that the party will not turn up on the doorstep. Before taking a booking make sure that you can cope with it. There is no point in taking a booking for a meal for 80 if you can only seat 60, so make sure you know how many people you can accommodate for different formats – sit down, finger buffet, horseshoe, theatre style.

Make sure you have all the equipment you need (don't forget you need enough for the function and the normal running of the pub), including cutlery and crockery. There is nothing worse than having to collect teaspoons from the first guests served with coffee before you can give the last guests theirs.

When it comes to calculating room hire charges remember to include all the additional costs that holding the function will incur. However, also remember that people in your functions room paying for drinks and food means income you would not have if they were not there. Is it, perhaps, worth offering the room free if the group are having food and drinks?

Marketing your functions room is essential. It is unlikely that your bar customers will have seen the room, so no one will know it's available unless you tell them. How you market the room will depend on what you are using it for. If you are hiring it out for meetings, private parties or weddings, put up a wall display in the pub with photos of the room laid out in different formats and brief information. You should also have a small brochure or leaflet available in the pub. The local tourist office may also carry the brochures for you, as this sort of use constitutes 'business tourism'.

If you are using the room for entertainment, put up posters, hand out leaflets, and contact the local papers and radio stations to get in their (often free) listings sections.

If you want to try to get clubs to use the room, then write to them and invite them to come and have a look. Maybe offer a discount on drinks or some snacky good to all committee/club/society members attending meetings.

Word of mouth is still one of the best ways to advertise a functions room. If you have customers from local businesses, tell them you have a meeting room available and get staff to tell as many people as possible about the room.

One last thing to remember is to make sure the room is always clean, tidy and laid out in a basic format. You never know when someone will ask to see the room – and first impressions always count.

GARDENS

If you have a garden or outside area you should try to make the best possible use of it. The garden 'decor' is as important as that of the bar and will depend on your trading patterns and customer profiles.

There is a huge range of furniture available. The type of furniture you choose should be determined by the type of pub you are running and the image you want to give. All-in-one wooden 'picnic-style' tables and benches are relatively cheap and long lasting and may be appropriate for large grassy areas. For patios there are many styles of seating available. Plastic tables and chairs are cheap but will not be appropriate for an upmarket wine bar, while cast-iron furniture is expensive but has a quality feel. You may decide that you want to build brick seating or incorporate it with flower beds, which will ensure that it doesn't get stolen.

Planting can also have a huge influence on the appearance of an outside area. Even the smallest, most ill-placed piece of concrete can make a pleasant patio area with a bit of imagination. But do consider the maintenance of any planting before trying to recreate Kew Gardens: a well-planned garden of evergreens providing good ground cover will produce a good-looking, maintenance-free and indestructible environment. Flowers and bedding plants may look spectacular but need much more maintenance and care and may easily be damaged by customers. It is up to you to assess how green your fingers are, how much time you want to spend in the garden and how much destruction your customers are capable of!

Whatever you plant, make sure that it is not poisonous, especially if you have a family trade.

(On the subject of plants, hanging baskets or window-boxes on the front of the pub look fantastic when new, but remember that they need maintaining and watering. Nothing makes your pub look less cared for than dead plants hanging around the front door.)

The type of custom you aim to attract and the size and nature of the garden will determine whether or not outdoor lighting is worthwhile. If you have a family trade in the evening and play equipment, then good lighting will be essential to ensure the safety of the children.

Outdoor heating can extend the length of time that you can use your garden, both later into the evening or further into the colder months. It is important that you fully understand the initial costs, including getting a gas supply to the units, how many units you will need to be effective and the ongoing cost of running the units. Bear in mind that you are in effect trying to heat the whole town.

As mentioned previously, it may be possible to turn an outbuilding or barn into a functions room. Alternatively, it may be worth considering using the space for a children's room, family room or games room. Similarly, a large outside area could be used for other entertainment. You may be able to encourage additional custom by having a bouncy castle for children – or why not try a bucking bronco or pole jousting for big kids? If you are a more traditional operation, you could try boules, bowls, bat and trap or Aunt Sally. Giant-sized versions of such games as Jenga and Countdown are now also available and can be a good selling point.

Barbecues are popular during summer months. They can be a moneyspinner and attract a great number of people. You need to take into account the risks of a barbecue, which include fire, storage of food at safe temperatures, cross-contamination of food and the possibility of customers burning themselves. (See also Chapter 7.)

If your outside area is large then you might consider organising bigger events. A large car-park could be used for Sunday morning car boot sales. A large garden could be used by a local group, eg Scouts or Guides, for a fete. While the later will not raise money for you, it will bring customers into your pub. Other ideas for a large garden could be a fun day or a fireworks display, but these take quite some organising and have huge health and safety implications.

209

THE NEW CONCEPT IN LIVE HI-TECH ENTERTAINMENT

The Lodge, Goyt Mill, Marple. Stockport SK6 7HX

Well known in the Licensing trade as leading suppliers of Karaoke equipment to the home and leisure industries have available, their 1999 catalogue, packed with a host of new products and 60 pages giving a selection of over 1200 discs.

Introduced for the first time are:

Premier 99 Multi CD Player -
MULTI-FUNCTION 3 DISC CAROUSEL KARAOKE PLAYER
Plays Videos, Graphic & Audio CD's - Also Plays MIDI CD Supplied
With UP To 3700 Mixed Language Songs Disc or 350 English Songs Disc - Keychange
2 Mic. Inputs - Echo - Multiplex - Tempo Control - Video or Camera Superimpose.

JVC 3 TRAY Karaoke Player -
TRIPLE TRAY 3 DISC CAROUSEL KARAOKE PLAYER
Video & Graphic CD Player - Also Plays Audio CD's - Digital Echo - Keychange
Multiplex - 3 Mic. Input - Surround Sound - Switchable PAL/NTSC.

TOMBOX 100 Cd Storage Unit -
100 Disc Storage System - Stackable - Dustfree - Available With Or Without Backlight.

RADIO LINKED Video Camera -
Black & White or Colour - Switchable 4 Camera System

Video CD Karaoke is now replacing the large expensive 12" laser format. The Latest players accept Audio CD, Graphics CD, Video CD and a range of feature films with 2/3 microphone inputs, echo and keychange.

Their rechargeable Radio Microphone avoids the expense of replacement batteries and is the most compact unit available.

Ten working systems, together with a range of accessories which includes lighting, large screen TV and Disc storage are always on show at their studio in Stockport, where visitors are always made welcome.

Should you require a personalised alphabetical listing of your choice of songs or are unable to find your favourite song, the computer will do the work for you.

A full range is also available via the internet at:

www.karaoke-uk.demon.co.uk
or Email: mailord@karaoke-uk.demon.co.uk
or Telephone: 0161 449 0441 For a catalogue and full price listing.

Whatever you do with your outside area is going to increase your workload. You are in effect extending your pub and creating greater sales opportunities. You must ensure that you consider all aspects of what you are doing and take into account issues such as theft of equipment, pub security and the health and safety of customers.

MULTIPLE USE

Multiple use of the pub will be most appropriate to those situated in small villages, towns or communities. It is a way of getting the greatest use out of your assets as well as providing a service to the community. If you have the space available it may be possible to incorporate another business within the premises – perhaps

an off-licence. This would not need any additional space as you could offer the facility from the bar, providing that your Justices Licence permits off-sales.

An expansion of this idea would be to provide a local shop. If your pub is in a village with no shops, or where a standalone shop is not viable, there is an opportunity for you to generate additional sales by opening a small shop within the premises. You may also consider operating a sub-Post Office facility within the pub.

First, though consider whether you really want to run a shop/sub-Post Office. Do you have the expertise? Other considerations are: is there enough local demand to make it worthwhile, will the cost of conversion and equipment be returned, will the Post Office accept your application to operate a Post Office facility, what additional hours will you need to work and do the returns justify the extra effort needed?

Alternatively, you may be able to let spare space – for instance, a lounge bar or upstairs meeting room that you don't normally open at lunchtime – to visiting services. This will require little additional work on your part but will generate additional income.

Services that may be interested in this type of arrangement could include chiropody, Citizens Advice Bureau or an MP's surgery. (This use doesn't just apply to spare trading space: there have even been cases of pubs with surplus kitchen capacity producing meals on wheels under contract to the local social services department.) This is going to depend very much on your locality and the willingness of the service providers.

A longer-term approach, which again will involve little ongoing work on your part, would be to lease any spare space that you do not want to use to another party, eg let a disused outbuilding as a shop or studio or, if it's large enough, a micro brewery. This will be subject to any restrictions laid down by your landlord, if you are a lessee or tenant, and planning restrictions.

OUTSIDE BARS

With an outside bar you are renting your services to a private individual or group to operate a bar for a function. To run an outside bar you need all the equipment required to run the bar in your pub. Pumps and coolers can be hired, although some

breweries will provide them free of charge. You will need to buy extra glasses, fridges, optics, optic stands, ice-buckets, etc. You will also require some kind of bar (a good sturdy trestle-table will suffice) for venues such as marquees that do not have one already, and a way of providing ice.

When deciding whether or not you want to offer outside bars you must consider issues such as storage, transport, responsibility for running the bar and stock control. You will need a substantial amount of equipment to run an outside bar effectively and you must have somewhere to store it (it doesn't look very fetching in the middle of your lounge floor), as well as some way of transporting it. It is unlikely that a car will be large enough and so you will need to consider buying or hiring a van. When you run an outside bar you have to apply for an occasional licence for the event. This is tied to your full licence and you are personally responsible for the people at the function, in the same way that you are in your pub. You must therefore ensure that you have a responsible and trustworthy person to run the bar at the function and maintain stock control.

BREWING ON THE PREMISES

In the last decade more than 300 pubs have started brewing their own beer. A small brewery can be installed in any suitable outhouse or part of the main building for £12–20,000, but the local Customs and Excise office should be consulted before plans are laid.

Planning permission is also essential, even if no buildings are altered, because installing a brewery represents a change of use for which permission is required, and there is a possibility of brewing creating nuisances – especially smell and increased traffic – which residents have a right to object to.

The purpose of brewing on the premises is not usually primarily to trap the brewers' and wholesalers' percentage, which the costs involved can easily wipe out. Rather, it is a marketing device that attracts destination trade.

Any publican contemplating brewing should therefore take into account not only the additional time and effort that will be involved in the actual production of the beer, but also the time and effort needed for the marketing which will make it all worthwhile.

Having said that, it can be a lucrative addition to a pub operation, especially if the brewery is visible – perhaps through a viewing panel – from the bar.

It is very much easier to make cider on the premises. It is legal to make for sale up to 7000 litres of cider of not more than 7.5 per cent alcohol by volume (abv) a year without paying duty, which cuts out the paperwork and makes the business more profitable.

The process is also very much easier than brewing: you can either mill and press your own apples or buy the juice in. All you then need are enough fermentation vessels. You may not even need yeast, since most apples come with a ready supply of their own. The juice should not cost more than

£1,000, and the return should be £7500–10,000.

LETTING ROOMS

Many pubs have either spare bedrooms or an outbuilding that could be converted to letting rooms.

Before deciding whether to let them, ask frankly whether they are suitable. Rooms the size of a cupboard will not make good letting rooms – people expect to be able to get through the door and take more than two steps before they end up in bed. Is the room big enough to accommodate a wardrobe, bed, dressing table and sanitary ware? You will be able to charge more for rooms with *en suite* shower and loo, but all the rooms will need at least a handbasin.

If you do not have the room to accommodate *en suite* bathrooms, you must provide sufficient toilets and bathrooms within easy reach.

If your letting rooms are above the pub, do consider your own privacy. The last thing you will want is to come face to face with a stranger on your way to the loo in the middle of the night. Similarly, there is the security issue. Guests will expect to come and go as they please and will therefore expect their own key. You must ensure that guests cannot roam around the whole pub in the middle of the night helping themselves to your stock. You must also make sure that a guest who forgets to shut the door properly does not present a security risk.

Before going ahead with any alterations you will need planning permission. If you wish to be able to serve alcohol to your guests outside licensing hours you will also need to make an application to the Licensing Justices.

You need to remember that fire regulations will apply to furnishings and doors in letting rooms. You should also bear in mind that it will be cheaper in the long run to buy better quality fixtures and fittings at the outset. They are going to get a great deal more wear and tear than in domestic accommodation – you can live with a dodgy wardrobe door but a paying guest will not, and they are not as careful with your furniture as they are with their own.

Next, consider the work that is required to operate the service. There is the time needed to service the rooms, wash laundry and serve breakfast. (These will involve getting out of bed earlier in the morning, and you must decide whether this is something you want to do!)

If you have letting rooms and serve breakfast to guests it may be worthwhile opening to non-residents for breakfast, depending on your location. Obviously if you are in the middle of nowhere, with no passing trade, it won't be; but if you are on a busy road or in the centre of town, it might be. Even if business from non-residents is slow, you are not losing anything by offering the service.

In marketing your letting rooms you need to be clear who you are trying to attract and how you can reach them. An advertising board outside the pub is essential. If you have local businesspeople as customers, tell them about your rooms and give them a guided tour. If you are close to businesses that are likely to have visitors from out of town, try to get to talk to the person who

books the accommodation in your area (this is often a secretary and you will be surprised what an invitation to join you for a free meal, before or after viewing the rooms, will do).

You are unlikely to reap benefits from advertising in the local press. After all, the people most likely to see your advert live in the area. But if you are aiming your accommodation at specific customers it may be worthwhile advertising in a related publication, eg if you offer fishing or there is good fishing nearby, advertise in a fishing magazine. An advert in *Yellow Pages* and a listing with Talking Pages are probably going to provide a good source of bookings.

Most tourist information offices hold lists of local accommodation. You should try to get on this list, even if you are asked to make a 'contribution'. It is also worth being included in other guides. Some of these provide free listings based on the standard of your accommodation, eg *Room At The Inn*, published by the Campaign for Real Ale. Others require you to pay to be included, and you should be extremely wary of these – all too many are con-tricks. You pay your money, but nothing ever gets published. If approached by a 'sales representative' for a paid-entry guide, demand to see previous editions.

There are several organisations that offer a recognised grading system, eg AA and RAC. These schemes generally operate on the basis that the standard of your accommodation is assessed and then you pay to be accredited, have a listing in their guide and use the relevant logo.

Having your accommodation accredited by an organisation guarantees guests a certain standard of accommodation and service and therefore offers some peace of mind when they are booking.

SEASONALITY

The seasonality of your business will depend very much on your location.

If you have a country pub it is likely that good weather will bring the customers and the summer months will be your most profitable. However, in a town or city centre trade is likely to be much more evenly spread throughout the year, with a dip in January and the summer months. Wherever your pub is located it is likely that Christmas and New Year will be your busiest times of the year and January will be your quietest.

You must be prepared to amend your staffing and purchasing habits as trade increases and decreases. Some pubs will see a 50 per cent drop in trade from one week to the next in September, an increase greater than this in December, a fall of over 50 per cent in January, increasing again for the summer. In this situation it is essential to have flexible staffing arrangements.

You must also be prepared in terms of stock levels. You must be realistic about trading levels while trying not to run out of anything: the tendency at Christmas is to fill every spare inch of the pub with stock to make sure you don't run out, but when January comes you will have great difficulty selling the excess and end up with wasted stock.

However, there are many fixed outgoings – loan repayments, vending machine hire, rent, business rates, etc – that are not seasonal. It's up to you to make the most of opportunities to bump up cash flow in the quiet periods – for instance, Burns Night falls in January, and St Valentine's Day falls in February. A winter ales festival may also give a cash boost on an otherwise dead weekend in January or February. (Of course, this is also a good time for your annual holiday – the quiet trade means you can leave a responsible member of staff in charge, rather than going to the expense of hiring a relief manager.)

SALES OPPORTUNITIES

There are many ways to increase trade that will cost you nothing. These are linked to your staff and their training. They are simple and in some cases serve the double purpose of increasing your sales and offering a service to customers. If a customer has half-an-inch of beer left in his glass, offer him another. If they were wavering over whether or not to buy another, you will more than likely sway them. Similarly, when clearing glasses from a table (and if you have the time), offer to fetch customers another drink.

Ask any customer who orders a short: 'Large one?' If they say no, fine; if they say yes (and they often do), you've chalked up a 100 per cent sales gain. Train staff to do the same.

If you have a menu, it is pointless tucking one copy down the side of the till waiting for someone to ask for it. Make sure you have menus on all tables and the bar. Try to offer the menu whenever you can.

Make sure that you and all your staff know what the products are

MUSIC LICENSING FOR PUBLIC HOUSES

A great many people do not realise that simply owning a record, tape or compact disc (sound recording) does not give the automatic right to publicly perform or broadcast it. Phonographic Performance Limited (**PPL**) is the national licensing body committed to making people more aware that a licence is required by anyone publicly playing commercial sound recordings on their premises.

One of the current activities of **PPL** is to provide information on copyright music licensing to owners of businesses. Whilst many businesses have already recognised the need to secure a **PPL** licence for the use of sound recordings at their premises, many more remain unaware of the obligations.

PPL works on behalf of nearly 2040 different UK record companies and controls the public performance and broadcasting rights in some 7500 labels. Their member companies include all multi-nationals, independent and small specialist producers. **PPL**'s repertoire covers all areas of music and probably encompasses over 95% of all sound recordings commercially available in the United Kingdom, including imports and compilations.

Luckily for all concerned, separate applications to hundreds of record companies do not have to be made and one licence from **PPL** is all that is required.

The licence from **PPL** is not to be confused with the one issued by the Performing Right Society (PRS). They work on behalf of the music composers who own an entirely separate copyright and their licence is needed in addition to **PPL'S**.

It is widely acknowledged that proprietors will often play music to create the ideal ambience for their customers. If sound recordings are used in public then the owner of the premises is legally obliged to obtain a licence from **PPL**. Sadly many businesses do not realise this, or are ill-advised and can end up being faced with legal proceedings for copyright infringement and expensive solicitor's bills.

In terms of the cost, there are broadly speaking two types of licence. The first is for the use of sound recordings for background music that attracts an annual licence fee at just over £1.30 per week. The second type of licence is where sound recordings are played as a featured attraction to the premises, such as a dance, disco or DJ presentation. In these instances, fees are charged on a sliding scale that depends on the hours of record use and attendances.

Market research by Gallup into the use of recorded music in retail and social venues showed just how beneficial the playing of recorded music was for business. For example, four out of five publicans and restaurateurs agreed that recorded music was good for business and three out of five managers in all such outlets said that recorded music made their customers stay longer.

In thousands of premises, recorded music is played to entertain customers. Its importance should not be undervalued by ignoring the legal requirements in regard to copyright music licensing,

For further details, please contact our General Licensing Department at PPL, 1 Upper James Street, London, W1R 3HG. Telephone: 0171 534 1000.

and, in the case of food, what they contain. Always promote the products on sale positively, regardless of personal preference. Staff have been known to say to customers: 'I don't know how you could drink that.' Don't let yours do that!

PROFESSIONAL PRESENTATION

It is important that the presentation of your pub is at all times professional. Gone are the days when it was acceptable to have the pub looking good only when you opened the doors. Every customer who walks through the door expects the pub to look the same as when it has just opened, even ten minutes before closing. They do not know that three coach parties have just left, nor do they care.

This requires ongoing maintenance throughout the day. It may mean sweeping up cigarette butts at the end of busy periods or making sure that, if you have a sweet trolley, the last customer of the day does not get a choice of two dried-up gateaux. Do not forget any areas of the pub; including the garden and toilets (especially the toilets).

It is easy to open the pub and not actually go outside for days on end. Make a point of going outside and walking 100 yards down the road, then turning back imagining you are a customer. You will be amazed at what you notice – smudged chalk boards, old fag ends, crisp packets, dead hanging baskets, etc.

Point of sale and advertising material will be much more effective if it is presented professionally. This does not mean running up huge printing bills. Simple things like not sticking posters over the top of pictures and having a holder for leaflets rather than spreading them across the top of the cigarette machine do make a difference. Always ensure that your posters and point of sale are up to date and not damaged. There is little that looks worse than an out-of-date, nicotine-stained, dog-eared poster on the wall.

Remember to change your advertising regularly. Customers become blind to advertising material after about four weeks, and it becomes useless. I can name one pub where the A-board hasn't been changed for two years. Work out where in the pub most people will see material. Toilet doors, above the urinal in the gents, the back of WC cubicle doors and entrance lobbies are all good places. Once you have worked out where the most prominent positions are, then stick to them. A pub completely plastered in posters and point of sale material looks cheap and tacky.

SESSION BY SESSION OPERATIONS

Throughout the day and week your pub will have different trading patterns. You should try to change your offer to the customer as the trading patterns change. Aim your offer at a particular time of the day and week for the customers that you are trying to attract.

Music plays an important part in this. You should change the style and volume of the music as your customers change. It is pointless playing full-volume heavy metal at lunchtime if you are trying to attract office workers and shoppers; conversely, a younger evening trade won't stay

SATVISION Plc

The company has been involved in the sales installation and service of large audience communication environments since the early eighties. Its clients list is endless, serving many large corporations and over 3000 independent entities within the commercial market. Its expertise in front/rear video projection systems, commercial satellite communications, interactive multi-media high bandwidth networks, video & audio systems is possibly unrivalled in today's market place.

SATVISION Plc has been a BS5750/ISO9002 accredited company since 1993. We are proud of our reputation within the industry for our immediate service response and customer satisfaction.

Your purchase of a product from **SATVISION Plc** will guarantee you satisfaction and endless opportunities to profit from or just enjoy, your investment.

TRADENORTH Plc

Is a wholly owned Sales Aid Lease & Finance Company. Created solely for use of Satvision Plc and its clients around the UK. (Its investments within the UK market place total nearly £10 million), increasing rApidly as the business expands.

Large screen video - audio systems linked to high bandwidth multi-media communications offer the most cost effective form of entertainment available for the wider audience. Tradenorth offers an immediate response in-house service for clients, creating a smooth trouble free path for the installation of systems, which otherwise would nit be available to them.

The Services of **TRADENORTH Plc** are not confined to the independent entitles, but are used by many major companies to alleviate the problems of budgetary requirements at certain times of the financial year. Unique in its environment, a definite plus for our clients.

PLAYVISION from KAI-SAN Ltd

The creator of the Worlds First interactive, high bandwidth, multi-player games play platform. This platform enables multiples of game players to play in house, or form remote site to remote site, whether those sites are in their own country or other countries, is of no consequence.

This platform will facilitate all types of multi-player team games, enabling the creation of local, regional, national and international leagues and championships around the world, all played out from their home site, YOUR Pub or Club.

THE SATVISION GROUP PLC

The Northwest Teleport Centre, Stockport Road West, Stockport SK6 2BP England.
Tel: 44 (0)161 406 8066   Customer Service: 44 (0)161 406 8076   Fax: 44 (0)161 406 8073
E-mail: 100624,1600@Compuserve.com   Web Page: Satvision.co.uk

long if you're playing Mantovani. Remember: the music is not there for you or your staff but for the customers – even if it is not to your taste. You may even employ different staff to cater to different markets, or simply give them different lunchtime and evening uniforms.

It may be possible to increase your sales and profit by changing your product offer. If you have a large and not too price-sensitive business custom wanting to sample different cask ales early in the evenings, why not buy a polypin of a special guest beer and serve it direct from the cask, charging a premium price, every Friday from 5pm?

On the food side, your lunchtime customers may want a snack on the hoof while your evening trade want a full three-course meal.

Linked to the products you offer are the prices you charge. You may be able to generate additional custom by offering a Happy Hour at quiet times – but if your pub is really busy on Friday and Saturday nights and your customers are willing to pay, you can even put your prices up temporarily. (This is easier if you have the right kind of electronic till that can be pre-programmed to switch to the higher prices automatically).

CONSISTENT IDENTITY

Whatever type of pub you decide to run, what services you offer and the customers you aim for, you must try to present a consistent message to your customers. If you are running a traditional pub, do not fit it out in chrome and glass or put up a neon sign outside. This will give confusing messages to customers. Decide what you are going to be and stick to it. Do not try to be all things to all people or you will end up being nothing to anybody. Do not let one area of your business jeopardise main areas of your trade. If your clientele is predominantly senior citizens and your local bikers club wants to hold its annual convention in your car park, think about what effect this will have on your regular trade.

STAYING AHEAD OF THE COMPETITION

Once you have decided what type of pub you want, what services you will offer, what style of operation you are going to have, what products you are going to stock on the bar and what food you will offer, remember it is not set in tablets of stone for the next 25 years. You must constantly review what you are offering the customer. This is the only way you will stay ahead of your competition.

Constantly introduce new ideas. These could be small things like trying a new beer, changing the staff uniform or introducing a jellybean machine, or more substantial changes like introducing a play area. Use your own imagination, but listen to new ideas from staff and customers too.

Evaluate the chances of success of new ideas before you commit to them. If a new idea doesn't work then see if you can make changes to make it work and, if you can't, learn from the mistake.

Finally, whatever you decide to do with your pub, make sure that it is what *you* really want to do. Ideas you are unable to fully commit yourself to will not work. Do everything wholeheartedly. Your biggest success will come if you can stamp your personality on your pub.

Most important, if you enjoy what you are doing, your customers will enjoy themselves and your pub will be a success. Good luck!

 Health and Safety Notes

In considering ways of promoting the pub regard should be had to its locality and the potential for noise issues.

People aggrieved by noise from your pub can complain to the local environmental health department. If an investigation into the complaint satisfies the local authority that a statutory nuisance exists or is likely to recur, a notice can be served requiring an abatement of the nuisance or preventing a recurrence. Failure to comply with an abatement notice may lead to prosecution in the Magistrates Court. There is a right of appeal against a notice. The principle of 'best practicable means' applies (see notes on nuisance under 'Food').

While the majority of nuisances are dealt with by the local council, the Environmental Protection Act 1990 allows people to complain directly to the Magistrates Court and magistrates can make an order in relation to the nuisance and impose a fine.

To avoid the above it may be useful to liaise with your neighbours, to check the noise level yourself by walking around outside the pub during events, and to stick to those sort of entertainments that create the minimum of disturbance. If noise problems arise this could have implications for your entertainment licence (where applicable) and could be brought to the attention of the Licensing Justices.

If you are providing accommodation for either customers or staff, fire safety is a particular issue and advice on appropriate measures to take should be sought from the fire officer. In some instances a fire certificate will be required. Fire is an issue to include in your health and safety risk assessment. In carrying out the assessment you will need to consider whether adequate precautions are in place and whether the necessary checks are being made to maintain those precautions.

Other fire-related issues to consider include general maintenance requirements and the checking of electrical appliances provided such as kettles, hairdryers and irons. The Health and Safety Executive has provided a booklet aimed specifically at electrical safety in hotels and tourist accommodation. This is available from your local environmental health officer or directly from HSE Books, reference IND(G) 164L.

If you provide accommodation for lodgers for whom it is their permanent place of residence, a 'house in multiple occupation' may be created. If so, specific housing legislation applies and advice should be obtained from the environmental health officer.

Legal Notes

The showing of videos requires the prior grant of a Video Performance Limited Licence. A Cinema Licence may be needed for video juke-boxes. Application for Cinematograph Exhibitions Licences are made to the local authority. Under the Cinemas Act 1985 exhibitions of moving pictures (other than TV or Cable TV) may not be given unless licensed. Terms and conditions may include a condition requiring the premises to close on Sunday, Christmas Day or Good Friday. There are exceptions in the case of occasional exhibitions (no more than six per annum), provided certain notices are given to the licensing authority, fire authority and police.

An Occasional Licence is for the sale of intoxicating liquor at premises other than the applicant's –

mainly outside bars. Application is to the magistrates, who have discretion to grant an occasional licence for a period not exceeding three weeks at any one time. There is no restriction on hours in the Licence as specified, even on Sundays, but an Occasional Licence is not available on Christmas Day or Good Friday. The premises become licensed premises for the purpose of the Licensing Act 1964 and therefore restrictions regarding young persons apply.

The Magistrates Court has discretion to grant Special Orders of Exemption for special occasions (extensions) upon application by the holder of a Justices' On-licence, adding such hours as specified in the order. There is a drinking-up time.

PART FIVE
BUSINESS SYSTEMS

STOCK AND FINANCIAL CONTROL

Paul Adams

You may have all the skills required for running a pub – welcoming customers, making sure they have a good time and even being able to throw out the inevitable drunk. However, there is one other skill that is just as vital – you also need to be able to control your business financially.

It is often not appreciated that you, the publican, are controlling a business with a turnover of between £150,000 and £500,000 or more. Many businesses this size will employ a bookkeeper or accountant, but the publican normally does the vast majority of the work himself.

Unless you have experience of preparing accounts you will need the services of an accountant to produce your accounts each year and agree your tax liability with the Inland Revenue. Their charges will be based on the amount of work they have to do and whether you trade as a limited company. The general rule is that the more work you do the less

the accountant does, and therefore the lower the charges.

The first decision you have to make is whether you should trade as a sole trader (or partnership) or a limited company. The major difference is that a limited company means your liabilities are limited to what you put into the company if it should fail. However, even if you are a limited company you may find you have to give personal guarantees for loans, or to the landlord if you have leasehold premises. If you are unsure of the best route to take it is worth paying for an hour's fee to discuss your circumstances with an accountant or solicitor. Whatever decision you take at this stage can have major effects in the future if all does not go well. Another word of advice if you are going into partnership: do have a partnership agreement drawn up by a solicitor before you start, so that all parties are clear on what share of profits (and work!) are due, and what happens if one party dies or decides to leave. Many accountants and solicitors have a field day sorting out partnership troubles that could have been avoided in the first place.

Before you start or take over your pub you must apply to Customs and Excise for a new VAT number or, in the circumstances, to take over the existing one. In addition, notify your local Inland Revenue office to make arrangements to pay over PAYE and National Insurance. You must also decide which bank to use for your business account. Generally, pubs generate the majority of their turnover in cash, so pay particular attention to the charges for paying in cash. If you already have a relationship with a bank then the old adage of 'better the devil you know' probably holds true. You may wish to consider Girobank: their charges for handling cash are normally lower as they constantly need cash to pay pensions, etc. In addition, Post Office hours are longer than high street banks', and there is nearly always a Post Office near your pub.

If there is significant food business you will probably have to accept credit cards such as Visa and Access. Consider this well before the intended take-over date as it takes at least three weeks to process the application. Remember that the service charges made by the credit card companies vary from around 2.75–4 per cent, so it's worth shopping around and considering whether to use an electronic terminal. Although you have to rent these, from about £10 per month, and they need to be connected to a telephone line, the service charges are cheaper than paper transactions and they auto-

matically check that the card is valid.

Quite often, the question arises whether giving a credit card over the bar for a series of drinks can be construed as supplying alcohol on credit (or slate). Strictly speaking, if no substantial meal is also provided, this is illegal, although there is some doubt and I have never heard of a prosecution.

Another important thing to arrange is insurance for the pub. Apart from buildings and contents insurance to cover the normal risks of fire and burglary, it is essential that you have employer's and public liability cover. Simple accidents that can happen to either staff or customers, even though you would think it was their fault, can result in hefty claims for injuries. Do shop around for pub insurance – there are many specific packages that give good cover and they are all vying for your business.

If you are considering taking a leasehold premises you need to be aware of what responsibilities and restrictions are being placed on you. The list of things you 'covenant' to do and not to do can be extremely onerous, and the landlord always has the whip hand if you end up in a disagreement. Make sure that your solicitor fully explains to you in simple terms what you are taking on.

RAISING FINANCE

Most people have to borrow money to help finance the purchase of a pub business, be it freehold or leasehold. A bank, finance company or building society will want to see projections of what profit you expect to

College Green, the licensed trade's leading broker and financial services provider

COLLEGE GREEN
INDEPENDENT

LICENSED TRADE SPECIALIST

College Green are well known as specialist financial advisers, offering tailor-made solutions with special benefits for the licensed trade. To maintain our reputation as your industry's financial adviser, we have now expanded - enabling us to offer you an even wider choice of personal and corporate Financial products to better serve the distinct needs of the trade.

A greater choice of personal and corporate products to suit your needs

Our expansion is prompted by the growing range of new financial products and the desire to provide you with the very best of these. As an independent broker, College Green, now part of Taylor Acland & Co Ltd, can recommend products from all the leading providers in the market place.

College Green Independent can now ensure that you receive the best possible advice on:

Life Cover
Trade Insurance
Mortgages,
Critical Illness Cover.

In addition we are currently providing Trade Insurance for over 500 Public Houses. Our "Taylor" made insurance products can also incorporate cover for the contents of your living accommodation, thus ensuring that College Green can provide your insurance needs lock, stock and barrel.

Reviewing your existing policies or planning for the future call us today on

Taylor Acland & Co. Trading As College Green Independent. Koinonia House, High Street, Cranbrook, Kent TN17 3EJ
Tel: 01580 714911 Fax: 01580 714493

MEMBER OF
BRITISH INSURANCE & INVESTMENT
BROKERS ASSOCIATION

01580 714911

Mon-Fri 9.00am - 5.30pm

Risk in the Licensed Trade

Risk is something we all live with, it is mostly accepted as an inevitable aspect of each day - crossing the road, driving a car, using electric equipment - going to a pub?

Of course, risks turning into accidents with serious consequences are fortunately few and far between and in any case we all tend to push the idea of "something happening" to the back of our mind in favour of more optimistic thoughts! And, of course there's always the insurance.....

True enough, there are many good quality competitive specialist insurance packages on the market, with a few insurers seeking clients like you aggressively. So what's there to worry about?

You should, with good advice from your broker, be able to protect yourself against the financial consequences of all the usual risks in the Licensed Trade. But what no insurance gives you back is the time and worry of dealing with an event that disrupts your business, and damages the reputation you are trying so hard to nurture and build.

That's the risk, and is the reason why some time and effort spent now in thinking about and avoiding potential problems will prove very effective in managing your risks, and will contribute to the stability and success of your business.

In this article, we set out just a few "risks" you may face as a member of the Licensed Trade, and offer a few practical tips to make sure you are doing all you can to control your own destiny.

Public Liability

Most of your public liability risk relates to your customers - not a surprise. It's easy to imagine common slips and falls in the pub but think as well about the car park, and consider installing lighting perhaps with a movement sensitive switch, to make sure customers feel welcome on arrival and safe on departure.

The amount of legislation about these days that relates to food safety is huge - and for good reason. There's no subject guaranteed to generate bad "word of mouth" as an allegation of "something I ate" that relates to your pub. We've all seen news stories relating to 'e-coli' where the consequences for both the customer and the business are truly catastrophic,

These days there is truly no room for complacency in the discipline of hygienic food preparation. This is an area of the pub business that can generate good profitable income, and so needs particular attention from you.

If you have a garden with children's play equipment, do make sure you check it as regularly as you would if your own children were playing on it, and try to introduce some soft ground covering below swings and slides.

Beyond these specifics, we suggest that "being a good neighbour" is also something to work on. Apart from being good sense from a marketing perspective, you can build goodwill in your community by being seen to care for your customer's welfare, and this will stand you in good stead in the event of troublesome or minor incidents that can easily be cleared up with a smile.

Employer's Liability

As an employer, you owe a duty of care to your employees to provide a safe place of work. And beyond your legal obligations it makes sound business sense to look after good quality people, who are hard to find and who are always the backbone of success in any service industry.

We mentioned food hygiene in the last section, as a risk to customers. Well, food preparation is itself a risky business - cooks and catering staff are very prone to injury especially when working under pressure,

Cuts burns and falls are all common risks in even the best kitchens, and as well as injury to your staff, you will find that

there's disruption to food preparation or servicing - again placing strain on the priceless commodity - "customer service".

There are always "new" risks around in the world and perhaps one for the future in the Licensed Trade is passive smoking, which would be a problem to customers but perhaps especially staff who may be in a smoky atmosphere very regularly. If you are considering air filtration or conditioning systems, this would be another good reason to install such equipment.

One last thought - you can take out "personal accident" cover for you and your staff, and the availability of a known cash amount in the event of specified injuries can help mitigate the likelihood of a lawsuit.

Theft

Just about the most aggravating risk of all is theft, there's something very immediate and personal about someone taking money or items you have worked hard to obtain.

Money itself is kept in various places, and is usually on the premises at night. Your safe, charity boxes, gaming machines are all targets, and you should take all the precautions you can to secure them. Place gaming machines where you can see them from the bar. If you can video-monitor the safe this can he a deterrent. Do also make sure you have a peephole fitted to external doors, and be sure before opening the door to visitors after hours or before opening.

Carrying cash to the bank is a time of obvious exposure to theft, and your insurance should protect you financially. But the trauma of an assault and robbery is considerable,and so varying the route you take, and the times you go are both sensible precautions, along with physical deterrents to the opportunist snatcher.

Perhaps you have valuable garden equipment or plants, maybe especially following a refurbishment. There's a limit to what you can do in this respect, but external automatic lighting and perhaps a guard dog can deter, or alert you to a problem.

Life and Investment

As some of you will know by now, the minute you put on an application for life insurance that you are involved in the Licensed Trade the Insurer treats you as if you are a beer drinking smoker and either declines or increases the cost of your cover.

At College Green we know that this is simply not the case and as Independent Financial Advisors we will find the right insurance, with the right provider at a competitive premium.

We operate a computer quotation system and can normally give you an idea of the premium within 24 hours, this could be useful if you are thinking of buying the premises or just planing your next move.

With regard to investment we offer advice, on either regular or lump sum savings vehicles. These could prove to be a prudent savings scheme if you are looking to expand or develop your business in the medium to long term. However, please remember the value of investments can fall as well as rise.

We also offer advice on Mortgages, Personal Equity Plans, Individual Savings Accounts, School Fees Planning, Inheritance Tax Planning and Child Savings Plans.

Pensions

College Green has obtained a reputation in the Licensed Trade for giving Pensions advice and this still goes on today, with the extra advantage now that as Independent Financial Advisers we must give best advice by law to you. This means recommending the right Product and Provider to suit your needs, As each client is different we will match your needs to the best plan.

Your needs could be any or all of the following, and if so we have the plans to match

- **Early Retirement**

- **Premium Flexibility**

• Portability and Investment Flexibility,

We also offer advice on Past Pension Rights and Pensions for staff.

Private Medical Insurance

After going through this Handbook this is probably the last thing on your mind.

However, if you are ill, who will carry out your duties?

The longer you are off or indeed carrying out restricted duties the larger the potential of a reduction in the takings and a reduction in your income.

As you will be aware with Private Medical Insurance you are often seen quicker by the consultant and then treated quicker which means you will be back to your full duties sooner and the reduction in income will not be as bad.

Starter plans need not be expensive and you may start to build up no claims discount just like your car insurance.

All insurers are checked on their attitude to the Licensed Trade first.

Some Final Thoughts

It's well worth keeping a record of purchases, and equipment you use in your business. Proving the amount of your loss is often a time-consuming and hassle-laden element of making a claim, and the more you can do to show a loss adjuster that you have a bona-fide claim, the easier and quicker will be your settlement.

An insurance broker has written this article, and so you'd expect us to say something about the value we bring. Well, when you are buying insurance on behalf of a business we believe that it's a real strength to have an advocate and ally, both to ensure that all odd examples we've quoted above are "insured", but also to help you through the process of making a claim. A broker who specialises in the Licensed Trade will be also able to offer you further risk management advice to avoid incidents happening in the first place.

By the way, you will also find that as soon as you enter your profession as "publican" in a proposal form, for example for motor insurance or critical illness cover, that many insurance companies suddenly get cold feet, so a good broker can be worth his (or her) weight in gold!

For further information Please contact: Gordon Taylor

College Green Independent Koinonia House High Street, Cranbrook Kent TN17 3EJ

Tel: 01580 714 911 Fax: 01580 714 493

231

make and also a cash flow statement. It is important that you understand the difference between the two – the profit and loss account records the income and expenditure of the business (such as sales and overheads) but excludes capital items (such as equipment and furniture), and only takes income and expenditure into account in the period to which it relates. Cash flow on the other hand reflects every movement of cash whether it affects the profit and loss account or not. For instance, the day before you take over your pub, you pay one quarter's rent of £5000 and £10,000 for the fixtures and fittings. Your profit and loss account at that stage will be zero as the rent was in advance and fixtures and fittings is a capital item. However, the cash flow will already show minus £15,000, as the cash has actually left your account.

Apart from the normal high street banks, you may wish to try other sources of loans. Some building societies now offer business loans, and there are lots of other financial institutions which also make loans. A good way of finding such funds is via the agent you are buying the pub through. The agent will also help with submitting an application and generally provide advice to smooth the raising of funds.

The bank manager will be particularly interested in the cash flow statement as, although you may be able to trade profitably, you still need working capital to finance the purchase of stock, rent, etc. You may even find that utility companies want a deposit if you cannot provide a history of paying for gas, electricity, etc at a previous address.

Quite often you will hear the request for a 'business plan'. This basically means you need to put in writing how you intend to trade the pub, what improvements and changes you intend to make, how much that is all going to cost, plus a projected profit and loss account and cash flow statement. You should also include descriptions of your own experience, whether in the trade or not, and provide assurances of your suitability to run a pub if this is your first venture.

STOCK AND CASH CONTROL

One of the major items in the pub business is to ensure all the cash gets into the till and that your stock only leaves the premises by being purchased. Unfortunately the pub business is notorious for employees stealing cash or stock, so you must be in a position to monitor the situation.

Obviously, if you run the pub without employing staff you can be sure that no theft of stock or cash is taking place. However, you still need to be vigilant – it is not unknown for a drayman to short deliver an item if he thinks he can get away with it. I remember one pub that always seemed to have a stock shortage – it took some time to discover that beer stock kept in a locked yard was being stolen overnight at the rate of a keg a week!

For the larger operation, with various staff involved, it is essential that a proper stock control system is in place. You must decide whether you feel capable of doing this yourself or will employ an outside stocktaker. The other decision is what type of tills you use – either a straight till or electronic point of sale.

The latter system means that every sale is recorded by product and size and the till looks up the price at which it is sold. For this system to operate effectively, all deliveries must be entered on the machine, plus any items given away, and allowing for any below normal sale prices, eg happy hour. Although this may seem time consuming, it does allow any shortages to be pinpointed exactly.

The alternative is to leave stock-taking entirely to an outside firm. Although I recommend stocktaking be carried out on a monthly basis, a lot of people feel quarterly is suffi-cient. The problem is that, if the stock control is going awry, you need to know as soon as possible. An outside stocktaker will count all the stock on hand and then record all sales and deliveries of goods. This enables them to calculate the amount of stock used during the period. As the selling price is known for each item, and allowing for wastage, pro-motions and any other adjustments, it is easy to calculate the amount of cash that should have been received in the tills.

Charges for a stocktake vary depending on the size and com-plexity of the job, but expect to pay from £60 upwards. If you feel con-fident enough and have the use of a computer you could purchase a stocktaking package that will enable you to do the same job. However, great accuracy in checking all the stock on hand and entering deliv-eries is required, otherwise you will end up with a meaningless set of figures. Personally, I think stocktak-

ing is best left to the professionals, so that you know you are getting an accurate result. The other benefit is that most stocktakers have a wealth of experience and can point you in the right direction for curing any problems.

Apart from losing stock due to pilferage, the other problem is to ensure you don't overstock your pub. Overall, you should aim to carry no more than two weeks' stock. This will vary according to your type of operation as, say, an extensive wine list will obviously take your stock-holding higher. As a general rule, to work out your weekly order you should use the formula of twice your weekly sale less the amount of stock on hand. For example, if you start the week with five cases of tonic water and finish with two cases, you have sold three cases. Twice the weekly sale is six cases, less the stock of two gives an order of four cases.

If you do over-order on some items which carry a best before date you can still sell them, probably at a reduced rate, as long as you make this clear at the time of sale. I would advise that you try to sell excess stock by reducing the price before the date in question is reached, rather than ending up with stock that has passed its expiry date before. Rotation of stock is important so that you don't end up with old stock buried under a pile of younger items.

SUPPLIERS

If you are a free house you can obvi-ously source all your products from any brewer or wholesaler. The market is highly competitive and you should shop around to get the best deal.

Discounts for a one-off account of say 300 barrels can get up to £50 per barrel, which is about 20 per cent off the list price, so you can see there are good deals to be had. However, price is not everything: you must consider whether the brands a supplier is offering are right for your customers, because if you can't sell it, then no amount of discount helps you.

With items such as wines, spirits and food it is probable that you can get lower prices from a cash and carry than a company that delivers to your door. You must consider whether your time and transport costs are worth more than the amount saved. That said, I know a lot of publicans actually enjoy visiting the cash and carry – it gets them away from the pub and they can see what new prodcuts/offers are on the market.

RECORDS AND BOOKKEEPING

Whatever level of financial knowledge you have, there is a minimum level of records you must keep.

There are three government agencies that you need to be aware of.

1. **Customs and Excise** is responsible for collecting VAT, and these days they are judged by how much extra they can find to collect when they visit you. They have extraordinary powers to enter your premises and confiscate records if they think fit, so they are people to be taken seriously. Hopefully you will not see that side of them, as they will be happy with the records you keep. You can expect a visit from a VAT Inspector within the first year of trading as you will be paying a fair amount of VAT over each quarter.

Although VAT on the face of it is simple, in that you charge VAT on sales and, before you pay this over you can deduct any VAT you have paid on supplies, it gets slightly more complicated. For instance, if you have a functions room and let it for a meeting and don't provide any other services, you needn't charge VAT. However, if you provide refreshments in the price, then you do have to charge VAT. Also when deducting VAT paid on purchases you must be careful to get a proper VAT receipt from the supplier showing not only his VAT number but also the VAT amount and VAT rate (unless it is a small amount). Remember, if you don't have the right documentation, the Inspectors will disallow such claims and then you have to pay up, plus interest.

The other highly important point with paying over your VAT is to adhere to the due dates. If you are a few days late they will issue a surcharge notice which lasts for a year. If your return is late during that coming year, you are automatically surcharged a percentage of the VAT due, plus a penalty.

2. The **Inland Revenue** gets involved on two counts: the collection of PAYE and National Insurance on a monthly basis, and your tax liabilities on any profit you make.

You can expect a visit from the Inland Revenue to check your PAYE and employee records, but

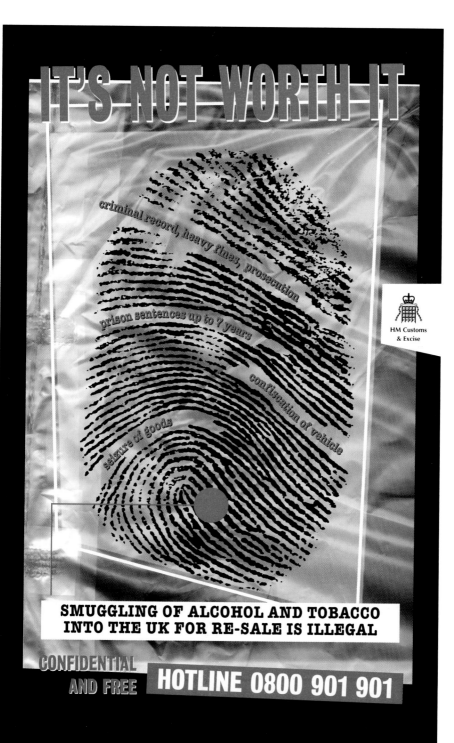

IT'S NOT WORTH IT

criminal record, heavy fines, prosecution

prison sentences up to 7 years

confiscation of vehicle

seizure of goods

HM Customs
& Excise

SMUGGLING OF ALCOHOL AND TOBACCO
INTO THE UK FOR RE-SALE IS ILLEGAL

CONFIDENTIAL
AND FREE   HOTLINE 0800 901 901

HM CUSTOMS & EXCISE RECEIVE £35 MILLION BOOST FOR NEW OFFENSIVE AGAINST ALCOHOL & TOBACCO FRAUD

The smuggling of alcohol and tobacco into the U.K for resale has increased significantly with the introduction of the Single European Market on 1 January 1993 and the newly introduced right of EU citizens to travel freely within the member countries. As a result of this HM Customs and Excise has had to develop and improve its investigative and intelligence capabilities to enable continued success in tackling this illegal activity.

On the 28th July 1998 the Financial Secretary Dawn Primarolo announced a massive offensive on alcohol and tobacco fraud and smuggling, with £35 million extra over the next three years.

"This activity will simply not be tolerated. Tougher use of existing criminal prosecution powers and stern guidelines on sentencing issued by the Appeal Court also send a message to law breakers that smuggling does not pay."

These new measures lend further support to the Governments commitment to fighting fraud.

"this package will give those on the front line the tools needed to crackdown on smugglers and protect law abiding traders"

Whilst the abolition of duty-paid allowances of alcohol and tobacco benefits many travellers to the UK, it actually poses a huge threat to UK revenue. From 1993, passengers could bring in as much as they liked so long as it was for their own use and not for commercial purposes.

The following Minimum Indicative Levels (MILS) which are enshrined in UK law by the Excise Duties (Personal Reliefs) Order 1992, were drawn up to provide guidance to both passengers and the Department of the type of volumes that would satisfy this requirement.

CIGARETTES	800
CIGARILLOS	400
CIGARS	200
TOBACCO	1 kg
BEER	110 litres
WINE	90 litres

(Of these not more than 60 litres can be sparkling wine)

FORTIFIED WINE	20 litres
SPIRITS & LIQUERS	10 litres

(over 22% volume)

Alcohol & tobacco fraud is the importation of duty paid or duty free goods from another

EU state and re-selling them without paying the required UK Duty and (where appropriate) VAT.

The mass availability of such goods sounds enticing, but as the latest figures indicate its effect on the taxpayer is the loss of £885 million per annum in revenue.Furthermore, alcohol and tobacco fraud undermines the legitimate trade and lines the pockets of profiteering criminals, who are often found to be placing an extra financial burden on the Government, by claiming housing or unemployment benefits.

This activity is illegal and alongside combating fraud at the front-line Customs are anxious to change the public perception that the smuggling of excise goods is a victimless crime.

Customs stress that people who buy smuggled goods are depriving themselves and their community of funding. This can have the effect of jeopardising, for example, the financial stability of their local hospitals and schools and threatening the businesses of local shops and pubs which they use.

Initiatives to combat excise fraud and smuggling, outlined in the Alcohol and Tobacco Fraud Review, can now be taken forward. The review was prepared in partnership with the trade. Ministers have accepted the joint recommendations and have provided funds for this year and the three years.

Customs plan to place additional officers at ports and inland to pursue those organising, distributing and selling illicit goods. The impact of more than 100 extra officers will be significant. Smugglers will encounter stop checks more frequently and Customs will be able to concentrate attention and resources on problem areas.

The Minister also announced a number of other initiatives to counter fraud which range from the identification of products on stock records and on commercial documentation, to the registering and assuring of proprietors of excise goods.

Customs will also be consulting with the trade regarding the possible use of electronic tagging of alcoholic products and the possibility of marking tobacco products to help identify those goods intended for export. It could then be an offence to sell unmarked tobacco products.

In addition, the Beer Orders will be amended to remove the anomaly where brewers cannot refuse to supply companies they suspect of being involved in revenue fraud. Some of the measures will require negotiation through the European Union before they can be implemented. These will be taken forward by Ministers in Brussels, through the EU High Level Fraud Group.

These new measures will complement an existing set of policies announced in April, when Customs revealed a new package of hard-line measures to tackle alcohol and tobacco fraud.

The new policy, which works on the 'THREE STRIKES AND YOU'RE OUT' principle, is designed to hit the finances of those organising smuggling trips and hit their operations by taking vehicles off the road. The restoration fee for vehicles used in smuggling is £250 or a sum equal to 50% of the duty on the seized goods, whichever is the greater. On the second offence, the charge will be levied at £1000 or a sum equal to 100% of the duty up to 'trade-in value' of the vehicle. On the third offence, Customs will reserve the right not to return the vehicle to its owners at all.

The new policy includes a firmer line on prosecution and will result in more criminal court action being taken against smugglers. Customs will also press for the use of all criminal sanctions available including compensation orders for the revenue evaded and curfew orders to prevent smugglers from venturing abroad. The Court of Appeal recently issued sentencing guidelines to Courts for cases involving the smuggling of alcohol and tobacco.

From 1 May 1998:
• offenders may receive a custodial sentence of up to 7 years on a guilty plea;
• offenders using vehicles may be disqualified from driving;
• holders of liquor licences may have them revoked and deprivation orders for vehicles and goods may be considered.

Customs are continuing to strengthen their links with other Government agencies, such as the Benefits Agency, Inland Revenue and Trading Standards. Previous joint ventures have proved highly successful in tracking down and reporting those found profiteering from their smuggling activities.

Customs are determined to crack down on alcohol and tobacco fraud. If you suspect that someone is involved in alcohol or tobacco fraud Customs would like to hear from you. They have set up a **CONFIDENTIAL FREEPHONE HOTLINE 0800 901901** and are waiting for your call.

they vary tremendously, so you could wait years. Be careful though, as they can go back for six years and charge you for any mistakes made during that period. The records you must keep for PAYE and NI are detailed in the Employers' Pack which you will be issued with when you register with them.

With regard to the Inland Revenue and your tax liability, this is normally done through correspondence with you or your accountant. However, if they are not happy with the figures or answers to queries, they have the power to go through everything with a fine tooth-comb. Bear in mind that they can issue an assessment for tax and it is down to you to prove that it is wrong!

3. The **Contributions Agency** is the department which checks to make sure National Insurance is being paid on employees' earnings and any benefits you provide. They take great delight in identifying any benefits given to staff that should have NI charged on them. For instance, if you pay for a taxi to take staff home at night, this is a 'benefit' and should have NI paid on it.

If they visit you, they usually check the PAYE records as well, just to help out the Inland Revenue. Why the PAYE and NI departments aren't combined into one is anyone's guess!

Computers

Computers soon become irreplaceable for your record-keeping and financial control once you have tried

them. As mentioned above, you can get stocktaking packages off the shelf and you can choose from a number of accounting packages for small businesses such as Sage or Pegasus. They all come with pretty good instruction manuals, and as long as you follow them carefully you can use the information either to produce accounts yourself or pass them over to your accountant to finish off. If you do the latter, check with the accountant if they have a preference for which package you should use.

You can also use the computer to calculate wage payments. Keeping manual records is OK and pretty straightforward (guidance manuals are produced by the Inland Revenue), but it does take quite a lot of time to calculate the PAYE and NI due on each person's wage, whereas the computer does it in seconds. The machine will also produce the year-end returns up to 5 April each year for submission to the Inland Revenue.

An added bonus is that the computer is able to produce menus and posters whenever you like and to an extremely high standard. There are many such 'desktop publishing' programs around and most new computers come with a suitable package.

MAXIMISING PROFITS

The major effect on profit is obviously the amount of sales and the gross profit you can make out of those sales. It is difficult to give you any meaningful guidelines on what gross profit you should make, as it varies so much between different parts of the country on selling price and what discounts you can negotiate on purchases. On wet take these can vary from 40 per cent to over 60 per cent, and on food anything from 30 per cent up to over 70 per cent.

Another large slice of expenditure for a reasonably sized pub is wages for kitchen and bar staff. Most managed houses work on a budget of 10 per cent for staff (excluding managers) where there is little food involved, but this can increase dramatically where the food take is high. Remember that, although food gross profits can be very high, the wages costs for preparation, cooking and serving can mount alarmingly if you don't keep tight control.

Many of your overhead costs such as rent are fixed, but there is scope to reduce other costs. Most fair-sized pubs can now shop around for gas supplies and can make savings of at least 33 per cent over standard British Gas tariffs. There will shortly be the opportunity to do the same with electricity.

Another major cost can be rates. As far as pubs are concerned, the Inland Revenue Valuation Office fixes the rateable value based on the amount of business the pub is doing. This is reviewed every five years and can result in the rateable value going either up or down. If you think the rateable value is too high you can appeal and have it reassessed. This is a specialist field and I would advise you to use one of the many experts available. However, be careful who you choose as there are many firms that charge up-front fees and never obtain any reductions. My advice is to stick to the rating departments of the licensed valuers – they are all members of professional societies which ensure proper care is taken.

Finally, if things do go wrong and the business ends up in difficulties, take professional advice from your accountant or solicitor. He should be able to advise on what action to take to help with further financing or, at worst, how to minimise the financial burdens. If things go badly wrong, and you have borrowed money from a bank or other institution, you will need all the help you can get, as they always have the power to take any action they like to protect their interests rather than yours.

Legal Notes

It is forbidden to sell or supply intoxicating liquor for consumption on any licensed premises unless it is paid for when sold or supplied, unless the liquor is sold with a meal and paid for together with the meal, or it is sold or supplied to a person residing in the licensed premises and is paid for together with the accommodation. This also applies to liquor sold to guests of residents.

Credit or debit cards may be used as the transaction is completed once they are accepted.

INFORMATION TECHNOLOGY FOR PUBLICANS

Jill Upton

Faced with the challenge of new technology, people always tell me they know nothing about computers. Whether that's true or not, it helps to remember that you don't need to understand the internal combustion engine to use a car. The same goes for computers: they are essentially a tool to help you get from A to B faster, and with better information.

What really frightens people about computers is not the computers themselves but computerspeak. For some reason the computer industry communicates in a tangle of technical jargon and acronyms, which – perhaps deliberately! – simply creates confusion. To outsiders, it may seem essential to know all the latest buzzwords just to have a conversation; but believe me, it isn't.

The golden rule for businesspeople with little or no experience of computers is: ask questions, keep on asking questions, and don't stop asking questions until you get all the answers you need. And insist on getting understandable answers, even at the expense of appearing ignorant. If a sales person can't explain the jargon, maybe they don't understand what they are talking about either!

INTEGRATION

There seems to be very little information in the computer industry specific to public houses. Whereas the sector-specific requirements of hotels, hospitality suites and clubs are all well researched and categorised, there is no material under the simple heading 'Pub'. So I have undertaken some research of my own, visiting publicans and interviewing as many as I could in order to gain an understanding of current options and directions for information technology in the licensed trade.

When asked, in this rough exercise in sampling, what were the benefits of computerisation, pub tenants and managers were all agreed that it had increased their turnover through better control of takings, stock and profits.

It soon became evident that while it is possible to benefit from computerising stock control or the business's accounts in isolation, gathering all the information and then typing it all into the system, the real benefits came from having an integrated system.

Such a system would be based on a personal computer (PC) and printer plus cash drawers with touch pads, and a printer in the kitchen. These pieces are all called 'hardware' and are cabled together to create a 'net-work'. The 'software' then controls the information entered at the tills, interprets it, and displays it across the whole system as required. This is called an electronic point of sale (EPOS) system.

The advantage of a fully integrated EPOS is that the information gathered by the keypad on the till can be used in all sorts of different ways. The information gained from the original single entry will provide the data you need for everything from stock control and accounts to making major management decisions.

FROM CASH REGISTERS TO COMPUTERS

Once upon a time it was enough to take the cash out of the till, count it

Coining in the Profits

A BT Payphone like all other coin operated vending machines can generate high levels of revenue in relation to the amount of space it occupies in a pub. Providing a BT Payphone is a much appreciated customer service, which can generate more business and provide a considerable income in its own right.

All BT Payphones are sophisticated vending machines that offer a host of useful features such as a multi-lingual display, volume control for noisy environments and a new coin facility that can be used to take tokens or new British (even European) coinage.

Ursula Butler, BT's Private Payphones Marketing Manager commented, "*at BT we are continually looking at ways to build upon our expertise in both coin operated arid cardpay private payphones, to give our customers more choice arid revenue-generating opportunities*"... "*Publicans have realised for a long time how profitable a BT Payphone can be, so it is important to ensure that our products, such as the Contour range, meet and hopefully exceed their expectations on what a payphone should deliver*"

The range starts with the Contour 50 and 100 which simply plug into an existing phone socket, leading to the tough Contour 200 with its metal casing, vandal proof cash box and armoured handset. Top of the BT Cardpay which accepts BT Phonecards, BT Chargecards and most major credit/debit cards.

Mr and Mrs Evans of The Wildfowler Inn, Swansea, who recently won a Contour 50 as part of a competition run on Soundwave radio remarked "*we know that our payphone has always been both a popular and profitable asset in the pub. We're sure our new Contour 50 will continue to generate profits for us and provide our customers with an excellent service*"... "*We've certainly found the easy to follow instructions on tariff settings a great help, as we now know how much we're charging per minute and therefore how much revenue it's bringing in*"

BT Payphones pride themselves on offering customers a choice. This means you can either purchase a BT Payphone outright or lease one through BT's Fixed Price Agreements (from 18 months to five years). These offer the benefit of inflation-proof rental for the duration of the agreement and come complete with BT's comprehensive back-up service.

For more information on special offers or on how you can benefit from a BT Payphone call us free on

0800 44 22 55

up and put it into the bank. Then along came electronic tills, which did the adding up for you, printing out a list of transactions and totalling them for banking. These early business machines still relied on the mental ability of bar staff to add up the round in their heads and calculate the correct change – probably easier at the beginning of the evening than at the end!

Soon the tills got a little cleverer, and drinks could be coded and prices entered. Bar staff could then enter the round drink by drink, and the till totalled the transaction and calculated the change from the amount paid. As well as making transactions at the bar quicker and more accurate, these tills could also produce simple lists of the day's or week's business, showing the total amounts of drinks sold.

Now there are PCs, and the picture is transformed. Unlike previous advances the PC is not just a smarter adding machine, but is the centre of an information network linking several tills and actually using the information entered on the till keypad. The till is still there, but is merely a terminal serving the PC, the printer and the systems running on it.

These are collectively referred to as the 'back office' system, and the clever publican can use it to monitor every aspect of the pub's performance: for instance, looking at the volume of transactions by time of day to see if the bar staff are employed at the right times.

The back office also controls stock by monitoring usage, allowing accurate forward planning of purchases and avoiding over-ordering. If purchases as well as sales are processed

through the system, then all the pub's accounting information will be automatically updated. Abnormal transactions like refunds and credits can be highlighted and monitored. Gross profit and cash flow can be monitored as they happen, and predicted.

All this equipment is expensive (to find out just how expensive, see below), but at a time when margins are ever narrower and business is ever harder to attract, it is becoming essential to have better management information to make informed judgements about the business.

Here are some ways in which the information provided and collated by your PC can help you control costs, either by giving you the data you need to make management decisions or taking over routine but time-consuming and error-prone tasks:

◆ employing staff at the right times
◆ reducing stockholding
◆ detecting pilfering by tracking sales data such as voids, complimentary items, refunds and wastage
◆ saving your expensive time by;
  – preparing your banking
  – stocktaking
  – automatically calculating staff wages
  – working out your accounts and VAT.

These benefits are available to you if you run more than one pub: if you are a multiple tenant, say, or if you own a chain of free houses, because a single back office system can run a huge number of EPOS tills, which need not be in the same building. The PC can be at a totally different location and the whole system can be connected using the telephone line. Obviously, this will incur call charges if BT is the telephone provider; but even here there are opportunities to reduce costs: for example, cable operators do not charge for local calls.

The control exerted by computerisation is not relaxed even on the rare occasions when you manage to snatch a holiday or while you are sick: the trading record of your period of absence will be there on your return, transaction by transaction, staff member by staff member. If one of your regular staff has been in charge while you were away you will be able to tell exactly how well he has managed. If you have used a relief agency the evidence of how it has performed is there in black and white, leaving no room for stressful, time-consuming and costly disputes.

INCREASING TRADE

A PC will not only help you to control the business you already have more efficiently and profitably, it can also help you win new business.

It will record precisely what trade there is, and how the overall volume of business fluctuates through the seasons, the days of the week, the time of day. It will also track what kind of meals and drinks sell best at different times, which will tell you what sort of crowd you are attracting through the different trading sessions – and whether you are losing their loyalty in time for you to take preventive action.

It will enable you to spot weak points and strong points and plan your marketing on the basis of hard fact rather than vague impression,

accurately recording the results of promotions you have run and providing detailed knowledge of which are your best-selling and most profitable items, and the percentage gross profit item by item.

OTHER BENEFITS

The PC in your EPOS system should be running Windows '95. You can then buy Microsoft Office '97 or '98 Small Business Edition, which will cost about £235 and will provide:

◆ Word, for writing letters
◆ Excel, for spreadsheets for numerical analysis
◆ Publisher, a nice and easy desktop publishing product that will produce very professional posters, menus and leaflets.

If you are going to produce your own point of sale material, don't skimp on the printer: nothing less then an inkjet colour printer will maximise the benefits of the system.

These products are widely used, and training is available at most evening classes at local schools and colleges very cheaply.

THE SYSTEMS

The systems are not cheap, but according to my survey of pubs already using them they should pay for themselves in one to three years.

Below are some suppliers of specialist EPOS systems for pubs. The prices quoted include the hardware (PC, printer, two cash drawers and key pads plus a printer for the kitchen), software, cabling installation and training. The prices quoted are to buy, but lease options are available to spread the outlay, usually over three or five years, bringing the cost down to £1000–£3000 a year.

Checkout:	cost – £7000–£9000	
	tel – 01582 471112	
FBH Viewbase:	cost – £6000–£8000	
	tel – 01823 335292	
Clarity:	cost – £5000–£7000	
	tel – 01722 746200.	

All these systems provide the user with full management, stock and account information.

BUYING A SYSTEM

Just like anything else the salesman will sell the features, which may or may not be what your business needs. So before you see a salesman you need to do some homework.

First, decide what you need your system to do for your business, then talk to some suppliers.

Check out other pubs that have already installed PCs. Ask why they needed a system and compare their requirements to your own. If they needed a system for different reasons and are happy with what they bought, it won't be right for you.

If you need help through the process, contact an independent systems consultant like IT Works (01525 862266) with the expertise to help you specify the best system for your business.

And one final tip for anyone buying a PC for any reason: before you commit yourself, ring your intended supplier's after-service hotline. It's a fair bet you'll need it once the PC is installed; if you find it takes all day to get through, and if you do get connected it's to someone who doesn't understand the manual any more than you do, choose a different supplier.

PART SIX
FOR YOUR COMFORT
AND SAFETY...

CHAPTER SEVENTEEN

FIRE SAFETY

Glen Gorman

Fire is a peculiar monster, if you take a little time to think about it. One of the oldest forces harnessed by humanity, and one of the most useful, yet it is taken more for granted than almost any other element in our lives. How often do we give a thought to the power fire has? Handled safely, fire will not give rise to any problems; but introduce a few combustibles and a little carelessness, and you summon a monster worse than your worst nightmares.

Appreciating the power of fire is part of controlling it. Knowing what devastating effects it can have on property and lives is a step on your way to a better understanding of basic fire safety – not just knowing what measures to take, but understanding why you have to take them.

For instance, how long do you think it would take the average living room, furnished with everyday items – three-piece suite, coffee table, TV, video and so on – from time of ignition to blazing inferno? Ten minutes? Five?

In fact, in tests a fire started in an armchair by an unextinguished cigarette takes less than four minutes to rage totally out of control, with a heat so intense that furniture at the other end of the room will ignite even before the flame reaches it. Unconvinced? I can show you the video.

Make no mistake, fire is an extremely dangerous beast if let loose. But it is not often that victims of fire die from burning. The majority of fire-related fatalities are the result of smoke inhalation.

Smoke has many constituents, including carbon monoxide and cyanide gas, depending on what is burning.

Carbon monoxide has an affinity for red blood corpuscles and will attach itself readily to them when you breathe it in, preventing the corpuscles from taking up oxygen from the air. It gives you a pleasant cherry-pink complexion – and it kills you. Cyanide gas attacks your nervous system: death can result from a short contact with very small amounts.

There are other deadly constituents of smoke: in fact most of the materials in your home will give off deadly gases, depending on their make-up, but by far the worst comes from what you are probably sitting on right now. Foam-filled furniture when subjected to heat or flames gives off fumes that are both flammable and poisonous. The situation has been improved by recent legislation governing newly manufactured furniture, but there is still a huge amount of pre-legislation around.

Fire and smoke kill and do not discriminate. Young or old, male or female, day or night. I remember a case in Blackpool in the late 1980s where five people, some of them children, died in a hotel fire despite the best efforts of my colleagues to save them. It was two o'clock in the afternoon.

I hope that you now appreciate the destructive power of fire in your pub, which is probably also your home, and, armed with your understanding, will grasp the importance of fire safety. But before going into detail, there are certain generalities to be considered.

It is no good installing fire safety devices and instituting model fire safety procedures if no one takes any notice of them.

Take the humble self-closing fire-resistant door. Its purpose is to check the passage of fire and smoke, but it can only do this if it is closed. Consider this scenario. Five bedrooms, all fitted with perfectly good self-closing doors, open on to a common corridor leading to an escape stairway.

One bedroom has a fire; but the occupant has gone to the bathroom, leaving the door propped open. The smoke detector sets off the fire alarm and the other four occupants attempt to make their way to safety – only to be faced with a thick wall of choking smoke as soon as they leave their rooms. How do they make their escape? They don't. They die on the corridor from smoke inhalation – and all for a door left open.

There is no room for complacency with fire safety. Staff have to be properly trained by a competent person. Guests have to be adequately informed of fire routines. If you are responsible for fire precautions it is up to you to enforce them, because in the event of fire your guests' – and your family's – safety is in your hands. Should any contravention be found on inspection it could mean a hefty fine. Should death or injury occur as a result of laxity it will be on your conscience for the rest of your life.

STEPS YOU CAN TAKE NOW

There are several very simple common-sense steps that you can take right now to improve fire safety in your pub. At night, before going to bed, check you have unplugged any electrical appliances that don't need to be on. Don't empty ashtrays until morning or, if you do, make sure the butts go into a metal container. Don't run electrical flexes under carpets where you can't see if they're getting worn: they can set fire to the carpet. Fit correctly rated fuses in plugs – 13 amps for any appliance incorporating a heating element.

Make sure chip-pans are never more than one-third full of oil, or when you lower the food-basket the oil will overflow and flame on the burner. Never leave a chip-pan or frying-pan unattended on the hob: it only takes minutes to reach ignition temperature. If you do have a chip-pan fire, never try to put it out with water: water turned instantaneously into steam expands at a rate of 1700:1, so every cup of water you throw on to a blazing chip-pan will come right back at you as 1700 cups of scalding steam, compounded by droplets of burning oil.

When you go to bed, close all internal doors. Imagine you're asleep in bed. Downstairs, a fire breaks out, and thick smoke starts pouring upstairs. What stands between you and the smoke – between your children and the smoke? Certainly not your bedroom doors, if you've left them open. The smoke will kill you while you sleep. Close your doors and multiply your chances of survival.

There are many, many more equally simple measures – far too many to list here. Call in at your local fire station tomorrow, and they will be glad to tell you more.

FIRE SAFETY LEGISLATION

If your pub provides sleeping accommodation for six or more staff and/or guests, and any of those are above first-floor level or below ground-floor level, then your premises fall within the scope of Section 1(2)a of the Fire Precautions Act 1971 and will have to have a fire certificate. If you are in any doubt contact your local fire safety department (it's in the phone book) which will be more than happy to advise you – free. Remember, under Section 7(1) of the Act it is an offence to operate a

premises without a fire certificate, and if you have a fire certificate it is your personal responsibility to ensure compliance with its requirements.

This is not just bureaucracy. This could save your life.

It is important to understand that your fire certificate is a legal document. It is not just a single piece of paper but a booklet containing information about your premises, with the fire safety requirements you must adhere to contained both in writing and on a plan along with any other relevant documents issued by the fire safety department.

Any other documents issued to you – an inspection report, for example, are also legal documents.

You may not alter or add to your fire certificate, which must be kept on the premises to which it relates and be available for inspection at any time.

The fire certificate will detail certain measures with which you must comply. These will vary from premises to premises, depending on individual characteristics, so if you are comparing fire certificates with other publicans, do not be surprised if theirs is different from yours. If, on inspection, you are found to be in contravention of any of these requirements you will be advised on what to do and given time to put matters right. If you fail to comply you will be prosecuted and fined. If matters are judged so serious as to be a danger to life the court may restrict the use of the premises or even close you down completely, using powers under Section 10 of the Act, until you have complied with the requirements of your fire certificate.

Some basic requirements

One requirement will always be to have a fire alarm system throughout the premises complying with BS5839 and fitted by a competent installer.

Each exit from the premises and each floor will have to have a break-glass call point to actuate the alarm (in public bar areas these can be fitted behind the bar).

Escape routes and rooms leading off them will have to have automatic smoke detectors. There are two common types: the ionisation type and the optical type. The former detects the invisible products of combustion and is thus very sensitive. False alarms can be frequent, as the ionisation type can be set off by steam from kettles or bathrooms, aerosols, and even small insects. The optical type detects larger particles of smoke and is less prone to false alarms. Both types are available as self-contained units for domestic use, but your fire certificate will require them to be linked into your general alarm system.

In the kitchen and other areas that can become smoky a heat detector will be required. These either go off when a preset temperature is reached or, where the area to be protected is naturally hot – ie the kitchen – they can detect anomalous or significant increases in temperature.

You will be required to test your alarm system and record the results in a log, which must be kept with your fire certificate and must be available for inspection. Most fire safety departments will also require a six-monthly test by a competent person other than yourself, who will supply a certificate of testing.

Escape routes and windowless areas will require emergency lighting installed to BS5226. This must also be tested and certified every six months.

Walls, doors and partitions that form part of the escape route must have a minimum of 30 minutes' fire resistance. Glazing in these areas must give the same fire resistance and be glazed shut. Doors opening on to escape routes must be self-closing and should never be propped open. New doors opening on to escape routes must be fitted with intumescent strips, which expand when heated to seal the gap between door and frame, and smoke seals that will operate when the fire is less hot but still producing smoke.

The escape route is the lifeline for your guests, any live-in staff, yourself and your family. It must be kept clear of obstructions and combustible materials at all times of day and night.

If your pub is less than 11 metres tall or has less than four floors you will only need one escape route, but it must be treated as a sterile area – that is, there should never be any furniture, equipment or anything else there except fire safety equipment. Doors across the escape route must be free from any fastenings – in thick smoke you may not find the handle in time to save your life. Doors leading from the escape route to the open air may never be locked other than by an approved mechanism that works without the use of a key or card – a push-bar is common. These doors should never be blocked from the outside.

If your pub is taller than 11 metres or has four or more floors, then a second escape route must be provided to serve the upper floors – either an external fire escape or doors communicating with neighbouring properties.

All staff or guest bedrooms will need a comprehensive list of instructions on what to do in case of fire or when the fire alarm sounds. This should be prominently displayed – beside a mirror is a good spot, because everyone looks in the mirror, don't they? The back of the door is a bad place, especially if there are coathooks there.

You will need portable fire extinguishers, the number of which will be stipulated according to the floor area and nature of risks in your pub. Mainly these will be water extinguishers, mounted on wall brackets, protected from vandalism and improper use, and tested annually by a competent service company. In the kitchen you will need at least one fire blanket and a CO_2 extinguisher. If you are in doubt about the proper use of extinguishers, ask at the fire station.

When the alarm sounds

All staff must be trained in what to do in case of fire or on hearing the fire alarm. Day staff need to be instructed every six months, night staff every three; and the dates of instruction need to be recorded in your log book. This can take various forms: fire drills, walking the escape routes, maybe discussing different possible scenarios. It should be the job of one responsible member of staff to ring 999 on hearing the alarm.

It is always good to have a fire action plan with one or two alterna-tives. Plan A, for instance, could relate to a fire where everyone could escape easily and unaided, whereas Plan B could outline action when residents are prevented from leaving their rooms by smoke in the corridors. Practice makes perfect, as they say; and if you design and learn these drills well, you may one day find yourself leading your staff, guests and family to safety calmly and efficiently.

When there really is a fire, the first thing to do is to sound the alarm. Never assume someone else will do it. If the fire is obviously small – for instance, in a wastepaper basket – and you feel confident enough to tackle it safely, do so. Otherwise, close the door on it and institute the relevant fire action plan. Never put yourself at risk, and once the building is evacuated no one should re-enter it for any reason unless allowed to do so by the senior fire brigade officer present.

The person nominated to ring 999 should do so at once and should never wait to investigate – the seriousness of the fire will already have been established by whoever sounded the alarm. The nominated person will be asked a number of questions by the 999 operator and should be prepared in advance to answer calmly and audibly. They may seem a waste of time in an emergency, but the more detailed information the operator can pass on the more quickly the fire brigade can respond. In most cases two appliances will arrive within five minutes of the 999 call, and these early minutes can be vital in containing the spread of the fire. Do not be afraid that the call may turn out to be a false alarm – provided you are calling in good faith the brigade would rather you called straight away than delayed; and if false alarms are occurring because of a fault in your system you will be advised to call a maintenance engineer.

Never silence the alarms. If you do, people may assume the emergency is over and start heading back to their rooms and possible disaster. Never reset the alarm panel: it can guide the fire crew to the seat of the fire.

Once the pub has been evacuated take a roll call. If anyone is missing inform the fire crew immediately and tell them where the missing person or persons were last seen and what room they should have been in.

How to save your own life

If you ever find yourself unable to get out of an upstairs room because of smoke in the corridor, there are steps you can take to improve your safety.

Make sure the door is properly closed and use any available sheets and towels to seal any gaps around it to keep the smoke out. Then open the window and shout for help, and if it is safe to do so wait near the window until help arrives.

However, it may be the case that the fire is so serious that you are going to have to leave the room by the window unaided. In this case, stay calm. Drop out anything that will soften your landing – the mattress and pillows, any bedding you haven't used to seal the door, and any available chair cushions.

Make sure the window-sill is free from sharp objects such as broken glass, and take a good look at the lie of the land below.

Children can be lowered out to passers-by or dropped as gently as possible on to the cushioning below.

To rescue yourself, lower yourself out of the window to full arm's length to reduce the distance you have to fall by as much as possible, point your feet downwards so they don't catch on anything, and let go. Be sure to bend your knees and roll as soon as you reach the ground.

This may all seem terribly dramatic and is indeed highly unlikely ever to occur, especially if you have been vigilant and meticulous where your fire safety precautions are concerned. Still, by knowing what to do you may one day save your own life.

CONCLUSION

What you have just read is by no means the ultimate compendium of fire safety in your pub, but more of a guide to what you might encounter, with, I hope, just a little insight into how dangerous fire can be.

There are other legal requirements that need to be taken into account – you need to be aware of your responsibilities under the Health and Safety at Work Act 1974 and the Licensing Act 1964, for example. If you want further detailed advice on fire safety contact your local fire safety department or pop along to the nearest fire station.

There are also private safety companies all over the country – but expect to be billed for their services. The quality service you will receive from the fire brigade is mainly free – and very willingly given!

Health and Safety Notes

Fire safety is a particularly important issue and advice on appropriate measures to take should be sought from the fire officer. In some instances a fire certificate will be required.

Fire is an issue to include in your health and safety risk assessment.

In carrying out the assessment you will need to consider whether adequate precautions are in place and whether the necessary checks are being made to maintain those precautions.

CHAPTER EIGHTEEN

SECURITY IN LICENSED OUTLETS

Brian Taylor

Crime of all sorts is, sadly, a very real problem for today's licensees and pub operators, and it is something that cannot be ignored. Publicans and brewers carrying out refurbishments have their spending priorities, and are sometimes reluctant to spend money on sound practical security considerations.

I once heard of a situation where thousands of pounds had been spent on a refurbishment which, to the customer's eye, was extremely attractive and turned the pub in question into the place to be. But the back door was not steel lined – which was unfortunate, as it allowed access to the cellar where the free-standing safe stood. The burglar alarm was of the type that could be deactivated by cutting the telephone wires. Local thieves who had been keeping watch on the refurbishment soon noticed the lack of high grade security.

The pub duly reopened, attracting hundreds of free-spending customers into its delightful bars. The takings for the opening weekend were placed in the safe. During the night the thieves forced the substandard rear door, deactivated the alarm, moved the safe, sawed through its hinges, and helped themselves to the takings.

Following the attack, the pub now has a sophisticated security system.

This chapter looks at ways in which security measures can be effective in pubs, ensuring that the premises, cash and stock are protected from criminals and providing safety and peace of mind for staff and management.

In addition advice is given on spotting and coping with drug dealing, how to prevent burglary, secure cash carrying, machine security, defusing potentially violent situations, and dealing with extortion. The subject of doormen, registered or otherwise, is also discussed, together with details of the pilot schemes being operated by police forces throughout the country.

STRATEGY

A clearly defined security strategy must be drawn up for each pub, backed by commitment, determination and persistence from publicans, breweries, and the police.

When analysing the need for security in licensed outlets we should look first at perceptions of security among both the general public – and the criminal fraternity.

Banks and building societies, by the nature of their businesses, are both overtly and covertly very security conscious. Bullet-proof screens often separate customers from staff and, even when high profile security has been relaxed to allow open-plan reception areas, the cash is transferred by air tubes and stored in a secure vault. In contrast, pubs have an open, welcoming air, with direct over-the-counter contact with customers and no evidence of security measures.

Pubs are attractive to criminals because they deal in cash, which in business hours is held in cash drawers behind the bar and at night is stored on the premises. Gaming machines, juke-boxes and cigarette machines also contain cash.

Before defining a strategy, account must be taken of the nature of the risk. Risk is defined as the probability of damage, injury or loss, not just a catalogue of actual crimes or incidents; and the risk assessment process must include realistic evaluation of the location of the premises, the design and construction of the building, any past incidents, and the value of the building and its contents.

Risk varies. It is higher at some times of day than others. It may change if extensive alterations or additions to the pub are carried out or new and valuable equipment or stock is introduced. Good risk management tries to anticipate these variations by being proactive.

A balance must be struck if security is not to interfere with the smooth running of the business. The difference between a pub and an industrial site is that conventional crime prevention measures – topping fencing with razor wire, say – are not always compatible with the relaxed and friendly atmosphere most pubs seek to create.

There is no single answer. Each preventive measure should support and reinforce the others in a balanced package. Some measures demand more effort than money, and not all rely on electronic or physical protection. In an ideal world there would be funding for all crime prevention measures in pubs, but security is not always the top priority, and when cash *is* available there is a danger of concentrating resources and hardware on one risk to the exclusion of others – a situation that must be avoided.

The simplest way for a publican to assess the crime risk in his pub is to ask the following questions.

1. If I was locked out, how easy would it be for me to get back in?
2. When I am alone in the pub outside trading hours and someone knocks, can I see who it is?

Let us start at the beginning.

The front door

If there is a knock on the door and you can't see who it is, then fit a wide-angle door viewer without delay.

There are many instances of publicans hearing a knock at the door outside business hours, being unable to see who it is, calling out, and receiving the reply: 'It's the postman'. Of course, everyone opens the door if they believe the postman is standing there waiting to deliver letters or a parcel. Only when the door is opened, the 'postman' turns out to be a criminal armed with a sawn-off shotgun. What happens next is ugly – and could easily have been avoided by the installation of a wide-angle door viewer.

Door viewers should be supported by door chains or doorstop devices, both of which are cheap to buy and simple to install, and ensure that the publican and his staff are in control of any attempt at unauthorised entry into the pub outside normal business hours.

Another all too common method of entry arising from the publican's inability to see who is at the door when the pub is shut occurs in the momentary relaxation between the cleaners leaving and the pub opening.

The burglar alarms had been turned off while the cleaners were working and the publican is enjoying a cup of coffee and reading the newspaper, and there's a knock on the door. Because there is no door viewer, the publican assumes that one of the cleaners has forgotten something. He opens the door – and there confronting him are the men with the baseball bats. Another crime that could have been prevented by a door viewer.

So often it's the simple devices that protect staff and management

from criminals, together with a sound, well-thought-out 'best practice' list of security measures.

Alarms

Most pubs are fitted with intruder alarms, but the style and standard of those alarms causes concern. Publicans often look for the cheapest deal; but when you consider the cash, staff and stock you have to protect you will see that it is worth spending a few pounds more on appropriate and effective alarms.

All police forces adhere strictly to an Intruder Alarm Policy, and publicans are advised to seek out the terms and conditions of that policy with their intruder alarm installer or crime prevention officer.

Some publicans do not realise that the police will not respond to a bells-only intruder alarm that is not connected to a control room. If yours is such an alarm, get it replaced with a system that is fitted to a suitable specification.

Intruder alarms must be designed to fit the specific needs of the pub, and not to suit the installers' standard package. There must be a combination of door and contact detectors, together with movement detectors which should be fitted so that some parts of the system can be deactivated when others are active. For instance, the alarms covering the public areas must be deactivated during normal business hours, but alarms covering the liquor store and safe should remain activated.

Many intruder alarm installers fit movement detectors, which are excellent in factories or offices where members of the public do not normally have access. But in pubs, unless they are anti-masking detectors (which prevent 'customers' from deactivating them so that they won't set off the alarm when they return after closing time as burglars), they are useless.

The living quarters should also be protected by alarms. The minimum requirement in these areas is a panic button at the bedside or other convenient place. The same applies to cash offices and areas where the publican or a member of staff counts and stores the cash takings.

Many of the older alarms are fitted with digital dialling systems that call the control room if the alarm goes off, and criminals have learnt simply to cut the telephone wires. Today's systems are fitted with BT Red Care, which rings the control room if there is any attempt to cut the wires. The difference in cost between the old and the new can be £1000 – but remember that the cost of fitting a cheaper system is wasted if it doesn't work when it's needed, along with the cost of the stolen cash and stock.

Under no circumstances should an intruder alarm be fitted by an installer who is not NACOSS approved, NACOSS being the National Supervisory Council that sets standards of equipment and service for the intruder alarm industry.

Safes

Safes are a must in all pubs, and if you have a vintage safe that has served the pub for years it's time to replace it.

There are many styles and shapes of safes, but whichever you choose the one thing to be sure of is that your safe is not free standing. Safes should be firmly fixed to the floor – either bolted or set in concrete. The room or cellar where the safe is housed should be protected by movement detector units, security cameras and a smoke cloak device, which fires a smoke cartridge when activated, quickly filling the area with a heavy cloud of smoke which completely disorientates the thief.

Inside the safe you can fit a smoke dye unit, which activates if the safe is tampered with, rendering the money useless to the thief. Critics say that money in cash bags is not affected. That may be so, but the thief himself will be covered in sticky dye. Smoke cloak and dye cartridges are an excellent deterrent and the fact that they are fitted should be freely advertised in the pub.

Similarly, time-lock safes are a great deterrent, especially if it is advertised in the pub that the safe cannot be opened by management or staff. Those who argue that restricted access to the safe can be inconvenient to the running of the pub ought to take into consideration how inconvenient it is to be forced to open the safe at gunpoint.

Lighting

Effective lighting in and around a pub is a must as part of an integrated security programme. Lighting does deter thieves, both in car-parks and at other vulnerable points such as cellar flaps, rear doors and windows.

Security lighting should in the main be movement activated, which is both efficient and cost effective. Many publicans have found to their cost that regulars are soon deterred if the family car is stolen or broken into in a pub car-park where there is no lighting or any other security measure.

The same principle of lighting applies to areas used for storing stocks of kegs and bottles. They are easily raided by thieves for lack of security locks or lighting.

Remember: lighting is friendly to customers but a deterrent to thieves.

Anti-climb paint

As part of your security strategy, look at any drainpipes that could give access to flat roofs or windows leading into the pub or living accommodation. If you feel that thieves can easily gain access by climbing up the pipes then a simple remedy is anti-climb paint, which can be bought from any good ironmonger.

Security cameras

Security cameras are a great deterrent to drugs users and dealers and extortionists, among others, and are arguably the best form of total security. They are fast becoming a standard item of pub equipment, both inside and out, but can be a minefield to buy and install.

Sales representatives may over-quote the number of cameras you need, while in many cases failing to stress the need for adequate lighting as part of an integrated security programme, and you can end up with a system which is more expensive than it need be and not as effective as it should be.

Publicans with access to brewery security managers should take advantage of their expertise before deciding on the lighting and security cameras required for the pub. Security cameras are not cheap, but they are very effective when they work in conjunction with 24-hour video recording equipment.

Fast scan is a new generation of video surveillance whereby security pictures are transmitted by a telephone link to a control room, allowing staff to watch a burglary or other crime actually being committed.

Security cameras are also one of the best preventive measures against pilfering by staff members. Many instances have been recorded on video when members of staff left alone in the pub, mainly in the late afternoon or early evening, have plied their friends with 'free' drinks. In other cases customers are seen to be given change from receptacles other than the till – handbags, purses or pockets. These crimes have easily been detected using high-specification security cameras and video equipment.

Machine security

The contents of gaming and other machines can be vulnerable to theft during the day, and security is a key consideration when planning where to put them.

Machines should be placed so as to be fully visible from behind the bar – awkward angles can be overcome with mirrors – or within the range of any security cameras inside the premises. As an added deterrent alarms can be fitted to sound in the event of tampering, and padlocks or security bars can be fitted to the cash box doors.

Machines should be regularly inspected for signs of damage and attempted pilfering.

Licensees should keep an eye on machines during opening hours. Individuals fiddling with the coin mechanism or groups forming around machines should be watched. A discreet way of doing this is to regularly collect beer glasses and empty ashtrays from the area.

Customers with frequent claims for non-payment should be monitored. If the machine supplier says the claims are invalid, the licensee will have to use his best judgement and tact in deciding whether to pay future claims.

The identity of visiting supplier representatives should always be checked – bogus collectors and engineers who steal the machines or the money in them do exist.

Overnight, the contents of gaming machines should be put in the safe. The cash box should be left open to make it clear to any intruders that it is empty. To deter criminals looking for a potential target during the day, a notice can be stuck on the front of the machine advising that it is emptied every night.

Most gaming machine theft involves stealing the contents, but the machines themselves can be targets too. To improve security, machines can be bolted to the wall and covered at night with special cages.

Guard dogs

The presence of a dog in a pub always makes a thief think twice. The only problem with dogs is that health and safety rules exclude them from the kitchen, cellar and bars. There are no problems in a dog patrolling the back yard, provided that notices are properly displayed giving a warning to trespassers. Dogs prone to attacking or biting people should always be chained in the yard and not allowed in public areas.

Dogs in general are a great asset to crime prevention providing that they are under the proper control of the owner and do not become a health hazard within the perimeter of the pub by fouling public areas or being allowed into areas where food is prepared and served.

Carrying and storing cash

As discussed earlier, cash should be kept in a safe fitted with a smoke cloak and time lock and supported by an intruder alarm and security cameras. All of these work very well until the cash has to be taken to the bank.

Ideally only contracted cash-carrying companies should be used to transport cash, but many publicans and breweries prefer that cash is deposited personally. Common sense and economic best practice must be the watchword here, and whether or not to use a cash-carrying service must depend on the following criteria:

◆ the area through which the cash is to be transported
◆ the amount of cash likely to be built up over a given period, including weekends
◆ those days when the greatest amount of cash is taken

◆ the safety and understanding of the staff being asked to transport the cash
◆ the number of staff available to transport or deliver cash, which should never be one person only.

The usual well-publicised precautions such as varying routes and times do need to be implemented.

Many publicans favour the use of taxis, and I recommend that only licensed hackney carriages be used. Without wishing to get into any arguments with owner-driver taxis, there have been unfortunate instances when criminal attacks on publicans and staff have been traced back to persons who were not holders of a licensed hackney carriage licence.

Approved cash-carrying bags with a wrist chain and dye cartridge are an excellent method of transporting cash. Several types of this specialist equipment are available, costing around £80 each and £25 per replacement dye cartridge.

Some publicans believe that using cash-carrying bags marks them out as a target, and a carrier bag or sports bag is less conspicuous. In that case, simply carry the cash-carrying bag inside the 'disguise' bag, but with the the wrist-strap correctly attached so that in the event of a snatch the smoke dye cartridge will ignite.

I have heard many negatives from publicans and staff about cash-carrying bags but, for the safety and protection of users, these bags are the only alternative to the takings being collected by a contracted cash-carrying service.

Prostitution

For many years bars were frequently centres of prostitution. That is not the case these days, although some city-centre pubs do attract this trade. In most cases it is easier to detect than the drugs trade, and easier to control.

Publicans must remember that their liquor licence can be revoked if they allow prostitution on their premises. Even allowing touting for business can lead to a court appearance (although it is a misconception that publicans may not serve prostitutes who are 'off duty', so to speak).

Tackling violence in pubs

There have been many studies over the years relating to assaults and violence affecting pub customers and staff. In this section the subject of defusing violent situations is discussed, and the preventive methods now adopted in many licensed outlets outlined.

During the 1970s and 1980s closed circuit television (CCTV) with recording facilities was not a common method of dealing with violence in pubs. However the 1990s have seen an increase in the installation of CCTV, rewarded by a dramatic reduction in the incidence of violence in public houses.

People appear more aggressive in many aspects of life these days, and pub customers are no different. Violence can be sparked by the most minor incidents. Pub management and staff cannot be physically screened off from the customers, so dealing with violence calls for a mixture of training and experience.

It is usually the same person or group of persons who cause violence and create difficulties for pub staff.

One of the best preventive methods is becoming a member of a local pubwatch scheme. Problem customers are identified and discussed and can find themselves barred from all the member pubs – an extremely effective deterrent, and a message to all that antisocial behaviour will not be tolerated.

Meeting violence with violence is not the answer and, while staff may sometimes have to defend themselves, experience shows that a violent situation can be defused by a calm approach with the assistance of all the pub staff.

We all know of publicans who can 'handle themselves' in violent situations. The majority, though, prefer conventional methods of defusing situations – remaining calm, maintaining eye contact, and talking common sense.

Brewery management should develop and implement a company strategy regarding violence in pubs, and training programmes should be made available to free trade management and staff as well as managed house and tenanted staff. It is imperative that a combination of preventive devices, such as security cameras and staff training, are given high priority to ensure safety for staff and customers alike.

Extortion

Extortion is the securing of money, goods or favours by intimidation, violence or the misuse of authority, and sadly pubs like other businesses can be victims of it.

Criminal elements are most likely to target pubs in certain areas, especially where there is weak management and no sign of support for the publican from either the brewery or the police. The whole issue requires careful and skilful handling, not only to stop the loss of revenue but also to prevent the violence and distress caused to the management and staff.

The crime of extortion occurs every day in Britain, but few are willing to report it to the police. It can take various forms, from a small-time bully obtaining free drinks by threats to much more organised racketeers exacting large sums of money by terrorising the publican and staff, all of whom often know the violent capabilities of the perpetrator. If the extortionist's demands are not reported quickly a cycle of terror begins which becomes harder and harder to break.

The cycle normally starts when a number of local criminals (who know the pubs where they are least likely to meet resistance, and who all have reputations for violence) enter the pub at once, demand a round of drinks, and refuse to pay, threatening either personal violence or damage to the property. This will probably not happen at peak drinking times, but when the pub is least busy and when there are only one or two inexperienced bar staff on duty who lack the experience or training to cope.

If they succeed at first, their demands escalate, and one of the typical indicators of an extortion problem is a worsening stock and cash shortage in a pub where such problems have not previously been recorded.

Despite the fear of personal injury or damage to property, and however well grounded those fears may be, reporting approaches at the earliest possible opportunity is the only way to avoid months and years of suffering the financial loss of paying protection money and losing trade, and the misery and humiliation of having to endure the extortionist's threats.

Many police forces now have a wealth of expertise in dealing with extortion which, together with sophisticated technology, only needs the victim's cooperation to resolve these crimes. Fitting security cameras is one of the best deterrents to extortion. There have been cases of extortionists demanding the videotape from the camera; police experts will often install covert camera equipment instead.

There is a new phenomenon, used mainly by drug dealers to get their feet in the doors of youth venues (especially clubs and discos), known as 'extortion in reverse'. Several cases have been logged of publicans who maybe run a successful weekend disco in the lounge bar being approached by one or two smartly dressed men who ask permission to visit the disco and assess it, as they are thinking of operating similar ventures elsewhere. They even say they will pay for the privilege.

The publican, seeing no harm, agrees, and pockets the cash. Other visits follow, and on each occasion the publican is paid some cash. But in fact the visitors are dealers who have been busily setting up a drugs ring in the disco – which the publican can't report because, having accepted cash, he's implicated.

Once they've established that the publican is trapped, the dealers stop

paying him – but the dealing goes on. That's extortion in reverse, and the message is to learn from the folly of others and under no circumstances allow yourself to be conned into accepting payments.

Drugs

Busy, unsupervised pubs make the ideal place for drug dealers and their clients to operate unnoticed. But misuse of drugs on licensed premises, whether it be possession for one's own use or supply for another's, is a criminal offence; and so is allowing one's premises to be used for the purposes of drug abuse. It is therefore the responsibility of publicans and their staff to be observant and make every effort to spot people engaged in drug trafficking as soon as possible.

If drug abusers or suppliers are allowed to become entrenched in a particular pub it takes a great deal of effort to root them out. Any suspicions that persons either known or unknown are using licensed premises for the purposes of drug abuse must therefore be reported to brewery representatives at once. Identifying them isn't always easy, but there are signs publicans and their staff should watch out for and, if spotted, never ignore.

◆ Drug abusers and suppliers usually try to take over a small corner or private alcove in the bar. There won't necessarily be a large crowd of them, maybe only two or three – the supplier himself and a couple of minders or lookouts. They will usually act furtively.

◆ A constant flow of strangers or persons who are not regular clientele will visit the pub where the dealer is operating. They will not buy a drink and will stay only long enough to make a purchase.

◆ users of cannabis, who normally smoke the substance in hand-rolled joints, will leave sweet-smelling cigarette ends in ashtrays. The harder drug users who inject will leave used needles in bins in the toilets.

If there is any doubt in the publican's mind about how genuine certain customers are then the advice of the police should be sought immediately. It is a misconception that a police investigation of drug abuse in the pub will cause massive disruption to trade. Generally speaking, and in the majority of such circumstances, this is definitely not the case.

Usually, when the police receive information (which will always remain confidential) that certain licensed premises are being frequented by drug abusers or suppliers, a short, low-key undercover operation will be mounted. Experienced plain-clothes officers will soon spot the persons involved, and will quickly call uniformed colleagues to arrest them. The whole operation can be over in minutes, without any disruption to trade whatsoever.

Doormen

Since the early 1980s there has been a marked escalation in certain types of unsocial behaviour affecting the licensed trade. Drug abuse, the carrying – and use – of knives and other weapons, drunkenness and its consequent violence, protection

racketeering, even political terrorism have all afflicted publicans and their businesses to varying degrees.

To protect their staff, customers and property, brewers and publicans have for many years employed doormen to monitor access and weed out customers who, in their judgement, would cause problems.

In the past doormen sometimes had as bad a reputation as the people they were supposed to be excluding. In time the police, the local authorities and the Licensing Justices got together and decided it was time to set standards for doormen.

Being a doorman has now become a legitimate profession. Proper training has to be given, and a certificate is issued to successful candidates, who are officially registered as doormen.

The main aims of doorman training and registration schemes are to:

◆ regulate the employment of all people engaged in maintaining order in licensed premises

◆ insist, as a condition of the licence of all premises that employ door-staff, on a commitment to certain standards on the part of those employed

◆ provide a framework within which licensees, police and local authorities can improve relationships and reduce crime, especially drug abuse and violent assault, and prevent door staff from being subverted by criminals.

Doorman registration schemes are generally administered by local authorities and implemented by making it a condition, through the Local Government (Miscellaneous Provision) Act 1982, that holders of Public

Entertainment Licences should not employ or engage any person not registered with the local authority in any capacity concerned with the maintenance of order.

The use of unregistered doormen where a registration scheme was in force would be a breach of condition of the Public Entertainment Licence, rendering the holder liable to prosecution and revocation of the licence.

Applications to become a registered doorman are considered by a local authority committee with regard to the suitability of the applicant, and taking into account any history of involvement in serious crime – for example assault, possession or supply of drugs, or sexual offences. However a previous conviction, depending on the type and severity of the offence, is not an automatic bar to registration.

The police are involved throughout the procedure as a vetting body.

Having been accepted into the scheme the applicant becomes a registered doorman or supervisor and is issued with a lapel tag bearing a registration number and a laminated ID card complete with photo, signature and registration number. Registered doormen are required to wear the tag and carry the card while on duty.

As well as vetting, there is compulsory training given by police trainers including race relations advisers and the drugs squad, the fire brigade and the St John Ambulance Brigade. Subjects covered will include fire safety, licensing law, first aid, drugs awareness, power of arrest, use of reasonable force/restraint techniques, and interpersonal skills, and training is followed by formal tests.

Registered doormen convicted of an offence or accused of inappropriate conduct such as a breach of code of practice or habitual association with criminals can be brought before the committee which originally appointed him, where his registration will be reconsidered.

Properly trained and dedicated doormen are excellent representatives of the licensed trade. Because of the type of training they receive, they can give a genuine service to customers, advising, warning, assisting and protecting.

CONCLUSION

Publicans may sometimes feel isolated, but the truth is that they are not alone. If they are unsure about any aspect of safety or security they can and must turn to their brewery or to the police, where sound advice will be given.

Never act alone or think you can tackle a major security problem on your own. Help is readily available. Don't be negative about costs: security in a pub is as important as short-term profit, because without security tailored to the needs of your pub, profitability will soon decline.

Legal Notes

If a person is convicted of an offence committed on licensed premises, and the court is satisfied that the person used or threatened violence, the court may make an order prohibiting that person from entering those or any other named premises without the express consent of the licensee. The order can be from three months' to two years' duration as specified by the court. A breach of the order is punishable by a fine and/or imprisonment.

In addition to a licensee's ordinary rights to refuse entry to his premises, under the Licensed Premises (Exclusion of Certain Persons) Act a licensee has the right to expel from his premises any person he suspects has entered his pub in breach of an exclusion order. The police must assist if requested.

A licensee has a legal duty not to permit drunken, violent, quarrelsome or disorderly conduct to take place on the premises, or to allow prostitutes to solicit or remain longer than is necessary to take reasonable refreshment.

If a customer refuses to leave when asked to do so by a licensee, employee or police officer in uniform, he may be prosecuted.

A licensee or member of his staff must not sell intoxicating liquor to a drunk.

So far as door staff are concerned, more and more licensing committees are insisting upon door security staff being registered with the local authority. You should make the appropriate enquiries at the town hall.

The only authority the police have to officially close licensed premises is under Section 188 of the Licensing Act 1964, which provides the power to any two Justices of the Peace for the area to order every holder of a Justices' Licence for the premises in or near the place where riot occurs, or is expected, to close for such time as may be ordered. It is an offence punishable by a fine to ignore this order. Wherever possible it is always preferable to cooperate with a request reasonably made by the police.

**CHAPTER
NINETEEN**

SMOKE SIGNALS

Oliver Griffiths

Smoking is an accepted part of everyday life in the licensed trade. Indeed, pubs often seem to be the last haven of the smoker. There are fewer than a dozen non-smoking pubs in the entire country, and almost 50 per cent of all pub customers – and a higher proportion of regulars – enjoy a cigarette with their drink. A ban on smoking either through legislation or through staff litigation would be devastating – and yet both of these options have featured on the front pages of the national newspapers in recent months.

In fact, so much has been written about smoking since Labour came to power that it's sometimes difficult to know what is really going on. Government ministers have come out strongly for a ban on smoking in public places (including pubs), and there have been leaks about a ban through the 'back door' by using tightened health and safety rules. There have been court cases, including the case of Nurse Sparrow referred to below, and reports on the level of risk posed by being exposed to second-hand tobacco smoke. So

what does it all mean and, crucially, what can you do about it to safeguard and develop your business – to get rid of the smoke without getting rid of the smokers?

The first thing to note is that nothing in the regulations on 'passive smoking' has actually changed in recent years. No Act of Parliament has been passed, the health and safety regime remains unaltered, and the high profile 'landmark' passive smoking case was decided in the employer's favour. So why should you care? Why do anything about smoke in your pub? Because what has changed, and will continue to change, is the degree of sensitivity to pollution of all sorts among staff, customers and regulators. Sensible, planned action now will reduce or eliminate any future liability, improve your working environment, help to avoid excessive costs to your business in the future and probably pay for itself very rapidly in increased business. Much of this is evident in the recent Sparrow case.

Ms Sparrow is a nurse who worked in an old people's home. The home had both smoking and non-smoking areas. Ms Sparrow, due to staff shortages, had to work for part of her time in one of the smoking areas – and took her employers to court because she believed that this exposure had caused her to have asthmatic attacks, which had led to her resignation. The parallels to working in a smoky pub are obvious. And perhaps the key reasoning in the judgment finally going against her was that the management had taken all reasonable, practical steps to reduce or eliminate her exposure as soon as they knew of her concerns about the environment. Staff shortages made it essential for her to visit the smoking area. It was felt that a smoking ban was not feasible given the often confused state of the elderly patients, and the window could not be opened for safety reasons.

For pubs, these reasons do not usually exist. Smoking is allowed in most or all areas; it clearly is possible to ban smoking (whatever the economic consequences!); and proper ventilation is always feasible and usually fairly inexpensive to install. The issue therefore hinges on the duty of care of the employer for staff welfare – and this can usually be discharged by getting rid of the smoke while retaining the custom of smoking customers. Neglect of this duty of care may result in a court case which will be expensive whether or not you win it.

To resolve this problem you need to look at your employment practices and your physical facilities.

First, employment practices. It is your duty to make a risk assessment for each of your staff when you hire them. People who are asthmatic or have other respiratory problems may be concerned about working in a smoky environment – it's important to be sure that you can accommodate them satisfactorily and that they are aware of the conditions in which they are going to work. Clearly it is in their, and your, interests to keep them away from smoke as far as is possible.

Second, the physical facilities. In most pubs, and especially smaller pubs, staff will be expected to go ~into areas where there is smoking. These areas do not have to be unpleasantly smoky and can easily be cleaned up by taking the following steps.

1. Renovate any existing, or install new, ventilation equipment. These fans are often loosely called extractors; but they have to be balanced to work correctly, both blowing fresh (supply) air into the pub and drawing stale (extract) air out. As an absolute minimum these should conform to the guideline of 8 litres per person per second; this represents about one 12" supply fan and one 12" extract fan per 50 customers and staff. To minimise complaints about draughts, place fans 8–10' from the floor and use diffusers to spread the supply air further. There may be concerns about heat loss as air is extracted; this can be greatly reduced by using variable speed fans (and possibly sensors to control them) and running them on low when the pub is not busy and high when it is. Heat recovery systems can also be used to save some of the heat being extracted, and integral

heaters can warm the air being blown in.

2. Position the fans to blow smoke away from staff (never extract smoke above or behind the bar!), non-smoking areas, and from dining areas. The extractor fans should be positioned in or near the smoking areas. Keep them running all the time, again varying their speed according to demand.

3. If this doesn't clear the smoke, put in more ventilation or, if this is difficult, install air filtration above the smokiest areas. Air filtration can be a very useful part of your strategy, but it can never do away with the basic need for ventilation because it doesn't bring in fresh air or dilute the carbon dioxide build-up. If you decide to use air filters remember that they pull smoke towards them, so site them so that they don't draw smoke over non-smokers or staff. They should also be easy to access so that filters can be changed regularly.

4. Position a non-smoking area nearest the clean air supply (by the bar or in the dining area). Use signage that is as prominent as possible and, ideally, permanent so that customers can easily see what is required of them. This will greatly help staff to police the policy. Non-smoking areas need not be fixed; the amount of smoking tends to increase over the day, so a flexible area that is larger at lunchtime and smaller in the evening may work best.

5. Keep the systems working by ensuring that your staff know how to control the equipment

and enforce the non-smoking area, and by getting sound cleaning and maintenance contracts for fans and, especially, aircleaners.

This may all sound expensive, but in four test pubs the average cost (excluding installation) for reaching this basic standard was just £2300. This can be spread out over easy payment periods and even partly written off against tax by use of lease purchase agreements. In the test pubs the investment paid for itself in increased business in 10–15 weeks. Drink sales rose by 12 per cent and food sales by a massive 32 per cent, confirming that while customers often don't complain about tobacco smoke; they much prefer to eat and drink where the air is cleaner.

These increases in business came initially from the changing habits of existing customers. The test pubs found that customers who had previously just enjoyed a drink were staying to eat, and customers who had previously left early because of the smoke now stayed longer. Girlfriends and wives who had given up on the pubs because of the smoke started to come back. These changes in the business have continued with the smokers remaining – but with more and more non-smokers joining them, and food sales becoming ever more important. A year on, two of the original four test pubs are expanding and the other two have had continuing growth, with cleaner air an important part of the business. The fear still remains, though, that investing in clean air now will be a waste of money because the Government will require something totally different in some forthcoming legislation; thus the wise head will wait to see what the government is going to do before acting.

This is not so: ventilation and no-smoking areas are at the heart of the government's own guidelines, and in fact the suggestions in this article are all based on the government's 1992 Code of Practice.

So is smoking an asset or a liability for your business? Well, as about half of your customers are smokers they are probably among your greatest assets – but their smoke can be a liability. Acting now to reduce smoke meets the demands of both staff and customers better, improving the environment and even attracting more business. If you would like to know more about how to get rid of the smoke but not the smokers please write to AIR, Freepost LON8895, London NW1 1YU; tel: 0171 209 5089; fax: 0171 267 6177.

AIR-HANDLING TECHNIQUES

Ventilation

Every room requires ventilation to bring in oxygen and to dilute the carbon dioxide (CO_2) that builds up when people breathe (whether they smoke or not). Ventilation brings in air from the outside, either by simply opening the doors and windows or by installing fans in walls, windows or ducts. It can also help to remove smoke, smells and unseen particles in the air. Ventilation is also the most cost-effective way of providing a cooling effect in hot conditions. Fans are fairly basic technology and are generally very reliable. They need

little maintenance and infrequent but regular cleaning.

Air filtration

This does not usually bring in fresh air from outside; it just cleans the air that's already in the room. It doesn't replace the need for ventilation but it is an optional extra. Air filtration units usually comprise, at their simplest, a fan and a filter: the fan pulls the dirty air through the filter and then pushes the cleaned air out the other side. This is a very dirty business in a smoky room, and the filters quickly get clogged up. Air filtration can be very effective at removing tobacco smoke, but requires regular maintenance and cleaning. As the systems just recirculate air already in the pub, they cause no heat loss.

Air-conditioning

The principal purpose of air-conditioning is temperature control. The idea is very simple: warm air is taken from the room, passed through a cooler, and then pumped back in. There may be some filtering, but it is not usually effective against tobacco smoke. The heating and cooling process is relatively energy intensive, and systems are often therefore expensive to run.

FRESH AIR SPECIFICATIONS

Ventilation, either mechanical (fans) or natural (windows/doors), is always required. The minimum amount required depends on the number of people in the room and hence the volume of CO_2 they breathe out. Each person requires about 3.5 litres of air per second, but most standards require ventilation at more than twice this level (8 per person per second or about 30 cubic metres per person per hour).

To work out how much ventilation is required as a minimum, calculate the number of people it takes to fill the bar and multiply by 30. This will be the total number of cubic metres of air you will need to bring in each hour. To find the number of fans required simply divide this number by the capacity of each fan (usually described in cubic metres per hour in the supplier's catalogue).

As a rough guide, a modern 12" fan should draw in enough fresh air for about 50 people (30 people for a 9" fan).

APPENDICES

LICENSING JUSTICES AND LICENCES

Intoxicating liquor must not be sold by retail without a Justices' Licence. Licensing Justices are chosen from among local magistrates. They sit as a licensing committee and consider licensing applications at their licensing sessions.

Licensing Committees must hold not less than five meetings in the 12 months beginning with February in every year. Each Petty Sessional Division fixes its own meeting dates in good time prior to the February meeting, which must be held in the first 14 days of the month and is known as the General Annual Licensing Meeting (sometimes referred to as Brewster Sessions). Other meetings throughout the year are known as Transfer Sessions.

Application to the Licensing Justices must be submitted in accordance with strict rules set out in the Schedules to the Licensing Act 1964. In addition most licensing committees issue their own policy guidelines which are available on request from the office of the Clerk to the Licensing Justices. It is essential for any prospective applicant to obtain a copy of the local policy document. A few courts make an administration charge for this document.

Licensing Justices generally have discretion to grant or refuse applications made to them for new licences. They also deal with most other licensing applications including, for example, applications to transfer or renew existing licences, or for approval of alterations to licensed premises, or for the grant of additional hours by approving Special Hours Certificates or Extended Hours Order. They also hear applications for revocation of Justices' Licences.

In considering applications, the Licensing Justices may grant a Justices' Licence to anyone (who is not disqualified) as they think may be fit and proper to hold a Justices' Licence.

PERMITTED HOURS

The usual permitted hours are:

◆ 11am to 11pm Mondays to Saturdays inclusive
◆ noon to 10.30pm Sundays and Good Fridays
◆ noon to 3pm and 7pm to 10.30pm Christmas Day.

There is a 20-minute drinking-up period at the conclusion of permitted hours.

Where a Supper Hour Certificate applies in an area set apart the permitted hours are:

◆ 11am to midnight Mondays to Saturdays inclusive
◆ noon to 11.30pm Sundays, Good Fridays and Christmas Day.

There is a 30-minute drinking-up period.

Extended Hours Order (Section 70 of the Licensing Act 1964)

Where there is a Supper Hour Certificate and music or any other entertainment is provided for diners, an Extended Hours Order may be granted allowing service up to 1am. There is a 30-minute drinking-up time allowed.

Special Order of Exemption (Section 77 of the Licensing Act 1964)

This may be granted for special occasions, eg wedding receptions, upon application. NB: this is not granted by Licensing Justices but a Magistrates' Court (or by the police in London).

DIFFERENT TYPES OF LICENCES

Justices may limit the manner in which a licensed premises may operate by imposing the following restrictions:

◆ beer, cider and wine only
◆ beer and cider only
◆ cider only
◆ wine only (Section 1 of the Licensing Act 1964).

SUPPER HOUR CERTIFICATE

The usual permitted hours for licensed premises cease at 11pm weekdays and 10.30pm on Sundays, Good Fridays and Christmas Day with a 20-minute drinking-up time. However, in a restaurant or an area of a public house set aside for dining, it is possible to extend the terminal hour by one additional hour subject to the sale or supply of alcohol being ancillary to a meal.

A Supper Hour Certificate is obtained by application to the Licensing Justices at any Transfer Sessions upon not less than seven days' notice. The fee is £25.00. The court will usually require a plan of your premises and the detailing of the area to which the Certificate is to apply.

You are required to display a notice in the part of the premises explaining the effect of the Certificate.

Where a Supper Hour Certificate applies there is a 30-minute drinking-up period. No new drinks can be supplied during the drinking-up period.

A Supper Hour Certificate will also add to the permitted hours on

Christmas Day the period 3pm–7pm for those taking table meals.

SPECIAL HOURS CERTIFICATES

Where a Public Entertainment Licence is in force, then provided all or part of the premises are to be used for the purpose of music, dancing and substantial refreshment, to which the sale of intoxicating liquor is ancillary, Licensing Justices may grant a Special Hours Certificate which has the effect of extending the permitted hours until 2am the following day (3am in London).

The Certificate has been used by publicans for many years as a way of extending their permitted hours, running their premises until 11pm as straightforward pubs, and after 11pm providing music, dancing and substantial meals to take advantage of the Special Hours Certificate. Although Special Hours Certificates have an end time, the courts have for many years granted the Certificates without specifying a commence-

ment time. The assumption was that they could operate from any time during the day at the discretion of the licensee provided they began no earlier than 11am.

However, much confusion and difficulty has now been introduced by a case called Shipley.

Essentially, as a result of Shipley, a Special Hours Certificate must now state a commencement time. Normal permitted hours will not apply, and the pub must remain dry until the time specified in the Special Hours Certificate. Worse, the Special Hours Certificate is now to be taken to mean that music, dancing and substantial meals to which intoxicating liquor is ancillary must be available throughout the time the pub is open.

In short, until Shipley is resolved, it is no longer possible to run your premises as an ordinary pub from 11am to 11pm and as a disco with meals until 2am, as in the past: it's either a pub, or a disco with meals, but not both.

GAMING

Gaming by means of machines with a limited payout – skill with prize machines (SWP) and amusement with prize machines (AWP) – may also be available on licensed premises subject to the grant of a permit from the Licensing Justices under Section 34 of the Gaming Act 1968. Usually a permit for up to two machines will be available. The licensing committee may require a plan of your premises indicating where the machines are to be located. Any more than two machines will usually require a separate special application.

It is permissible to hold certain small lotteries, including raffles, in public houses. However, the promotion of lotteries is guarded by strict legal rules and licensees are strongly advised to obtain professional advice (from, for example, the local authority's licensing department) before allowing lotteries to be held on their premises.

There is a general prohibition on gaming in places to which (whether on payment or otherwise) the public has access. However there are concessions for dominoes and cribbage, which may be played for money (along with any other game that is authorised to be played on those premises). These do not include games of skill such as darts, pool or billiards, where players wager with each other on their skill.

Other card games or gambling games must not be permitted without the Magistrates' court's authority, and even where gaming is authorised 'high stakes' are not permitted. Unfortunately there is no definition of what stakes may be considered 'high'. Guidance can be sought from the justices, the police, or the Gaming Board, which issues guidelines from time to time.

A race night or bingo evening may well attract the attention of the authorities, and must not be 'the only or the only substantial inducement for persons to attend the event'. Even if considered lawful, the whole of the proceeds of the entertainment, after deducting expenses, must be devoted to purposes other than private gain.

In any event you must not permit any person under 18 years of age to take part in any permitted gaming. Bingo also constitutes gaming so you will need a Special Order from the Justices. Be careful, as on summary conviction there is a fine up to £5000.

DISABILITY DISCRIMINATION

It is an offence under the Disability Discrimination Act 1995 not to offer people with disabilities the same facilities and service available to others without justification.

While there have been no prosecutions yet (and so no one knows what constitutes justification), two things are certain. First, the pub trade has been slow to adopt either the physical alterations or the changes in mental attitude necessary to offer an adequate welcome to people with disabilities. And second, once the alterations are in place, important financial benefits will follow.

◆ Proper facilities for people with disabilities will attract not only those customers themselves, but also their able-bodied friends, and are therefore a potential traffic builder of considerable importance.

◆ Lunchtime specials for organised parties of people with disabilities from day centres, etc create the potential for large sales at otherwise slack times.

◆ Facilities suitable for people with disabilities will also attract two other customer groups: the elderly infirm and patients released from hospitals with legs in plaster or other temporarily disabling conditions. These customers will also bring able-bodied companions.

Community pubs that have installed facilities for people with disabilities find there is another important benefit: their reputation as a place of welcome for the whole community is enhanced.

The most obvious facilities for people with disabilities are wheelchair ramps and specially adapted lavatories. However, wheelchair users want to be able to take advantage of all the pub's services, so all areas and services should be accessible to them.

◆ Doors should be wide enough for wheelchairs and free swinging.

Double doors are ideal for external access.

◆ Aisles between seat backs should be wide enough for wheelchairs.

◆ The bar and food servery should be low enough for wheelchair users to use: they want to buy their round too. A shallow well behind the bar will save the staff's backs!

◆ The toilet should include a handbasin at suitable height with elbow taps.

◆ An ordinary toilet mounted on a concrete plinth is much, much cheaper than the tall-pedestal toilet specially developed for wheelchair users, and just as effective.

◆ Make both of the toilet arms movable: not all wheelchair users are right handed!

◆ If you have a tampon machine in the ladies' loo and a condom machine in the gents', install them in the disabled toilet as well: people with disabilities have the same needs as anyone else.

◆ Keep the access to the disabled toilet clear, and don't use the toilet itself as a cleaner's cupboard. People with disabilities want to feel wanted, not just 'catered for' as if they were some sort of afterthought.

Remember too that wheelchair users are not the only people with disabilities: sight- and hearing-impaired customers also benefit from a comparatively simple level of special provision.

Staff should be able to serve customers with varying degrees of hearing impairment. If you have a member of staff who can sign, so much the better; if not, at least train the staff not to keep saying 'Eh?' and 'You what?' Smoke alarms should have a built-in strobe light to help the hearing impaired.

Braille menus for sight-impaired customers can normally be made up locally for a nominal charge. Emergency lighting should have extra-strength bulbs.

Staff should be prepared to serve half pints in pint glasses to customers with Parkinson's or other tremors or spasms without crass jokes about long pulls. Staff should not gawp at customers with facial injuries or deformities; if staff set the tone, other customers will soon follow.

Essentially, offering a welcome to customers with disabilities is no more than an extension of the kind of mentality a successful publican will possess anyway: a mentality that considers what people want and need in order to have a good time, and a willingness to provide it.

Advice on making alterations is available from the local council's social services department. However, publicans who wish to get on with it are advised not to wait for grants that may or may not be available and that usually come with strings. Alterations need not cost more than £1000, and can cost much less if the publican is a handyman able to install ramps, etc himself.

Finally, remember that installing the above facilities does not change your business into a sort of disability theme pub aimed at wheelchair users: it makes it truly a pub for everyone.

APPENDIX
FOUR

ALTERATIONS AND REFURBISHMENTS

Before undertaking any refurbishment or restoration work, and before starting any alterations, however minor, there are serious licensing, planning, and health and safety issues to take into consideration.

The most important point to bear in mind is that S20 of the Licensing Act 1964 requires the approval of the Licensing Justices before any alteration to the internal layout of licensed premises can be made. This includes seemingly trivial changes, for instance the installation or removal of a screen affecting the licensee's ability to supervise drinking areas.

To be specific, alterations which:

◆ give increased facilities for drinking in a public or common part of the premises,
◆ conceal from observation a public or common part of the premises used for drinking,
◆ affect communication between the public part of the premises where intoxicating liquor is sold and the remainder of the premises or any street or other public way

require the prior consent of the Licensing Justices.

Failure to seek the approval of the justices is a serious matter; if you are in the slightest doubt as to whether their approval is required consult your solicitor or the clerk to the justices. Courts, unlike councils, do not have the power to grant back-dated consent, so look before you leap.

The justices' interest is primarily in the orderly running of the premises; the local council has a much wider range of interests in alterations, including such considerations as public safety, traffic generation, noise nuisance and conservation. Failure to gain the appropriate consents before starting any work has very serious consequences – you may well be forced to return the pub to its previous state at your own expense – so it is important to ensure that appropriate enquiries are made at your local council before making any commitment.

Planning restrictions can take many different forms. For example, the local council may limit your trading hours, impose parking restrictions, or place conditions on the way the premises may operate to fit in with the nature of the neighbourhood. The planning process is also designed to allow all relevant bodies – environmental health department, fire service, highways department, conservation societies – the opportunity to give their opinion on your plans, and, although these procedures will be infuriatingly time consuming, the effort it takes to follow them is as nothing to the trouble that can arise from ignoring them.

Find out in particular whether the pub is in a conservation area and, if it seems to be of historical or architectural interest, whether listed building controls apply. (Owing to recent changes listed building controls may now apply to internal features such as snob screens, elaborate back fittings or decorative windows.)

Do not quietly destroy apparently historical internal features in an attempt to pre-empt the planning process: someone, somewhere – whether a statutory body or a conservation society – will have a record of any item of interest, and you may be forced to have a replacement expensively hand made.

However, the listing process does not exist to ossify historic pubs as uncommercial museum pieces. The regulations are very flexible, and you are more likely to achieve your business goals by negotiating with the relevant statutory authorities and voluntary consultative groups than by confrontation.

When considering any alterations, it is also sensible to involve your local environmental health department at the earliest possible stage, to enable relevant food hygiene and health and safety issues to be agreed and schemed in before you spend money on work which may later have to be undone.

Health and safety in the customer area also needs to be considered including, for example, appropriate measures to avoid slips, trips and falls. Regard should also be taken of glazed doors and other vulnerable glazed areas such as conservatories. Safety glazing needs to be used where necessary for reasons of health and safety.

The local authority's powers to regulate the provision of customer toilets are contained in the Local Government (Miscellaneous Provisions) Act 1976. British Standard 6465: Part 1: 1995 gives guidance on the appropriate level of toilet provision. If alterations are made that increase the customer capacity, or if complaints are made regarding the adequacy of the facilities provided, or if an entertainment licence is applied for, then regard may be had to this standard.

If alterations are being made it would be advisable to discuss disabled WC provision with the Building Control Officer at your local council.

There is no specific requirement for staff to have separate toilet facilities, but this is preferable, especially for food handlers. Food hygiene legislation requires that toilets must be connected to an effective drainage system, must not open directly into rooms where food is handled, and must be provided with materials for cleaning and drying hands.

APPENDIX
FIVE

NOTICES YOU MUST DISPLAY

Notices which must be displayed in on-licence premises are as follows.

1. The name of the licensee(s), usually displayed above the main entrance.
2. Details of any hours subject to a Restriction Order.
3. Details of a Supper Hour Certificate or Extended Hours Order.
4. Details of the effect of any Special Hours Certificate.
5. Details of the hours under a General Order of Exemption.
6. The measure used for the sale of whisky, gin, rum and vodka, which must be 25ml or 35ml or multiples thereof; and the measures used for the sale of wine by the glass, which must be 125ml or 175ml; and of wine in carafes, which must be 250ml, 500ml, 750ml or one litre.
7. A price list. The law requires that price lists are clearly displayed in order that customers may know what the prices are for food and drink offered for sale. Where there are 30 items or less on a menu or drinks list the prices of all items must be shown. However, it is sufficient to display the prices of 30 selected items. All prices must be VAT inclusive, and any service charges or other extra charges must be indicated. See Price Marketing (Food and Drink on Premises) Order 1979.
8. The percentage alcohol by volume (abv) of a representative sample of alcoholic drinks. The abv of a representative sample of 30 drinks sold in the bar, or of all drinks where less than 30 are for sale, must be shown either on the price list or in another conspicuous place. (Mixed drinks and cocktails are excluded from this requirement.)

NB: All packaged drinks with an abv of more than 1.2 per cent must be labelled showing their strength. It is important to be clear of the distinction between alcohol-free and low alcohol drinks. To be alcohol free the drink must contain no more than 0.05 per cent abv, and to be low alcohol no more than 1.2 per cent abv. Such drinks must be labelled with their maximum percent abv.

9. A tobacco sales notice under the provisions of the Children And Young Persons (Protection From Tobacco) Act 1991.

10. Notice, where applicable, of the effect of a Children's Certificate.

**APPENDIX
SIX**

USEFUL ADDRESSES
AND PHONE NUMBERS

Academy of Food and Wine Service
Burgoyne House
Burgoyne Quay
8 Lower Teddington Road
Kingston
Surrey KT1 4ER
Tel: 0181 943 1011
Fax: 0181 977 5519

Advisory, Conciliation, and
Arbitration Service (ACAS)
Clifton House
83–117 Euston Road
London NW1 2RB
Tel: 0171 396 5100

Alliance of Independent Retailers
Alliance House
Bank Chambers
5–9 St Nicolas Street
Worcester WR1 1VW
Tel: 01905 612733
Fax: 01905 21501

Association of Licensed Free Traders
Dane House
55 London Road
St Albans
Herts AL1 1LJ
Tel: 01727 841644
Fax: 01727 852208

Association of Licensed Multiple
Retailers
11 Fairway Drive
Greenford
Middx UB6 8PW
Tel: 0181 813 2800
Fax: 0181 575 8678

Brewers and Licensed Retailers
Association
42 Portman Square
London W1H 0B
Tel: 0171 486 4831
Fax: 0171 935 3991

British Hospitality Association
Queens House
55–56 Lincoln's Inn Fields
London WC2A 3BH
Tel: 0171 404 7744
Fax: 0171 404 7799

British Institute of Innkeeping
Park House
24 Park Street
Camberley
Surrey GU15 3PL
Tel: 01276 684449
Fax: 01276 23045

Business Link
Tel: 0800 50020

Campaign for Real Ale (CAMRA)
230 Hatfield Road
St Albans
Herts AL1 4LW
Tel: 01727 867201
Fax: 01727 867670

Catering Equipment Suppliers
Association
Carlyle House
235–237 Vauxhall Bridge Road
London SW1V 1EJ
Tel: 0171 233 7724
Fax: 0171 828 0667

Chartered Institute of
Environmental Health
Chadwick Court,
15 Hatfields
London SE1 8DJ
Tel: 0171 928 6006
Fax: 0171 827 5865

City and Guilds
1 Giltspur Street
London EC1A 9DD
Tel: 0171 294 2468
Fax: 0171 294 2400

Confederation of Tourism, Hotel
and Catering Management
204 Barnett Wood Lane
Ashtead
Surrey KT21 2DB
Tel: 01372 278 572

Cookery and Food Association
1 Victoria Parade
331 Sandycombe Road
Richmond
Surrey TW9 3NB
Tel: 0181 948 3870
Fax: 0181 332 6326

English Tourist Board
Thames Tower
Blacks Road
London W6 9EL
Tel: 0181 846 9000
Fax: 0181 563 0302

Federation of Licensed Victuallers'
Associations
126 Bradford Road
Brighouse
West Yorks HD6 4AU
Tel: 01484 710534
Fax: 01484 718647

Federation of Retail Licensed Trade
91 University Street
Belfast BT7 1HP
Tel/Fax: 01232 327578

Fleurets
18 Bloomsbury Square
London WC1A 2NS
Tel: 0171 636 8992
Fax: 0171 636 7490

Health and Safety Executive
Information Services
Broad Lane
Sheffield
South Yorks S3 7HQ
Tel: 0541 545500
Fax: 0114 289 2333

The Hospitality Training
Foundation
International House
High Street
London W5 3DB
Tel: 0181 579 2400
Fax: 0181 540 6217

Licensed Retail Consultants
(Paul Cooper)
46 Front Street
Slip End
Luton
Bedfordshire
Tel: 01582 424484

Licensed Victuallers' Trade
Association (London & South-east)
The Royal Six Bells
22 High Street
Colliers Wood
London SW19 2BH
Tel: 0181 540 1275
Fax: 0181 540 2715

Licensed Victuallers' Trade
Association (Midlands)
Larkfield
Ashlawn Road
Rugby CV22 5QE
Tel: 01788 553353
Fax: 01788 535626

Licensed Victuallers' Trade
Association (West)
Lord Haldon Hotel
Dunchideock
Exeter EX6 7YF
Tel: 01392 832483
Fax: 01392 833765

Licensed Victuallers Wales
2 Derwendeg Station Road
Govilon
Abergavenny
Gwent NP7 9RG
Tel: 01873 830415

Music Alliance
29–33 Berners Street
London W1P 4AA
Tel: 0171 580 5544
Fax: 0171 306 4050

Office of Fair Trading
Field House
15–25 Breams Buildings
London EC4A 1PR
Tel: 0171 211 8000

Pannone & Partners
123 Deansgate
Manchester M3 2BU
Tel: 0161 909 3000
Fax: 0161 909 4444

Tony O'Reilly
317 Conniburrow Boulevard
Milton Keynes, MK14 7AF
Tel: 0402 293 360

Royal Society for the Prevention of
Accidents (RoSPA)
Edgbaston Park
353 Bristol Road
Birmingham B5 7ST
Tel: 0121 248 2000
Fax: 0121 248 2001

Scottish Licensed Trade Association
10 Walker Street
Edinburgh EH3 7LA
Tel: 0131 225 5169
Fax: 0131 220 4057

Scottish Tourist Board
23 Ravelston Terrace
Edinburgh EH4 3EU
Tel: 0131 332 2433
Fax: 0131 343 1513

Wales Tourist Board
Brunel House
2 Fitzalan Road
Cardiff CF2 1UY
Tel: 01222 499909
Fax: 01222 485031

APPENDIX
SEVEN

CHECKLIST OF ESSENTIAL CONTACTS

Solicitor: _____

Accountant: _____

Financial adviser: _____

Bank manager: _____

VAT inspector: _____

Local council Environmental Health Dept: _____

Local council Planning Dept: _____

Local council Trading Standards Dept: _____

Police licensing officer: _____

Police crime prevention officer: _____

Fire safety officer: _____

Licensing Justices clerk: _____

INDEX OF ADVERTISERS

Adnams & Co Plc 65
Allied Drink Systems Ltd 89
Amberstone Trading Co 93
BB Supply Centre 59
BFS Ltd 209–11
BHMA Ltd 176–7
BOC Sureflow 68–71
BT Payphones 242–3
Budweiser Budvar 59
Carling vi, 39, 204
Carlsberg Export 62–3
Cellarmyxer Trading Ltd 43–7
Chadburns Ltd 165–6
Cinders Barbecues Ltd 127–31
College Green Independent 227–31
Comware Technology Ltd 51
Delta Catering Equipment 133–5
Diversey Lever *Inside front cover*
Emperor Bar Equipment v
Everards Brewery 10–11
Filton Brewery Products 52–5
Heath Advertising 181–2

Henninger 40–1
HM Customs & Excise 235–8
Inn Profit Systems Ltd 57
Inn Relief Services 151–3, *Outside back cover*
Mayfair Services 185
Mitre Master Ltd v
Morland Plc 27–9
Newdawn & Sun Ltd 187–9
Phonographic Performance Limited 216–7
The Publican xiv
Pubmaster Limited x–xi
Satvision Insatcom Ltd 219
Sea Fish Industry Authority 117–25
Skelton Design 61
Strelly Enterprises Ltd 95–8
Tavern Group Limited 36–7
The Wolverhampton & Dudley 17
Tilmaster 67
Viscount Catering Limited 109–11
Westminster College 31
Whitbread Pub Partnerships 2–5